# CANADA:

## THE TREASURE &
## THE CHALLENGE

# CANADA:

# THE TREASURE &
# THE CHALLENGE

The Reader's Digest Association (Canada) Ltd.

ISBN 0-88850-074-2

Printed in Canada 78 79 80 81 82/5 4 3 2 1

# Foreword

For decades, intellectuals, educators and artists have sought
an elusive Canadian identity. How wrong they have been,
how out of step with reality. For they have overlooked
a most basic observation: Canada is home. Because this
is where we live, I believe, few Canadians worry about
who we are or what constitutes our national identity.
*Canada: The Treasure and the Challenge* makes no attempt
to define any such identity. Instead, weaving a tapestry
of yesterday, today and tomorrow, it simply gives us
Canada—in colorful stories and dramatic pictures.

    This book showcases Canadian imagination, a quality
which has played—and continues to play—a vital role
in our country's development. The nation's pioneering
spirit is as alive today as when settlers forged westward
across the Prairies, and adventurers hacked through a
bleak, northern wilderness in search of gold. Recent accom-
plishments have been no less bold. The CN Tower. The
CANDU Reactor. The Anvil Mine. The White Pass
& Yukon Route. All come to life on the pages of this
book, demonstrating clearly that Canada is no static society.

    Critics claim that Canada has sacrificed cultural
growth for material progress. I don't believe it. I recall
that during our Centennial we built some 2,500 permanent

As the Centennial Commissioner in 1967, John Fisher oversaw the planning of Canada's 100th birthday party. He has been a reporter, broadcaster, special assistant to former prime minister John Diefenbaker and executive director of the Canadian Tourist Association. Often called "Mr. Canada," he received the Medal of Service of the Order of Canada in 1967.

buildings, many of them concert halls, theaters, archives and museums. Our producers and actors are no strangers to Hollywood, our ballerinas take curtain calls at the world's great theaters and Canadian singers bring up the houselights in Nashville, London and Paris.

Yet the ties that bind us are under testing strain. They can be strengthened only if we learn to better understand our country and our countrymen. Canada offers this challenge to us all—to know her better. Past generations have met that challenge and, along the way, built a great country. But—as the following pages show—we are still a land of pioneers, builders, dreamers. Canadians today would do well to heed these words of poet Sir Charles G. D. Roberts, written almost a century ago: "Awake, my country, the hour is great with change!"

*Canada: The Treasure and the Challenge* reflects that change. And I hope Canadians read this book from cover to cover.

John W. Fisher, o.c.

# Contents

# A Poet's View of Canada

By Alden Nowlan

As a child in the backwoods of Nova Scotia I lived with my grandmother, an old peasant woman who played the autoharp and believed in witches. She used to tell me about the days when farmers in the Annapolis Valley produced everything that they used except tea, sugar, rum and tobacco. Since her father neither smoked nor drank he bought nothing but sugar and tea; everything else consumed by his family of 14 children came, either directly or indirectly, from his own land.

That fascinated me when I first heard about it as a child of eight; it fascinates me even more now that I'm a grown man. It's the kind of fascination that has kept *Robinson Crusoe* alive for 250 years: man's repressed desire to be utterly self-sufficient and, therefore, wholly free.

My grandmother also told me about the days of the sailing ships, when the highest honor that could be attained by a Maritimer was to be master of a three-masted schooner. A party of Nova Scotians would cut down trees, haul the trees to a mill, saw them into lumber, use the lumber to build a ship and sail the ship to the West Indies, or even around the Horn. From my grandmother I learned not only that such men had lived, but that in some enigmatic yet indisputable way they were connected with me.

My grandmother, in her way, was heroic. As a young woman she had gone into the woods alone with horse, axe and bucksaw to cut firewood to keep her five small children from freezing to death. As a very old woman, near the end of a life of almost medieval poverty, she danced the jig and sang ribald folk songs. She told me about the woodsmen as well as the sailors, about the white-water men in their hobnailed yellow boots and red flannel shirts, who drank Demerara rum and crossed wide rivers by leaping from one floating log to another. And I knew that the woodsmen, too, were somehow part of me, and I of them.

It was easy for me to relate to the past because so little in our village had changed. In the 1930s my native place can't have been much different from what it was in the 1880s, except that the ships had vanished and the lumbering was petering out, so that most persons were poorer than their grandparents had been. We had no telephone, no electricity, no central heating and no plumbing except a primitive sink.

It's frequently said that Canadians are not prepared to pay the price of true independence, not ready to accept the lowering of the standard of living that might result from our ceasing to be an economic colony of the United States. That may well be. But in the section of the country where I've lived practically all my life, the Maritimes, we have little or nothing to lose. We've been paying a price for being Canadians ever since Confederation cut us off from our natural markets in New England and tariffs forced us, in effect, to subsidize Ontario manufacturing industries.

Canada is not just two nations, but a federation of nations, and I don't think that's bad. I think we should celebrate rather than bemoan our diversity in a world that's rapidly being homogenized.

By and large, we have a voracious appetite for the exotic and flamboyant that we refuse to acknowledge, even to ourselves. Take Prime Minister Mackenzie King, for example. The man has been characterized as the apotheosis of Canadian dullness, a staid, gray mood of his country. Consider the facts. This staid, gray man surrounded himself with artificial ruins. He consulted fortune tellers and spiritualists. He refused to send a cable to King George VI assenting to Canada's declaration of war against Japan until the hands of the clock pointed in an auspicious direction—perhaps the only occasion since the fall of Troy when a declaration of war had to await the proper mystical omens.

We Canadians assessed this 20th-century Merlin, and agreed that he was dull. No, Canada has never been staid and gray, but a great many Canadian intellectuals have been color-blind.

Brendan Behan, when asked his opinion of Canada, is said to have replied, "Ah, it will be a grand country when they get it finished." As a poet, and especially as a writer of fiction, one of the things I like best about Canada is that it's still being created.

Several years ago I stepped out of the public library in Saint John, N.B., and looked out over the ugliest section of the city. I had never before realized just how hideous that section was. For a moment I felt an almost physical sense of revulsion, a disgust that amounted almost to despair. Then I thought, "Yes, it's hideous, all right enough; but, then, we haven't started to build it yet." As Canadian cities go, Saint John is old; but when compared with European cities it's only a coastal settlement. The real Saint John is only just beginning to be built, and that's true of most Canadian cities.

Perhaps, then, Canada is not so much a country as magnificent raw material for a country; and perhaps the question is not "Who are we?" but "What are we going to make of ourselves?"

Alden Nowlan, a poet and fiction writer, won the Governor-General's Award in 1967 for his collection of verse, *Bread, Wine and Salt*.

# A SOUND SENSE OF THE POSSIBLE

"Life is redeemed by achievement.
All its fun is in doing things."

Sir Wilfred Grenfell

# "Bravo CN Tower!"

By Larry Collins

On the cold, gray afternoon of April 2, 1975, a holiday atmosphere prevailed around the base of a slender lakefront tower reaching far above the Toronto skyscrapers. Concessionaires hawked coffee, hot dogs and balloons. Traffic slowed to a stop as motorists craned their necks upward. Spectators crowded office windows. The CN Tower was about to become the world's tallest free-standing structure at 1,815 feet.

At 1:50 p.m. Olga, a giant helicopter, whirled aloft with the last section of a 335-foot broadcasting antenna dangling from her undercarriage. For ten tense minutes the orange machine hung over the tower. Then pilot Larry Pravecek heard foreman Paul Mitchell radio: "All right. You're on!"

As Olga drifted clear, spectators cheered, horns honked. Minutes later, ironworkers lit a flare and unfurled a Canadian flag. Moscow's Ostankino Tower, at 1,748 feet, was no longer the champ.

Moscow's undoing began in 1967 when the CBC, looking for a better Toronto transmitting site, persuaded the Canadian National Railways to include a tower in its plans for "Metro Centre," a $1.5-billion lakefront development. Designers could not resist the allure of the revenues promised by a tower that could call itself the world's tallest.

The design and construction team under Malachy Grant, a veteran of Expo 67, strove for a tower that would be attractive as well as safe. One more tower sticking up like a chimney wasn't good enough. "We had to create a piece of sculpture," said Stewart Andrews, then president of Metro Centre.

The final design, conceived by two Toronto architectural firms, John Andrews International and The Webb Zerafa Menkes Housden Partnership, was a triangular column, deceptively fragile in appearance. Each leg of the Y-shaped base is 94 feet long. The legs taper up into a single column

54 feet in diameter at the 1,100-foot level where a seven-story sky pod, 113 feet high and 150 feet in diameter, sits. Above the pod, the tower rises uniformly, 34 feet in diameter, to the top of the 1,480 feet of concrete. The five-sided base of the antenna is 14 feet in diameter and the top is just two feet square.

The $52-million tower rests in soil exhaustively tested by Eli Robinsky, a Toronto engineering consultant. "The tower is founded on shale," he said. "We had to find a layer that would support the load uniformly. We didn't want another leaning tower of Pisa."

To find that layer, small-diameter borings up to 300 feet deep were made, then four holes, 30 inches in diameter, were drilled 90 feet into the rock. Robinsky, equipped with oxygen tank, lights and a camera, descended into the dripping depths in a small cable cage, taking hundreds of color photographs, conducting strength tests, and bringing back samples of rock for lab testing. He installed gauges 50 feet below the level where the tower's foundation would rest to test the "rebound" of the rock under the tower's 130,000-ton weight. He estimated it could never sink more than three eighths of an inch.

Finally, excavation for the CN Tower began on February 6, 1973. And it was soon destined to stand alone in a maze of railroad tracks. Antidevelopment pressures killed the rest of Metro Centre on the drawing boards. Into the cup-shaped excavation, 55 feet deep, the tower's concrete foundation was poured and strengthened with 500 tons of steel. Unlike some office buildings, which are laced to the bedrock by cables, the CN Tower is held only by gravity. Cables would corrode long before the end of the 300 years the tower is designed to last.

By June 1973, the Foundation Building Construction Co. was ready to begin pouring concrete

No conflict here. The gleaming
CN Tower, a monument to this modern
age, complements the stately beauty
of Toronto's early architecture.

Visitors to the CN Tower while it was under construction were seldom as cool as the men building it. A CN executive threw up after seeing a workman walk blithely along an unprotected girder over 1,100 feet of space.

With pinpoint accuracy, a $4-million helicopter named Olga—specially designed for aerial construction—lowers one of the 39 steel sections of the tower's 335-foot broadcasting antenna.

for the tower itself. The most economic way, it was decided, was to use a 35-foot-high, five-level slip form, lifted by a ring of hydraulic jacks. On the top level, concrete was poured into chutes. At the next level, an electric vibrator made sure no voids were left in the wall. On the third level, workmen with trowels finished off the surface. The lower levels provided access to the jackrods.

Rising above the slip form, a giant crane lifted tons of steel for the tower's framework. As the form rose, it also had to squeeze the tower's tapered walls into shape. This was done by another set of jacks that were adjusted with every added *inch* of height.

As they rose, often more than 20 feet a day, sidewalk superintendents wanted to know, "How can you tell it's straight?" The answer: with bomb sights. Three of them were attached to the slip-form deck and the cross hairs were trained on target lines along the center of the base of each tower leg. As

a further check, 200-pound drums on cables acted as plumb bobs in each leg.

Readings were taken every two feet. If an adjustment had to be made, the jacks lifting the slip form would be shut down on one side until the tower was again rising straight and true. When the last concrete was poured on February 22, 1974, the tower was less than 1½ inches out of line.

But the builders had bigger headaches. Malachy Grant had planned to finish the concrete by the fall of 1973, but bad weather and a strike of cement finishers extended work through the winter. "No one had ever been foolish enough to slip form in the winter before," said Grant. "We had to figure out a way to cure the cement before it was exposed to freezing temperatures as the slip form moved up." The answer was to install 25 heaters on each floor of the slip form, a giant propane heater at the bottom of the tower's core and a 32-foot insulated plywood skirt at the bottom of the form.

In the summer of 1974 came the next big job: raising the steel and wood forms with which 12 brackets would be cast to support the sky pod. The formwork, weighing 350 tons, had been built on the ground in six sections. But before it could be lifted by cables and hydraulic jacks, a serious snag developed. The steel in the 45 cables was too hard for the jaws of the hydraulic jacks to grip. There was no time to get new cables. The problem was solved by fitting the jacks with extra safety jaws that were replaced every 300 feet. Finally the steel frame was bolted to the tower and concrete was poured into the forms. Later a reinforced concrete ring, 120 feet in diameter, was placed around the edge of the brackets, holding them in place.

The nonchalant courage of the ironworkers was never more apparent than during the pod's construction. Ask any of them how they can catwalk along steel girders over 1,000 feet of empty space and you are likely to get a blank stare. "It's never registered on me," said James MacDonald, who worked for 13 months on the tower, walking up each day instead of taking the man-hoist. "This job was safer than most tower jobs. We had the slip form as a platform. Sometimes, of course, you'd work out of the crane bucket. That could be dangerous because the crane operator couldn't see the bucket and if the cable had got fouled on something, you'd have been gone."

Newfoundlander Philip Penney, an experienced foreman, shrugged off the danger one day just after backing down a wooden ladder on the edge of the upper observation deck. But did his wife worry? "Not as long as I brought home my paycheck every Thursday." (Ironworkers on the tower made a basic salary of about $10 an hour. MacDonald made $35,000 in 1973. The team installing the antenna mast made about $1,000 a week.)

Only one man died during construction – on the ground. A gust of wind picked up a piece of plywood that struck an inspector on the neck. Had he been hit anywhere else, he would have been unharmed.

The three men who operated the 47½-ton crane, Winston Young, Dominic Narducci and Ray Jobst, worked in shifts, enduring high winds and numerous lightning strikes. "It's like a high-powered rifle going off in your ear," said Young, a university graduate in sociology. "There's no time to be afraid. You can see the sparks flying off the boom."

Young was on duty on November 8, 1974, when ironworker Bill "Sweet William" Eustace, a former army parachutist, could restrain himself no longer. Sweet William parachuted from the end of the crane's boom, 1,530 feet up. Narrowly missing the sky pod, he landed safely and was fired. Young nearly got fired, too, but was excused when he said he wasn't in the crane's cab at the time.

When Olga arrived in Toronto on March 5, 1974, to tackle the last big problem, erection of the antenna, the March lion came with her. She had to wait a day and a half to lower the crane's boom to the ground; and the very next day, she was grounded because of icing problems. But in 18 flying days to April 2, the lift was finished.

Through it all the ironworkers risked their lives to help guide the helicopter and bolt the steel canisters, ranging from eight down to four tons, into place. Each canister had three prongs sticking up to guide the next piece into position once the helicopter had maneuvred it directly over top. After each lift, it took eight hours to bolt the canister with an air-operated wrench. At first the men worked from a platform that could be moved half way up the mast. Then they bolted from smaller scaffolds. They didn't wear safety harness because it would have impeded their freedom to move.

17

From the indoor observation deck in the sky pod, at 1,136 feet, the view ranges up to 100 miles. At night, the lights of Niagara Falls are clearly visible. When the view is obliterated by the weather, color patterns are projected on the clouds. Below: A visitor to the pod uses a zoom telescope that enlarges an object 200 times and gives her the impression she is moving toward it.

Looming high above the Toronto skyline, the CN Tower is hit by lightning more than 250 times a year—with no damage to the tower or its visitors.

The antenna was covered with a huge plastic radome so smooth that, with the help of some warmth from the electronic equipment, it allows no ice to form. Icing is a serious problem for towers in our latitudes. Blocks weighing up to 300 pounds are rumored to have dropped from Moscow's tower. "We had to build the whole tower so there was no place for ice to form," said architect Ned Baldwin. That meant a snow-melting system on the roof of the pod to keep it dry. Railings that could ice up were kept to a minimum.

The focal point for sightseers is the sky pod. To reach it, visitors have to cross a walkway over the railroad tracks to the tower's base, where a glass-faced elevator takes them up to the pod in 60 seconds. For the hardy who go to the highest of the three observation decks at 1,464 feet, by an elevator from the pod, the approach is gradual. From the elevator they have to climb 14 feet of stairs to a three-foot-wide platform with a glass wall, which slopes outward to let the viewer gaze straight *down* into space. Straight ahead, the view is 100 miles. And in the pod's revolving restaurant, which turns once every 90 minutes, no hostile maître d' can spoil your view. Tables on two levels seat more than 400 persons with those toward the center slightly raised.

Still, the tower has its detractors. In a letter to a newspaper, artist William Kurelek urged Torontonians to "guard against coming to a bad end because of vanity." Anglican Archdeacon Arthur Brown asked what the antenna would communicate: "Robbery, violence, sex in our television programming? Instant views of man's inhumanity from all parts of the globe?"

However, artist Harold Town wrote a rave review after a visit: "I was standing on something all Canadian, an engineering triumph—a tower built faster and better than any other in the world and as casually as a salesman demonstrating the erection of a pup tent."

As for the man on the street, he never had any doubts. "It's funny how some things spontaneously catch the public's imagination," wrote Peter Worthington, editor of *The Toronto Sun*. "... Bravo CN Tower—and all of you who put it there!"

# Canada's CANDU: A Nuclear Triumph

By Robert Collins

It stands gleaming and smokeless on the shore of Lake Ontario, like some harbinger of the future—which it is. One of the largest nuclear plants on earth, the Pickering Generating Station represents tomorrow's answer to the energy crisis. Nuclear reactors may be supplying half of Canada's electricity by the year 2000.

The white-domed buildings housing four reactors silently belie the awesome force inside them. A muted whine and a few flags of steam are the only signs of power. Fish jump playfully in the plant's warm, clean effluent. Eighty-one acres of park and wildlife sanctuary roll westward toward Toronto, 20 miles away. Yet inside Pickering's four reactors lie 464 tons of uranium—the energy equivalent of ten million tons of coal. They can generate 2,160,000 kilowatts of electricity, enough to supply 1.7 million homes.

Pickering is a genuine Canadian success story. Each year 100,000 visitors from around the globe come to admire these Canadian-designed CANDU (for Canada Deuterium Uranium) reactors, which many now believe provide the world's best method of generating nuclear energy. Whatever the

Visitors to the Pickering Generating
Station, on the shore of Lake Ontario, can picnic, watch birdlife or
toboggan on slopes near the CANDU
reactor domes. So safe is CANDU that
a person who stood at the boundary
of the Pickering grounds, day and
night for a year, would receive no
more radiation than on a return flight
across Canada.

Technicians in the Pickering control room closely monitor the power generating process with the aid of eight digital computers—two for each of the four CANDU reactors at the station.

A worker prepares a 50-pound uranium fuel bundle for insertion into one of four calandrias at Pickering. Each bundle contains the energy equivalent of 450 tons of coal.

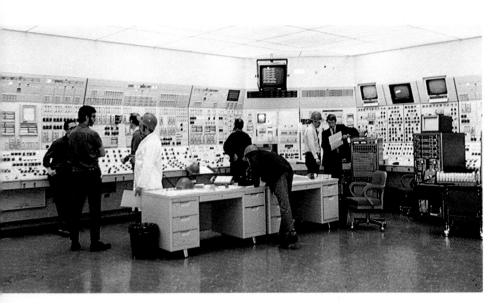

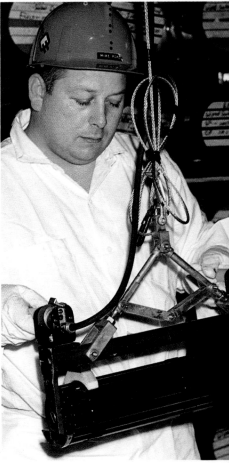

method, nuclear power is likely to become a major energy source over the next few decades. Oil and natural gas supplies are dwindling and, for sheer efficiency, nuclear energy is unbeatable: a pound of oil, two kwh; a pound of uranium, 29,000 kwh. Nuclear power is also cheap: over a 30-year period (allowing time to work off a nuclear plant's high capital cost) it comes out cheaper than coal.

To most of us, nuclear power is vaguely sinister. It's silent and invisible; we know it can kill. Just how does it work?

It begins with the tiny atom, and its nucleus of particles, called protons and neutrons. When an escaping neutron strikes the nucleus of a uranium atom, that atom splits ("fissions"), causing an enormous release of energy. Natural fission goes on in uranium all the time. But, traveling at up to 26,000 miles per second, the escaping neutrons generally pass right through other atoms without hitting the nucleus. Thus they don't split enough atoms to start a chain reaction. For that, the uranium must be surrounded by a "moderator"—water,

for example. The uranium neutrons then ricochet against the moderator atoms, slowing down, then bouncing back into the uranium fuel and splitting atoms. Given enough fuel, this sets up a chain reaction, providing steady heat. The heat turns water into steam that drives turbine generators to produce electricity.

Two main features set CANDU apart from other nuclear power systems. First, to hold the fuel and main coolant, CANDU uses hundreds of tubes rather than a single, large and harder to replace vessel. Heavy water once leaked from 69 pressure tubes of two Pickering reactors. Yet there was no danger to employes or the public, and the faulty tubes were easily replaced.

Second, CANDU plants are moderated by "heavy" water, which looks and tastes like ordinary water but has different freezing and boiling points. The best of all moderators, it enables CANDU plants to get a chain reaction out of natural uranium. The U.S. Light Water Reactors (LWRs) require enriched uranium. That means using about

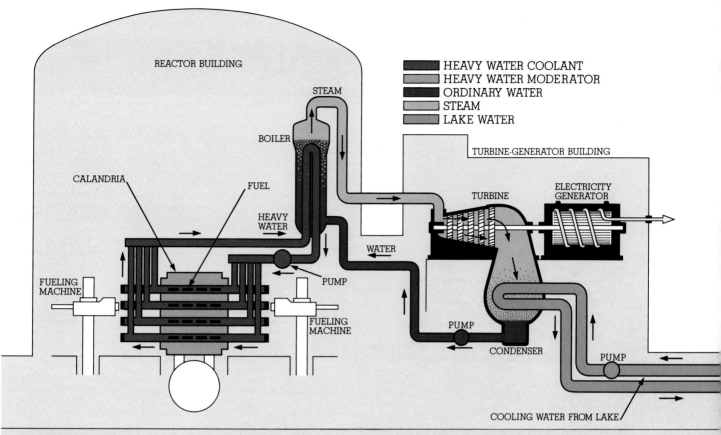

REACTOR BUILDING

STEAM

BOILER

CALANDRIA

FUEL

HEAVY WATER

FUELING MACHINE

PUMP

FUELING MACHINE

HEAVY WATER COOLANT
HEAVY WATER MODERATOR
ORDINARY WATER
STEAM
LAKE WATER

TURBINE-GENERATOR BUILDING

TURBINE

ELECTRICITY GENERATOR

WATER

PUMP

CONDENSER

PUMP

COOLING WATER FROM LAKE

·In the calandria, the heart of the CANDU reactor, heat is produced by nuclear fission of uranium fuel. Heavy water transfers the heat to 12 boilers (only one is shown here) and ordinary water is turned into steam for the turbines that generate electricity. After leaving the boilers, the heavy water is pumped into the calandria as a coolant. The steam that drives the turbines is condensed by cool lake water and piped back to the boilers to be recycled.

twice as much uranium as a CANDU reactor to produce the same amount of power—one reason why more and more countries are taking a second look at Canada's technology.

Let's examine CANDU, at the $750-million Pickering plant owned and operated by Ontario Hydro. This is the showpiece of an Atomic Energy of Canada Limited (AECL) program started in World War II. Then Canada began nuclear research in partnership with Britain and the United States, building a reactor at Chalk River, Ont.

Forced to go its own way after the war, Canada expanded the Chalk River plant, then in 1962 opened a nuclear power demonstration plant at Rolphton, Ont. Five years later, our first full-scale nuclear power station started up at Douglas Point, Ont. In 1971 AECL and Hydro-Québec completed Gentilly I near Trois-Rivières. That same year, Pickering went into operation.

To that point, Canada's unproven program had received scant attention abroad. The United States with its light-water reactors had the lion's share of world business. Pickering began to change that, as delegations arrived from around the world.

They found, as I did, a plant bristling with safety regulations. Helmets and identification badges containing a strip of film to register radiation are mandatory for everyone. All badges are regularly monitored for radiation levels and each employe carries a gauge to measure his own rate of exposure.

There has never been a radiation accident at Pickering. Men are constantly grooming the floors with a scrubber-vacuum machine. Employes wear freshly laundered working clothes every day. On leaving they walk through a contaminant detector that flies into a noisy fit at the slightest provocation.

As we moved through various zones, we thrust our hands and feet into monitors. Any fragment of radioactive dust would have sounded an alarm. In high-risk zones, blackboards carry up-to-the-minute radiation counts. Racks of disposable paper coveralls, rubber gloves and foot rubbers stand ready for use in the reactor buildings. Only qualified men enter the reactors, wearing masks and inflated plastic suits fed with fresh air through hoses from outside.

The heart of each CANDU reactor is the calandria, a massive 665-ton steel drum. Riddled with 390 horizontal fuel channels, it resembles a mighty Swiss cheese. Each channel houses a pressure tube containing 12 fuel bundles, lying end to end. A bundle consists of 28 half-inch diameter tubes of a corrosion-resistant alloy, each filled with uranium-dioxide pellets.

The calandria is housed in a concrete vault from four to eleven feet thick. Around it, the concrete walls of the reactor building are four feet thick. All four reactors are connected to a vacuum building—one with lower-than-atmospheric pressure. This massive structure, set on steel piles driven into bedrock, is topped with a storage tank holding more than two million gallons of water. If an accident in the reactor building raised atmospheric pressure up to one pound per square inch, valves would release the pressure into the vacuum building. If pressure in the vacuum building hit *six* pounds per square inch, water would spray down, condensing any steam and reducing the danger.

Nothing can happen in a CANDU reactor until 342 tons of moderator are pumped into the calandria. (This moderator never touches the fuel, which is sealed off with its coolant in a separate, insulated system.) Now the chain reaction begins. As billions of atoms split, the temperature of the uranium core builds as high as 2,000°C. The coolant water circulates around the fuel bundles and, pressurized to prevent boiling, leaves the reactor at 293°C. to move into a heat exchanger where ordinary water is turned into steam for the turbines.

What if the reactor somehow ran amok? A chain reaction can be slowed by lowering cadmium-steel shutoff rods into the calandria, to absorb neutrons. Or it can be stopped dead in 30 seconds simply by draining the moderator into a dump tank underneath. No moderator, no reaction. The chance of a major accident has been calculated at one in a million years.

But what if there *were* a major accident—say, a failure of all coolant systems, which would permit the hot fuel to melt right through the reactor into the earth and release poisonous fumes into the atmosphere? Virtually impossible, says the AECL. The fuel channels would still be surrounded by 342 tons of relatively cool (68°C.) heavy-water moderator, shielded in turn by a similar quantity of light water, which would absorb the heat.

What if an aircraft piled into this fortress of a plant? "You'd just have a badly damaged airplane," says Hydro.

What about leaks of radioactive gases into the atmosphere? The chances are remote. The air pressure inside a reactor is lower than outside (workers enter through an airlock) so air tends to seep *in*. Nevertheless, detectors constantly monitor the outside atmosphere for radiation leaks.

Suppose a crank sneaked in to turn radiation loose. Difficult, says Ontario Hydro, because each reactor can be opened only with a special key obtained from the control room, and only when the power is off. Nevertheless, a commando-type force could conceivably seize a plant and extract radioactive fuel bundles. What then?

"Anyone handling such bundles without protection would get a lethal dose of radiation," says an AECL engineer. "But the radius of a lethal dose drops off rapidly. If you wanted to menace the public, the fuel would have to be scattered into the atmosphere. This would be very difficult because the fuel pellets are highly compressed."

What *is* a concern, Hydro and the AECL admit, is the disposal of burned-out, but still radioactive, fuel bundles. At present, Hydro simply stores them.

Cesium 137 and strontium 90, both biologically dangerous ingredients, need about 1,000 years to decay to a harmless level; highly dangerous plutonium 239, at least 800,000 years. Machines pluck a few of the spent bundles out of the calandrias every day and send them through an underground tunnel into a concrete water bay which looks like an indoor swimming pool. There, with water shielding the radiation, they cool off.

By 2000 there may be enough nuclear wastes in Canada to cover a football field to a depth of 13 feet. The AECL will likely choose a three-phase disposal program: hold the wastes in water during the cooling period; then seal them in steel or other metal and put them in well-ventilated concrete bunkers from which they can be retrieved if we wish to reprocess the plutonium; some day, bury them in some impermeable geological structure.

Perhaps the greatest peril is the so-called "pluto-

nium curse." Plutonium is a by-product of nuclear fission. The amount remaining in spent fuel has a potential energy yield nearly equal to that of the original uranium, so future energy conservation will probably dictate that it be recycled. But plutonium is a highly toxic material in any form. It is deadly if inhaled, or if it enters the bloodstream. Many fear that as supplies of extracted plutonium increase, there will be a constant danger of accidents or theft. Transportation and storage of nuclear wastes, and access to plutonium, will demand safeguards beyond anything yet devised.

If we can deal with these awesome problems, the future looks bright for nuclear power. As nuclear energy becomes more important, we have in the CANDU system a proven model on which to build. Among the hopes, fears and uncertainties of a world entering the nuclear age, the CANDU story is emerging as a singular triumph.

# "By His Genius Men Sail Unafraid"

### By Ormond Raby

Shortly before Christmas 1906, a group of technicians at an experimental radio station near Boston, Massachusetts, were readying their equipment for the world's first radio broadcast. Suddenly, electric signaling devices fitted under their hats began an urgent "beep." The inventor of the tiny receivers—and of much of the transmission equipment that would make the broadcast possible—was in trouble.

Racing outside, they found their chief—his ample girth broadened by a hearty meal—stuck in the access hole of a 400-foot transmitting tower. Though they pushed and pulled, nothing would budge him. Finally, to the accompaniment of a barrage of oaths, they removed his vest and shirt, took off his trousers and, smothering his humiliation with axle grease, slid him out.

The ridiculous and the sublime were a constant part of the stormy career of Reginald Aubrey Fessenden, Canada's most extraordinary inventor. Though history books credit Marconi with radio's invention, Marconi's equipment was limited to broadcasting the Morse code. It took Fessenden to find the way to transmit the human voice across the Atlantic. Yet despite his genius—he was to pioneer the turboelectric drive, the electric gyroscope, the Fathometer and many other sea-safety devices—Fessenden is still unknown to many Canadians. For many years the *Encyclopedia Canadiana* dismissed his work in five lines—under an entry for his journalist mother, Clementina, who pioneered the observance of Empire Day in Canada. Fessenden's scientific contemporaries, however, were certainly aware of his presence. He towered well over six feet, was ginger-haired, bearded and haughty.

His restless mind was always at work. Many of his ideas came while walking alone in the woods, or out on the water. Colleagues recall seeing him floating on the sea, hat over his eyes, a cigar in his mouth, an ashtray balanced on his chest—thinking. Simple inventions like his aluminum tea bag and electrically amplified violin were tackled with high glee, and gave him the opportunity to refuel for the greater tasks on his mind.

Necessity, too, was often the mother of his inventions. When the paper mountain begat by his work threatened to engulf him, he devised a system of "microphotography." In later life he often marveled that the records of his 500 inventions could be stored in a box no larger than his hand.

Born in Bolton, Que., in 1866, he was the son of a poor Anglican minister and grandson of an equally impoverished inventor, Edward Trenholme. The parsonage had few worldly goods but it boasted an extensive library. By the time he was six, Fessenden had read the *Arabian Nights*. A year later, he was partway through Gibbon's *Decline and Fall of the Roman Empire*. At 11, already on speaking terms with destiny, he wrote his mother: "I think as God has made me beat boys of 18 in my studies, He means me to be of use in the way of learning."

Intellectually, life was a romp for Fessenden. As a student at Bishop's College in Lennoxville, Que., he studied at night and taught mathematics, Greek and French during the day. Tiring of Bishop's, he left before taking his degree, and went to teach in Bermuda, where he fell in love with Helen May Trott, the daughter of a well-to-do planter. In 1886, determined to make a name for himself in science and earn enough to support his wife-to-be, he quit his teaching post and set out to work with Thomas Edison in New York.

Persistence landed him a job in Edison's laboratories where incandescent light and the phonograph had already been created. Soon he was producing with the best of them, noting phenomena that others did not even suspect. He disputed with Lord Kelvin, a world authority on electricity, over the

In 1906, from this radio shack at Brant Rock in Massachusetts, inventor Reginald Fessenden made the first transatlantic voice transmission and the first radio broadcast. When Fessenden moved, it was usually at a half-run, a black Inverness cape flowing from his huge shoulders. He appeared, a friend said, "to come at you from down both sides of the street at once."

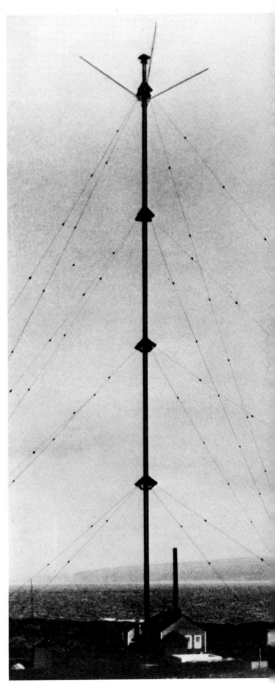

reason for rubber's elasticity. Kelvin believed that rubber particles stuck together because of the force of gravitation, not electricity. Young Fessenden thought the exact opposite, and proved his case in findings published later in a scientific magazine. After observing his research, an admiring fellow worker enthused: "When he takes hold of an idea, his mind glimpses it as if looking through a thousand windows."

Outside the laboratory, Fessenden could be as helpless as a babe in arms. Near the end of his employment with Edison, when the company was on the verge of bankruptcy, he asked Helen to marry him, first squandering his savings on a brooch and a Tiffany diamond. After the wedding when they sat in Central Park, hungry and without lodging, he confessed that he had forgotten to include such necessities in his planning.

Poverty pursued him for much of his life because he failed to exploit the money-making potential of his inventions properly on his own behalf. In 1897, only two years after Roentgen discovered X rays, Fessenden helped build the world's most powerful X-ray machine which could be used in delicate eye surgery, to find clues to cancer and, at the Carnegie steelworks in Pittsburgh, to trace hidden defects in armor plate. Astounded at his all-round genius, Andrew Carnegie offered Fessenden a partnership on two occasions, but he turned it down. To his colleagues' amazement, he set up a company to manufacture pocket X-ray toys, then wasted his time by peddling the playthings at Ontario fall fairs.

After leaving Edison, Fessenden returned to teaching. At Pittsburgh University he soon became the leading electrical engineering lecturer of his day. There, the question he had puzzled over since Bell's invention of the telephone kept coming to mind. "Why wires?" he asked himself. Sending voice along a wire was child's play compared to firing it electrically into space and forcing it to travel in a set direction. To find it again at the receiving end would be like seeking the proverbial needle in a haystack. He accepted the challenge, scrapped all prior knowledge in the field—including the mathematics—and plunged ahead.

In 1899 voicelike sounds whined through the air the length of his laboratory. Though excited, Fessenden felt the pressure of Marconi's already successful attempts to transmit Morse code several miles without wires. He quit his job, and with a contract from the U.S. Weather Bureau, set up an experimental wireless telegraphy station on Cobb Island in the Potomac to transmit weather reports in Morse to Washington, 60 miles away.

So began one of the most madcap races in the history of science, as first Marconi then Fessenden fought to prove the impossible possible and, in the process, make a fool of each other. On December 23, 1900, Fessenden took the lead by transmitting the human voice for the first time between 50-foot transmitting towers a mile apart. The following December, Marconi sent the three dots for the letter S winging from England to Signal Hill, Nfld. Fessenden's reply was to set up the National Electric Signalling Company, with the help of two Pittsburgh millionaires. He built a colossal tower at Brant Rock, near Boston, and another on the wild, western coast of Scotland and, in January 1906, made the first *two-way* broadcast in Morse across the Atlantic.

Determined to further outsmart Marconi, Fessenden established a testing station at Plymouth, 11 miles from Brant Rock, and began further experimental voice transmissions. He added the heterodyne to his growing list of inventions and could henceforth transmit and receive on the same aerial—and prevent atmospheric noises from drowning his signals. Then, in November 1906, he received a startling message from his assistant in Scotland. "At four o'clock in the morning," it read, "I was listening for telegraph signals from Brant Rock when, to my astonishment, I heard the voice of Mr. Stein telling the operators at Plymouth how to run the dynamos. . . ." The first transatlantic voice transmission had taken place by accident!

Elated, Fessenden announced a public demonstration, but before it could be staged, the tower in Scotland was destroyed in a storm. Undaunted, he decided to broadcast the world's first radio show, to the ships of the United Fruit Company, which he had equipped with radio receivers.

On Christmas Eve all was ready. A call signal was sent out in Morse, then Fessenden stepped to the microphone and announced the program. An operator switched on an Edison phonograph and Handel's "Largo" squealed out over the airwaves. An assistant, who fancied himself a singer, cleared his throat, opened his mouth, and froze—the world's first case of "mike fright." Fessenden leaped into the breach with a violin and vocal rendering of "O, Holy Night." A Bible text followed: "Glory to God in the highest and on earth peace and goodwill to all men." Then Fessenden rounded off the show by wishing his listeners a "Merry Christmas."

Within days, reports arrived from ships testifying to the broadcast's success. But Fessenden's triumph was shortlived. Marconi, ever shrewd, had obtained exclusive rights for radio transmission throughout the British Empire. Fessenden could not secure a permit to build so much as a tower in his native land. Then, in a dispute with his backers, he was fired. Going to court, he was told that he had surrendered title to his inventions as a condition of employment. For the next two decades, scarcely a week passed that he was not in court or preparing evidence for seemingly unending litigation.

Just when he was beginning to doubt if he would ever succeed, his old enemy, the Atlantic, provided him with a greater challenge. On the night of April 15, 1912, an iceberg holed and sank *Titanic*. Fessenden was doubly horrified. The means to prevent such disasters had existed all along. He had bounced radio waves off the ionosphere, why not off icebergs, or any underwater obstruction, to fix the relative position of obstacles in the path of a speeding ship?

Fessenden in full flight, running down the solution to a problem, was impossible to resist. Persuading the Submarine Signal Company to put him on staff, he was off to Newfoundland's Grand Banks within weeks to test working models of his "submarine oscillator." Out of this came an instrument for detecting the proximity of icebergs, and for determining the depth of water beneath a ship by measuring the time between the emission of an oscillator signal and its return as an echo.

By the start of World War I, Fessenden was well primed to carry out a personal vendetta against the Germans. Offering his services to Canada—including his inventions at no cost—he advanced on London sure that he had a solution to just about every problem confronting the Allies.

He took with him workable plans for detecting enemy artillery, and a new type of gunsight. When German zeppelins began bombing London, he reminded the British that a few years before he had shown them a way of detecting aircraft using a direction-finding antenna he had invented. No sooner was this device put into operation than he set to work on another problem. German submarines were sinking Allied transports almost at will. A means of dropping depth charges with accuracy had to be found—and fast.

After months of frantic activity—including time submerged in a submarine under actual battle con-

Adam Stein (standing) and Charles
Pannill (at the telegraph key) were
Reginald Fessenden's assistants
at Brant Rock. The supremely confident
Fessenden (right) often told them:
"Don't try to think. Leave that to me."

ditions—he came up with an echo-sounding device
to locate submarines underwater. The forerunner
of today's sophisticated sonar, it was one of the
major scientific achievements that helped ensure
Allied victory.

With peace in Europe, Fessenden waded into
his own war at home. Huge corporations were now
using his 300 radio patents and the contests hard-
ened, draining Fessenden's energy though not
damping his inventive fires. The echo sounder
evolved into the Fathometer and captains termed
it the single most important safety aid at sea. In
1919 he developed an early television apparatus,
proving that radio waves were the bridge needed
to transmit both voice and pictures. Then, in 1928,
he accepted an out-of-court settlement with the
Radio Trust of America. The struggle, however,
was crowned with typical Fessenden luck—bitter-
sweet: he gained almost a million dollars but lost
his health.

Now, in a final four years passed in the near-soli-
tude of his Bermuda home, the big body gradually
wearied. Stroke followed stroke, but his brain
remained active to the last. Immersing himself in
a "mental shower bath," he began writing a book
on the Greek philosophers and on Ptolemy who
followed, and he sounded a warning for contemporary society. "For hundreds of years the Ptolemies
endowed the scholars of Egypt, catering to their
every need. Yet from all this government paternal-
ism emerged not one original work of any importance. I see it happening today in all aspects of our
life. The elimination of self-responsibility and
incentive will inevitably produce a condition analo-
gous to the Dark Ages."

Fessenden died on July 22, 1932. His son, Reginald Kennelly Fessenden, provided a fitting epitaph:
*By his genius distant lands converse, and men sail un-
afraid upon the deep.*

# One Grade Only and That the Best

By Robert Collins

Samuel McLaughlin (standing) took over the family's Oshawa carriage business from his father, Robert (left), and with the help of his brother, George (right), directed the firm's switch from horse-drawn vehicles to motorcars. McLaughlin calenders (below: 1906, 1907, 1908) first scorned the automobile as a troublesome hazard, then touted it as "safe, strong and silent."

When I first met Robert Samuel McLaughlin he was sitting in his big office in Oshawa, Ont., chairman of General Motors of Canada, 98 years old and brisk as a jaybird. I complimented him on his obvious good health. "I exercise, hard, every morning," he said, with a gravelly laugh. "Here, feel my arm!" The biceps was firm. He thwacked his stomach with a blow that made me wince.

With the same gusto "Mr. Sam" went on to his 100th birthday on September 8, 1971. Everybody sent congratulations, from the Queen Mother to a Niagara Falls peachpicker and former blacksmith whose letter began "Dear Friend Sam . . ." When he died, four months later, every major newspaper in the land paid tribute and 20,000 mourners filed past his coffin. For Mr. Sam was that rarity: a man who was truly liked and genuinely loved.

His was the classic tale of the village boy, apprenticed in his father's carriage shop, who soared to success on such virtues as hard work and fair dealing. As founder of General Motors of Canada, he was this country's only automobile tycoon, a millionaire many times over who gave away at least $25 million in his lifetime.

Chrysler, Olds, Chevrolet—the *men,* not the cars—were his buddies, for McLaughlin was in at the birth of the North American auto industry. Governor-General Alexander of Tunis was a close friend and shooting companion. Millionaire industrialist E. P. Taylor was "Eddie," and C. D. Howe, the domineering politician of the '40s and '50s, was "Clarence."

But Sam also hobnobbed with librarians, storekeepers, garbage men and children. "Don't build a stone wall around me, I'm a person and I like people," he told a friend. In later life, he would throw open his 12-acre estate to visitors, and sometimes wandered among them, short and stocky, hat pulled low over his spectacles, head wreathed in clouds of Barking Dog Pipe Mixture. "Want to see the house?" he'd rasp, and lead some astonished stranger through his 45-room mansion.

Other afternoons, driven in his Buick or his $16,000 nine-passenger Cadillac, Mr. Sam went out to revel in the countryside. "Look, girls!" he'd urge his nurse, Margaret Nelson, or his secretary, Betty McMullen. "Look at that snow with the open water cutting through it! Isn't that beautiful?" And he persisted until they agreed it *was.*

Often on these drives, he would stop in Ennis-

Young Sam McLaughlin bicycled almost daily, sometimes pedaling the 60-mile round trip between Oshawa and Toronto. At county fairs he competed in bike races, winning numerous trophies—and so many pickle jars that, he once claimed, he had to get married to use them all.

killen, a village 20 miles northeast of Oshawa, where his boyhood home had been and where, as the third son of a carriage maker, he got an early introduction to his father's business. Robert McLaughlin, or "The Governor," as the boys called their father, was scrupulously fair, used only the finest upholstery in his work, the truest grain of wood, and imported Norway iron that cost five times more than any other. As an elder in the Presbyterian church, he sent his sons to Sunday school with freshly shined shoes, made them promise not to drink or smoke before they were 21, not to prowl the streets at night, and never *ever* to play poker.

When Sam finished high school at 15, he didn't intend to work for his father who, by this time, had expanded into Oshawa. His brother George, who did, reported it was no picnic. Brother Jack, a graduate chemist from the University of Toronto, was already on the way to his life's achievement: inventing the pale ginger ale that came to be called Canada Dry, and founding the company of that name. Sam thought of being a hardware merchant, lawyer, draftsman or maybe a champion bike rider.

But in 1887, after Jack wrote him a stern letter about family responsibilities, Sam did become an apprentice upholsterer and floor sweeper in the family firm. He worked Monday through Saturday from seven to seven for $3 a week less $2.50 room and board. When he'd learned to stitch, make cushions and was a journeyman at $1.75 a day, he quit to find out if he could hold a job where he wasn't the boss' son. He worked for three carriage companies in New York State, getting top wages and the latest knowledge of production and design, and came home with 15 cents to become foreman of the family business. He was 30 and a partner before he had the nerve to go to work at 8 a.m. "I was so guilt-ridden that I'd sneak in through the back door," he confessed later.

Soon, with Sam designing carriages and sleighs, the McLaughlins offered 143 models. Quebec liked the Concord body; Ontario favored boxlike shapes; the West called for buckboards and democrats; city people and Maritimers demanded the graceful phaetons, Stanhopes and fringe-top surreys. Often Sam worked after midnight, redrawing a design until he liked it.

Sam McLaughlin sits outside his Oshawa home in a 1908 McLaughlin Model F, one of the first motorcars made in Canada. The Model F sold for about $1,200—only 154 were manufactured—and could reach a top speed of 30 miles an hour.

Then, sputtering and snorting down the road, came the horseless carriage. (It had been around Canada since 1866 when Rev. Georges Belcourt of Rustico, P.E.I., drove his single-seated steam wagon for a half mile at an outdoor tea party.) And though the horseless was treated as a plague to be wiped out, to those with vision it was irresistible. Sam McLaughlin fell in love with the automobile after his first ride. "Right then, I knew we had to get a car company," he recalled afterward.

Unable to convince the Governor, who regarded the horseless as an instrument of the devil, Sam went on "vacation" to see the Pierce-Arrow, Thomas-Flyer, Peerless, Reo and Jackson auto plants in the United States. One day in a hotel dining room he met an old carriage-making friend,

35

William C. Durant, now the new boss of Buick. McLaughlin explained he was looking for a deal to make cars in Canada.

"If you don't find the car you want, come and see me," Durant advised. In a few weeks, Sam did.

When McLaughlin approached him, the imaginative Durant was making a lasting mark on the auto industry. Over the next ten years he put Buick into the black, established General Motors (acquiring Oldsmobile, Oakland and Cadillac and a score of other auto companies in the process) and started Chevrolet. He brought Charles Nash into the business. Nash in turn hired Walter Chrysler and went on to found the Nash Motor Company (later American Motors). Such was the man who now stood ready to help the McLaughlins.

Sam liked the idea of producing a Canadian version of Buick but they couldn't agree on the financial terms. Stubbornly, McLaughlin went home to make an all-Canadian car. His brother George was enthusiastic and the Governor was glumly resigned to it all. They fitted a shop with lathes, planers, shapers, everything necessary to make the first 100 models. Then their engineer went down with pleurisy. Sam wired Durant: could they borrow an engineer?

In reply, Durant, a small spare man with dark-brown piercing eyes, arrived with two top executives the next day. He pointed out that hundreds of small auto firms were going bankrupt; that volume production was the only route to survival. He offered Canadian rights to the Buick engine if the McLaughlins would design and build the bodies. "I think *that* will work," Sam said with satisfaction. In five minutes they drew up a one-page contract that lasted 15 years. The next year, 1908, the McLaughlins' company calendar did an abrupt about-face: instead of poking fun at the horseless, it showed cars and carriages as congenial partners.

The cherry-red McLaughlin-Buick benefited from the same meticulous care that had gone into the early carriages. Sam imported upholstery from England, mahogany for the dashboard from East Africa, white ash from Quebec and western Ontario for the bodies. He put two coats of paint on the wheels, and when his bookkeepers questioned such an expense, McLaughlin quoted the family motto, as he did thousands more times during his life: "One Grade Only and That the Best." The touch was so distinctive that one of his cars went on display in New York, at the U.S. company's request. Admiring crowds wondered where they could buy one like it, impelling a Buick executive to snap: "Get that thing out of here! It's not like *our* Buick!"

By now president of the thriving McLaughlin company and a director of U.S. General Motors, Sam was enjoying his new wealth. In 1899 he had married Adelaide Mowbray, whom he'd met in church. One day he drove around Oshawa with Charlie Nash to pick a new homesite. He paused before a green 12-acre tract on what were then the town's northern outskirts.

"If you can buy that, take it," cried Nash. McLaughlin did, and built Parkwood, with its 45 rooms, bowling alley, art gallery, barbershop, ballroom, elevator, pipe organ, secret stairway, and garden teahouse with its own full-fledged kitchen.

The McLaughlins still made carriages but business was waning. In 1915 Sam met Durant in New York over lunch and discussed Billy's newest creation, Chevrolet. Durant needed a Canadian distributor. Was Sam interested? McLaughlin was, but he couldn't handle another car and keep the carriage business. What would the Governor say to that? "You tell him, Sam," George said that night. "I can't face him."

Painfully, Sam told his father that the McLaughlins had to go wholly into motorcars if they were

The automobile made McLaughlin a millionaire many times over, yet the horse always held a special place in his heart. Left: Samuel McLaughlin on his 79th birthday. Below: During the Second World War, when gasoline was rationed and his factories were turning out military vehicles, McLaughlin saved fuel by traveling in a horse-drawn buggy. A three-time winner of the King's Plate, McLaughlin (holding King's Cup) discusses his horse Horometer's win in 1934 with Governor-General Lord Bessborough.

Tycoon E. P. Taylor called Samuel McLaughlin a "man with a voice of brass, a body of iron and a heart of gold." "Mr. Sam," as he was affectionately known, vowed that he would remain at his desk as long as he could be of "some value" to General Motors. He was there almost until his death at 100.

to survive. "I'm about through," the Governor said quietly. "Do what you think best." In a matter of weeks the carriage business was sold.

Within three years came another painful decision: sale to General Motors. Sam had five daughters but no sons. Neither George nor his sons wanted to continue. The Buick contract would soon expire, and Sam could never survive on his own. But if he sold to General Motors, Oshawa would always have its motor industry. So in 1918 he closed the deal, but at General Motors' request stayed as president of the Canadian corporation and, until 1967, as a director of the parent.

Sam was never the type to loaf. He had always been active and, at one time or another, had ridden on bicycle and horseback, swum, hunted, fished, golfed, curled, bowled, and played lacrosse, croquet, billiards and even a mean game of dominoes. Now he variously became a director in a half-dozen different companies, raised racehorses which, over the years, won three King's Plates and hundreds of ribbons, owned a prizewinning yacht and a 21-foot schooner, became honorary colonel of the Ontario Regiment, and crossed the Atlantic 26 times. And yet he remained, basically, the country boy from Enniskillen. Handed the traditional silver shovel for yet another sod-turning ceremony, McLaughlin once said, "I wish I had a *real* spade, like we used for digging potatoes when I was a boy."

In his lifetime, he gave away more money than anyone will ever know about, and his gifts were things people could use. He donated $500,000 to the University of Montreal and provided entire buildings for Queen's University, York University, the University of Guelph, the YWCA, the Girl Guides and the Oshawa General Hospital. He gave Toronto its planetarium; Oshawa its public library; two camps to the Boy Scouts; and enabled more than 500 Canadian doctors to study overseas.

In the latter days, with his wife of nearly 60 years and most of his old friends dead, Mr. Sam worked hard at keeping in touch. He gave many private dinners and an annual Chrysanthemum Tea, when hundreds of local people visited Parkwood. He met Queen Mother Elizabeth. ("She's the sweetest thing you've ever seen," he confided.) Though he bantered with everyone, Sam never abandoned his courtly manners. He apologized if even the mildest expletive slipped out in front of a stranger. He always removed his hat in an elevator, and he never issued an order without saying "please." From his nurse, who'd served him 25 years, to his senior gardener, with him for 50 years, the Parkwood staff adored him. Almost to the end, he continued

Sam McLaughlin's fascination with astronomy led him to donate $2 million for the building in Toronto of the McLaughlin Planetarium, one of many gifts he made to charities and other causes. At Parkwood, his 12-acre Oshawa estate, McLaughlin surrounded himself with superb gardens and valuable antiques—including this Steinway grand piano built in Germany.

to go to the office to attend to his business and charity affairs. "My old head won't let go," he said in 1968.

But his body finally let him down—after 84 working years—and he was buried in a coffin he'd chosen himself, made from the white ash and the metal tinted in "London Smoke" shade that once went into McLaughlin cars and carriages.

He left an estate of $37 million, with generous bequests. But anyone who ever met him prefers to remember the vital Mr. Sam. On my second and last visit, we discussed a book I was writing on pioneer motoring in Canada. He buzzed for his pretty secretary to bring some old catalogues. An aide, lurking in the wings, sprang to get them.

"No, she'll bring 'em," said McLaughlin with a rusty chuckle. "I like to look at *her*, too!"

Then he barked, "Come around here behind the desk," and lovingly traced the designs he had created more than 60 years before. "Look at that one! And that one! They were beautiful!" And they were.

He leaned back, pipe fuming, and looked around at the memorabilia of his life: plaques, scrolls of honor, a framed photo of his father, prints of calendars that marked the McLaughlin transition from carriages to cars.

"One Grade Only and That the Best," he said softly. "That was our secret." And that was also the secret of Mr. Sam, a once-in-a-century kind of man.

# Inuit Co-ops: The Little Five-Cent Idea

### By Lois Neely

I walked up the dirt streets of Tuktoyaktuk, on the shores of the Beaufort Sea about 25 miles east of the Mackenzie River delta. It was June. Racks of beluga whale were drying under the midnight sun. A bronzed Inuit was sitting at the door of his new two-bedroom prefab home sharpening a carving tool, with which he creates salable sculptures of ivory, bone or soapstone. And in the fur shop of the Nanuk Co-op, 20 Inuit women were cutting and sewing the handsome muskrat parkas for which the co-op is famous.

In August, at Cambridge Bay, 250 miles north of the Arctic Circle, snow was already gusting across the choppy gray ocean as the Beaver floatplane taxied to the dock with its load of freshly caught char, picked up daily from Inuit fishermen around Victoria Island. At the Ekaloktotiak Co-op's fish-processing plant, I watched Inuit women gut the char; others checked the cleaned fish as the conveyor belt moved by. From here the char would be flown to markets such as Montreal and New York, where it has become a gourmet item.

In September, 1,000 miles to the east, I stood on the shore of Hudson Bay watching the last ship of the year steam into Povungnituk with snowmobiles, groceries and ammunition. And I visited the workshops of the Povungnituk Co-operative Society, one of the largest producers of Eskimo art which, although almost unknown 20 years ago, is now eagerly sought by collectors and museums. This highly successful co-op also runs a department store, a grocery, a drugstore, a restaurant, a credit union and an oil supply business.

Today there are more than 50 co-ops in the Northwest Territories and northern Quebec. Across the North, the co-op movement is bringing about an exciting social awakening and, more importantly, is giving employment and a new sense of security to the Inuit people. It was not always so.

When Peter Murdoch walked from the aircraft into Povungnituk one March morning in 1955 he was depressed by what he saw. The new Hudson's Bay Company manager was only 25, but in his seven years with the company, this Newfoundlander had been in almost every community across the eastern Arctic. Yet seldom had he encountered such desperate poverty. Many of the men were sick and couldn't hunt. Moreover, foxes were scarce and seals unobtainable at that time of year. Families had little food and little seal oil to heat their igloos. Their only income was from the sale of their soapstone sculptures.

"How much money do you need each week to look after your families?" Peter asked the men as they came into the store. A credit of $20 a week was agreed upon, and during the following weeks Peter paid that sum to each family head. At the same time he encouraged the Inuit to improve the quality of their carvings, so that they could get more money for their work.

With enough food for their families, a new optimism pervaded the community. One day the men from one camp said to Peter, "Taking soapstone out of the earth is very hard work with our little hammers and knives. If we had bigger hammers, stronger chisels, we could get stone faster and carve more and better." But a set of such tools cost $125 to $150—an astronomical sum.

"Perhaps there is a way," Peter suggested. "Through the years, when men who live together have wanted something for the whole community, they have taxed themselves." And so "the little five-cent" idea was born. Of every dollar earned, five cents were put into a camp fund. Within six weeks the camp had its equipment.

*"Is it possible that a little five-cent piece could do so much?"* the Inuit wondered. Now their thoughts turned to canoes, for in Povungnituk they had

By pooling their talents and resources, the Inuit have found not only southern markets for their unique artwork, but also a means to buy such necessities as snowmobiles.

With a lump of sealskin, an Inuit artisan gently rubs paper to produce an impression of the inked stone-cutting underneath.

only skin kayaks. So they continued the tax, buying one canoe, two canoes, five canoes, then ammunition for the whale hunt.

And then came winter, a winter of exceptional cold, and there was no way the Inuit could earn enough money to buy dollar-a-gallon kerosene to take the chill out of their igloos. "Peter, could I take some money out of the camp account to buy kerosene?" one man asked. Here was a problem. The money belonged to the camps. But who was to authorize withdrawals? Peter called the men of the camps together and explained how an election was held. And so that winter of 1955-56, in a pork-and-beans carton from the back of the store, the first ballots were cast that enabled the Inuit to administer their own financial affairs.

During the previous year, bad weather had forced the Hudson's Bay ship to leave behind a new 30-foot whaler destined for Repulse Bay. For many months the Inuit eyed that boat with its six-horsepower motor. "Think of how fast we could get to the island to mine our soapstone," they said among themselves. "And to chase the seals, and hunt and fish farther up the coast. But the boat costs $1,800. . . ." They shook their heads sadly.

In the spring one of the camp leaders came to Peter. "We have $900 in our fund. Could we borrow $900 from the Hudson's Bay and buy that whaler?"

"Why borrow from the white man?" Peter countered. "Your own people have money. Why don't you borrow from one of the other camps?" Thus, a loan agreement was signed between the Inuit of two neighboring camps and the boat was purchased. Within a month the no-interest loan was paid off. But still the self-taxing continued, going up to 20 cents, then 30 cents of every dollar earned.

In 1957, Peter Murdoch left the Hudson's Bay Company to work for the federal government. But by then the little five-cent idea—or camp accounts system—had taken a firm hold. Moreover, an important newcomer had arrived in the community—Rev. André Steinmann, an Oblate missionary who had worked in the Arctic since 1938.

In the talents of the local carvers, Father Steinmann saw an opportunity to improve the conditions of the whole community. Out of an existing carvers' association, he founded the Sculptors' Society of Povungnituk, and set out not only to get the Inuit better prices for their work but new and independent sales outlets. Accompanied by a local carver, he embarked in 1958 on a promotion tour of the United States, and came back with prepaid orders worth $3,000. Next year, the society sold $17,000 worth of sculptures in the United States.

Inuit sculptors deftly use chisel, axe and hammer to shape soapstone into art. Workers in permanent settlements tend to produce larger pieces than did their nomadic ancestors, who carved trinkets from the tusks of walrus and narwhal.

Encouraged by such success, it was ready for Father Steinmann's next suggestion: the establishment in 1960 of the Povungnituk Co-operative Society.

Meanwhile, in 1958, officers from the Department of Indian Affairs and Northern Development had discovered an abundance of arctic char—that scrappy cousin of the salmon—around Ungava Bay. For three days the government officers talked to local Inuit, explaining how the char could be sold for cash; how the trees nearby could be cut and used to build houses and boats, and surplus lumber marketed.

The Inuit listened attentively. Early the following year, the people of George River established their own co-op to sell fish and lumber, and when the first boat arrived that summer, everyone was

on the beach helping to unload fishing equipment and materials to assemble the freezer the government had supplied. When the fall ship came in, the freezer was jammed with arctic char waiting to be taken to southern points. The George River co-op was in business.

The 23 Inuit at neighboring Port Burwell, also an impoverished community, quickly followed suit, establishing a fishing co-op and general store, with one of their own men as general manager. In 1960, under the guidance of federal development officers, co-ops were formed at Coppermine, Resolute Bay (about 125 miles southeast of the Magnetic North Pole) and Grise Fiord on Ellesmere Island. Then the dogsled telegraph took over, spreading the co-op idea across the 1.5 million square miles of

Prefabricated buildings such as this co-op bank in Povungnituk, Que., have replaced tents and igloos in many Inuit communities.

the Arctic. Northern Affairs staff in the Northwest Territories studied community resources for marketable products, then helped to organize the co-ops with financing from the federal government.

Over in northern Quebec, the co-op fever spread to one community after another. At Fort Chimo, co-op member Jeannie Snowball concocted the whimsical Arctic Ookpik from sealskin, and this comic snowy owl soon captivated hearts at Canadian trade fairs around the world. In most of the co-ops, the women sewed mukluks and mittens, and handsomely embroidered parkas. There was talk of sawmills and canoe factories, construction and fuel contracts, fly-in fishing camps.

In 1967, when Peter Murdoch visited Povungnituk on a CBC Radio assignment with author Farley Mowat, he was approached by representatives from the five co-ops then existing in northern Quebec. "Will you tie our work together for us?" they asked. "We need a center in the south to market our goods, to prepare purchases for shipment north, to promote our tourist camps, and to train our managers. And we need an audit service to help us with our accounts."

In May that year, under Peter's guidance, La Fédération des Coopératives du Nouveau-Québec was formed, and the results have been impressive. The federation now has more than ten co-ops and annual sales of Eskimo art, through its Montreal depot, average about $2 million. In addition, each year the federation's fish co-ops ship some 40,000 pounds of char and salmon to southern markets. Fishing and hunting camps earn roughly $500,000 a year, and trade in federation consumer co-ops—general stores, oil leases, restaurants—bring in more than $5 million annually.

The co-ops of the Northwest Territories have had similar success. Says Aleks Sprudzs, for many years supervisor of arctic co-ops for the federal government: "Co-op revenues have had a pronounced impact all across the North. We have seen seriously depressed areas transformed into economically sound, thriving communities as a direct result of the movement."

The emergence of Inuit women as strong community leaders is another by-product of the co-op movement. One of the earliest co-ops was the all-woman Fur Garment Co-op at Aklavik which has

Inuit catch arctic char—with their hands, if necessary—in a Cape Dorset river they have dammed with rocks. Once cleaned, the pink char is hung outdoors to dry.

been a great boon to women in need of financial support. Today Inuit women are moving ahead as artists and craftswomen, turning out elegant couturier fashions at Spence Bay, studying typography and lithography in Cape Dorset to print their own books. They are also sitting on settlement councils, chairing housing committees, organizing workshops, teaching school.

Emboldened by experience in co-op management, many of the Inuit men are also breaking new ground. They now hold taxi concessions in Inuit communities and own a luxurious fishing camp near George River. "These are Eskimos who had been sweeping floors and emptying trash baskets," says Peter Murdoch. "They did not have any idea they could compete in the white man's world. Now they are *employing* the white man!"

One evening I sat by the space heater in my Povungnituk cabin chatting about the old days and the new ways of the Inuit with Isa Sivuarapik, a fine carver. "The old ways?" he recalled. "I used to hunt the seal and the fox. I was always tired, and often sick. Sometimes I would be hungry, and my children would be hungry. Now I make money

carving for the co-op and I am happier. I can still go off and hunt, but my family does not go hungry. I would not want to go back to the old ways."

Having money of his own instead of being in constant debt has given the Inuit independence. If a man doesn't like the snowmobile the local store sells, he can bring in one from Montreal or Yellowknife. Inuit girls can order the fashions of their choice from catalogues. Some families are enjoying holidays "outside," like one couple from Gjoa Haven who took their children to Hawaii.

Yet the benefits have not been only economic. Since the first Conference of Arctic Co-operatives in 1963 at Frobisher Bay, co-ops have been an energizing, unifying force, bringing together people scattered over 4,000 miles of ice and tundra to discuss their mutual problems. "The Eskimo was forced too quickly into competition with the white man," explains Kayy Gordon, longtime missionary to the Inuit. "When they couldn't keep up, they began to believe they couldn't produce like the white man. Now with the co-ops, they are learning that they can achieve things—and earn a good living—by joining hands."

45

# Enterprise at Stand Off

## By Fred McGuinness

It was a most unlikely view from a picture window: the inside of a cavernous, 80,000-square-foot factory with hard-hatted men moving purposefully amid the din of sawing and hammering. Through the window, I watched one worker approach with his forklift truck. There was a shudder as he connected with the now-completed sectional house in which I was standing; then slowly we moved toward the hangar doors. Kainai Industries' unit No. 418 was off to market. For the Blood Indians of Alberta it was another day, another factory-built house.

As No. 418 disappeared through the doors, I learned from the plant manager that its living area was 1,320 square feet, with three bedrooms, 1½ baths, a carpeted hall and plywood-panel finishing throughout. Its equipment included a furnace, a water heater, a heavily insulated underside (the finished house will have no basement) and connectors for all utilities. It would be moved in two sections and, when bolted together, would form a 24-by-55-foot home for a Lethbridge family of six.

Later that day I watched the manager and his assistant straighten out a mammoth traffic jam so that house No. 418 could be moved into the storage lot. Blocking its way was the final section of one of the largest custom orders Kainai Industries has handled. When assembled on the property of the Drumheller medium-security jail, its 14 units would comprise self-contained living arrangements for 55 persons: single-occupancy bedrooms, dining facilities, baths, toilets, showers, washers and dryers, and a large open recreation room. The contract price on the "instant hoosegow," as the Indians called it, was more than $100,000.

Manned and run by Blood Indians near Stand Off, 30 miles southwest of Lethbridge, Kainai Industries is as striking physically as it is socially. The huge red-sided, silver-roofed steel building sits in isolation in rolling foothills, with the white-tipped Rockies for a background. Its principal products are two- and three-bedroom ready-to-move houses. Built to conform to the National Building Code, they leave the plant in 12-foot sections and, when delivered, sell for more than $15,000. This plant and its payroll represent a giant magnet, drawing visitors from all over North America to study this unique enterprise, and attracting to the tiny village of Stand Off social and commercial amenities which now include a $360,000 sports center, a newspaper, a radio service, a supermarket—all owned and operated by Blood Indians.

Three miles from the plant, Stand Off and its inhabitants are going through a revolutionary transition. A hundred years ago, Stand Off was of great historical significance. American whiskey traders used it as a base for sales of their rotgut liquor, reducing the Bloods from a once-proud people to a race of derelicts who sold their furs and guns for drink. The town's name derives from a skirmish in the very early 1870s, in which the traders were able to "stand off" U.S. Sheriff Charles D. Hard and his deputies from Montana (for then Canada had no police on the Prairies). Word of the fighting eventually reached Ottawa and spurred formation of the North West Mounted Police in 1873. Once the Mounties had driven the traders out, wise leaders of the Bloods were able to restore dignity to their people.

The Bloods have long been noted for their enterprise, and their willingness to coöperate with the white man—on the right terms. This heritage springs from a canny decision made in the early 1900s by Head Chief Crop Eared Wolf. When settlers pressured him to sell part of the 352,600-acre reserve, the wise old man rendered his judgment in graphic fashion. Picking up a handful of dirt in one hand, a handful of grass in the other, he declared: "The grass is for sale—but not the land."

Head Chief Crop Eared Wolf (seated, far right) spoke for the Bloods in the early 1900s when they were urged to sell land near Stand Off, Alta. Said the chief: "The grass is for sale—but not the land." Like him, today's Bloods are hard-headed businessmen: Kainai Industries, the tribe's house-building enterprise, earns more than $5 million annually. Below: Traditional garb on the Blood reserve near Stand Off.

On July 10, 1971, at Kainai's official opening, with
Prime Minister Pierre Trudeau present, Head Chief
Jim Shot Both Sides added some philosophy of
his own to his grandfather's memorable utterance:
"Ownership and control," he declared, "are the
keys to our social, cultural, economic and spiritual
survival."

The Bloods began this program of ownership,
control and coöperation early in the 1880s. Long
before the sodbusters learned the fertility of the
virgin plains, the Bloods had discovered it for themselves. Tribal records show that in 1882 they stored
70,000 pounds of potatoes and almost as many
turnips for winter provisions. Within a few years
they had added wheat, oats and barley to their regular crops. In 1894 the Bloods traded some of their
wiry mustangs for 35 head of cattle, the foundation
of a herd which now numbers more than 7,000.
Their first commercial contract was signed in 1891
when Chief Moon agreed to supply 40 tons of hay
to the Stand Off detachment of the NWMP, and
a year later Blood teamsters and laborers filled a
100-ton coal order from mines along the St. Mary
River.

In the years that followed, other members of
the tribe became mail carriers, scouts and log cut-
ters, and one brave, Many Guns, spent his life's
savings in 1936 on a 1½-ton truck to begin a cartage
company. In 1958, this same haulage contractor
was summoned to the Red Chamber in Ottawa
as Senator James Gladstone, first native Indian to
receive this appointment.

Despite their success as farmers, ranchers and
small businessmen, the Blood Tribal Band in the
1960s was faced with the need for more jobs for
their young people as modern machines reduced
the number required for agricultural work. The
band council appointed four members of its economic and industrial development committee to
uncover a major source of employment that would
benefit the entire reserve. To help them, the council
hired Rev. Denis Chatain, OMI, an Edmonton-
born expert in community development, and
together they analyzed the possibilities. The Bloods
had land, labor and money for investment. Whatever it was they were going to manufacture must
be sufficiently mobile to be distributed miles away
from isolated Stand Off. The product must be one
for which there was a substantial—and continu-
ing—demand.

Weighed against Alberta's booming economy
and the housing needs of its population, the conclusion was almost inescapable: ready-to-move home
construction. Once they had won approval from
the band council, the committee members, coördin-
ated by Chatain, fanned out looking for a partner
in the enterprise. For though the survey had listed
the tribe's assets, it also pinpointed its major defi-
ciency—skilled management.

The committee's assignment was to find a manufacturer who would not only help them set up shop,
but also train Indians eventually to assume total
responsibility. First discussions yielded only compa-

Blood Indians prepare ready-to-move houses in the 80,000-square-foot Kainai Industries Ltd. building (opposite page). Completed houses are loaded on flatbed trucks for delivery to market.

nies interested in using the Bloods as a labor pool. For almost a year committee members unsuccessfully visited major centers in Canada and the United States—only to meet success 30 miles away in Lethbridge with Haico Manufacturing Ltd., now Wickes Canada Ltd., manufacturers of recreational vehicles, farm equipment, steel buildings and grainers.

After negotiations lasting almost a year, the Blood Indian tribe formed a holding company,

Red Crow Developments Ltd. Red Crow became owners of Kainai Industries, built and equipped at a cost of $1,500,000, which it borrowed from the federal government, to be repaid from building rentals. Wickes provided management services and necessary working capital.

First of the Wickes personnel to join Kainai was John Chorm, who became plant manager. He was faced with a considerable task: the majority of his potential workers had no skills and no train-

Head Chief Jim Shot Both Sides
greets Prime Minister Trudeau at
Kainai Industries' official opening
in Stand Off on July 10, 1971.

ing of any type, and had never held regular jobs. Initial training was carried out in Lethbridge, with Blood braves making the 60-mile round trip each day in school buses. Once trained in the rudiments of carpentry and assembly, they became assistants for further training programs carried out in the factory.

"I soon learned that with an Indian crew the direct approach is not always the best," recalls Chorm. "In the first couple of months, many workers spent too much time in the toilets. I didn't think issuing an edict was the answer, so one day when we were having a staff meeting I told them I was going to paint numbers on the toes of their work boots so I could identify the slackers. They laughed, but the problem was solved."

Production began in December 1970. Within months, absenteeism ballooned to 28 percent. The

50

nomadic habits of the red man did not mesh with the white man's time clocks.

"Rigid time-scheduling wasn't working too well with an all-Indian crew," says Chorm, "but not because of lack of interest. Some started late in the morning, but they were the same guys who'd work half their lunch hours, or stay after five. This was our clue."

"We broke down the assembly organization into pieces just enough for one shift of four or five men. Then we picked a leader for each team. This way it didn't matter when they started. But they could not go home until they'd finished their project."

Soon the teams were maintaining their own discipline and finding a satisfaction in teamwork lacking on the assembly line. After six months, absenteeism was down to two percent.

In June 1974, Wickes relinquished its interests in Kainai Industries, and the Bloods took full control. Productivity remains high and workers produce about a house a day. Kainai generates annual sales of more than $5 million and turned its first profit in 1976.

Kainai's large payroll has attracted other businesses and services to Stand Off. The tribe's 40,000-square-foot administration building houses a branch of the Bank of Nova Scotia, the first branch on any Indian reserve in Canada. It also has a pharmacy, a public-health office, a supermarket, a post office, a restaurant and a branch of the Cardston medical clinic.

Now that they know they can find jobs back home after graduation, young members of the tribe who had sought employment outside are returning to Stand Off. One such was Geraldine Elehti, who attended secretarial school in Lethbridge after graduation, then worked with the Department of Indian and Northern Affairs, a chartered bank, an insurance underwriter and a radio station. She became company secretary of Red Crow Developments, then director of economic development at Kainai Industries.

Women have played a leading role in Kainai and in Blood band activities. At one time the Blood communications network had two female editors working on its radio broadcasts and its newspaper, *Kainai News*. Rita Tarnava, a non-Indian and former vice-president of administration and finance at Wickes, was a director of Kainai Industries. For her six months' grueling negotiations with governments to obtain training and incentive grants, the Bloods honored her by asking her to help Head Chief Jim Shot Both Sides drive the earthmover used at the Kainai sod-turning.

Others from the white community have made important contributions to Kainai's success. Fred Gladstone, president of Kainai and son of the late senator, is high in his praise of Tod Haibeck, president of Haico when the contract was signed, and Dick Rempel, who replaced Haibeck on his retirement. Few white men, Gladstone believes, would have coöperated so readily with the Bloods or had the vision to consider social as well as economic factors during the contract negotiations.

One non-Indian who is a close observer of the Bloods is Charles Price, a chartered accountant from nearby Pincher Creek. As the tribe's financial adviser, Price was heavily involved in the negotiations resulting in Kainai. The big breakthrough for Kainai, he believes, will come when other Indian tribes begin making their house purchases from the Bloods, an arrangement he believes will arise from the Indians' historic interest in bartering.

Meanwhile, Kainai Industries—owned, staffed and managed by Bloods—stands as a model of Indian enterprise, a fittingly modern adaptation of the Blood belief that for success you "sell the grass, not the land."

Working hand in hand has paid rich dividends for the Cyprus Anvil Mining Corp. and the White Pass & Yukon Route, one of the world's most picturesque railways. Built to tap the Yukon goldfields at the turn of the century, when passengers occasionally rode on flatcars (below), the White Pass & Yukon Route fell on hard times when the riches ran out. But the discovery of a $2-billion mineral deposit some 300 miles from the Arctic Circle and its development by the Cyprus Anvil Mining Corp. have given new life to the White Pass & Yukon Route. These are two stories of northern enterprise—the Yukon's scenic Gold Rush railway and, on page 56, the mining concern that helped it to survive.

# "The Railroad That Couldn't Be Built"

### By Paul Friggens

One summer morning not many years ago, genial, graying engineer Mark Lee climbed aboard his idling locomotive on the docks at Skagway, Alaska, pulled back the throttle, and set out on one of the toughest and most romantic railway journeys in the world. Running 110 miles from Skagway to Whitehorse, capital of the Yukon Territory, the remarkable White Pass & Yukon Route—"the railroad that couldn't be built"—follows the famed Trail of '98, over which gold-crazed hordes surged into the Klondike. It climbs some of the steepest railroad grades in the world to almost 3,000 feet in 20 breathtaking miles. At White Pass Summit the route passes through the rugged Pacific Coast mountain range where, in winter, courageous crews battle blinding blizzards and giant snowdrifts.

As it pulled out of Skagway, the train was a curious sight. It consisted of flatcars hauling tourists' automobiles and campers, and heavy freight; refrigerated containers with perishables for the Yukon; and, trailing incongruously at the rear, ten weather-beaten little coaches as authentically Victorian as when they were built back in '98. Now modernized for safety, they are still equipped with potbellied stoves, oil lamps and plush parlor-car seats.

Although the White Pass & Yukon cherishes its romantic link with the past, it is in fact a modern, heavy-hauling transport operation, and a world pioneer in containerization. Carrying everything from fresh lettuce and beer to petroleum products and mining supplies, the railroad is a lifeline for people living in Whitehorse and throughout the Yukon. But for nearly half a century, it was touch and go. Only lately has the company begun to enjoy modest prosperity, pay regular dividends and face the future with confidence.

Pulled by a pair of puffing green and yellow diesels, our train now began to climb a series of awesome switchbacks. I looked out at the green-clad mountains and snowy, shark's-tooth ranges ahead, and marveled that this Gold Rush relic was operating at all. "Biggest thrill I've experienced in traveling on three continents," an Australian tourist enthused, and the talk turned to how this engineering marvel was accomplished.

It is a colorful story. When news of the Klondike Gold Rush reached London, Close Bros., a British financial house, dispatched a survey party to see if a railroad could be built from the Yukon to the sea, opening a way to the goldfields, and averting the appalling human hardship as the grizzled gold-seekers toiled over the treacherous Chilkoot and White Pass trails. But, after surveying the incredibly hostile country, engineers decided the railroad could never be built.

Independently, Michael "Big Mike" Heney, a young Canadian railroad contractor who had worked on the Canadian Pacific Railway, surveyed the rugged mountain country, and came to a different conclusion. Meeting Sir Thomas Trancred, a British engineer, in Skagway's St. James Hotel bar, he argued into the morning hours and at length convinced Trancred that the railway *could* be built. In the end, the British entrepreneurs agreed to build a three-foot, narrow-gauge railroad and put the bold young Canadian in charge.

Work was started in May 1898, on what many said was the toughest railroad construction job ever undertaken. A thousand miles from the nearest supplies, sweating laborers blasted and hacked their way through the granite mountains. Workmen dangled by rope slings as they drilled powder holes in the sheer cliffs. At one place they drained a lake and laid rails across its bed. With nothing but black powder, horses, shovels and about 2,000 men, the "First Section" crew advanced laboriously toward White Pass Summit.

Meanwhile, "Second Section" crews pushed the rails from the northern tip of Bennett Lake to Whitehorse. On July 29, 1900, after two years' grueling assault on the mountains, the two crews met at Caribou Crossing—today shortened to Carcross—to drive the golden spike.

You're wonder-struck as you view this alpine feat today. Resurveyed a few years ago with modern techniques, the route was found to be amazingly well engineered. But there were still risks. In the railway's first serious accident in 1917, a landslide knocked an engine and three freight cars into a canyon, killing the engineer and fireman. "But miraculously, the coupling broke and the coaches with 15 passengers were not touched," a pioneer newspaper reported.

It was spectacular railroading then—and it still is. One afternoon in June 1965, engineer J. D. True suddenly felt the tracks drop from beneath his engine. A weak retaining wall had given away, leaving a gaping hole in the roadbed. True's locomotive plunged through, landing on a ledge more than 200 feet below. Jackknifing, the second engine tumbled nearly 1,000 feet to the river. True crawled out of the cab window and was off work for six months with a broken pelvis. Unbelievably, the brakeman riding the second engine was unhurt, while back on the mountain 56 passengers remained safe in their coaches.

Our diesels pounding on the nearly four-percent grade, we climbed steadily higher, while across the canyon we breathlessly counted 22 cataracts tumbling from a glacier to form Bridal Veil Falls. Twenty miles out of Skagway, our train reached White Pass Summit (elevation 2,888 feet) and we crossed the International Boundary.

Although it was now summer, great sheets of ice still clung to the railroad tunnels and snowsheds. Here it snows about 500 inches a year and train crews have to fight mountainous drifts and howling winds in sub-zero weather. Once, operating an old steam rotary plow in the winter of 1948, engineer Lee was engulfed in a thunderous snowslide. "It buried the whole rotary fleet and crushed the caboose like a matchbox," Lee recalls. "We were packed in like sardines! I was afraid the locomotive would blow up." At length, the caboose crew dug out, then rescued the others.

Today bulldozers keep the tracks clean, their daredevil crews among the railroad's unsung heroes. Paul Cyr introduced the bulldozer for this risky job one night when both rotary plows became buried in hard-packed drifts while a blizzard raged over White Pass. Starting out from a camp at Glacier Siding in the middle of the night, he plowed the six treacherous miles to White Pass, traversing en route a long, curving trestle arched 215 feet across a canyon. With no lights on his "cat," its tracks hanging over the edges, the nervy operator was guided across the bridge by an Inuit lad, Lloyd Takak, who rode on the 'dozer blade holding a flashlight. It took two days to plow out the rotaries, and bulldozers have been keeping the tracks open ever since.

Descending from White Pass Summit, our train picked up speed across a vast, lonely, boulder-strewn plateau left long ago by a retreating ice cap. We rolled by iceberg lakes, glacial streams and isolated railroad sidings until, at the weathered old wooden station on shimmering Bennett Lake, passengers and crew piled off to eat a memorable family-style meal in the old Bennett Eating House.

Our train sped on again, traveling for 27 miles beside Bennett Lake, a snowcapped range reflected in its azure-blue waters, and then through lovely forested country beside Miles Canyon where novelist Jack London used to pilot the gold-seekers through the white waters of the Yukon River. In the

The White Pass & Yukon Route's
green and yellow diesels pull automobiles, campers—even a bus—across
a bridge near Dead Horse Gulch.

late afternoon we whistled into Whitehorse, a lively
town that at the turn of the century was the end
of the line and the gateway to a fortune in gold.

"Travel first class from Seattle to the goldfields
in eight days!" the railroad then proudly advertised,
as it began operating paddle-wheel steamers on
the Yukon River from Whitehorse to Dawson.
But the Klondike proved less rich than imagined
and, as the gold petered out, the "stampeders"
departed and the young railroad fell on evil days.
One early president mortgaged his home in Victoria
to meet payrolls, and senior officials drew no salaries
during the winter months. "Working for the
White Pass was like joining a holy order!" recalls
an old-timer. But the valiant little railway never
accepted a dime of subsidy, either in cash or in
land grants.

As one lean year followed another, officials tried
everything to keep the company alive. Using 300

horses, they inaugurated connecting stage lines
and a pony express between Whitehorse and Dawson. During the late 1930s, the company pioneered
with the Ford Tri-Motor and the Curtiss Condor
biplane, establishing one of the early bush airlines.
But ultimately this too was abandoned.

"The company had almost gasped its last,"
recalled a former president, Frank H. Brown, when
World War II abruptly changed its fortunes. Gird-
ing its Pacific defenses, the United States decided
in 1942 to build the 1,523-mile Alaska Highway,
and to construct airstrips from which American-
built planes flew to the Soviet Union. From a
town of less than a thousand, Whitehorse boomed
into a huge military camp. The U.S. Army Corps
of Engineers leased the railroad for the war's dura-
tion, scouring the world for now scarce narrow-
gauge locomotives and rolling stock. For a time,
the military ran from 17 to 38 trains a day.

55

From mine to market: ore "concentrate" in steel containers is loaded aboard trucks near the Anvil mine and driven 240 miles to Whitehorse, Y.T. Then, trains operated by the White Pass & Yukon Route haul it 110 miles to Skagway, Alaska, where it is transferred to ships bound for Germany and Japan.

But the U.S. Army paid minimal rent and performed only scanty maintenance. Virtually broke at the end of the war, the company had fewer than a dozen working engines, and other equipment was in sorry shape. "When I first saw conditions in 1951," said Brown, "my inclination was to cut and run. Still there was our written obligation to maintain the Yukon lifeline."

Scraping together fresh capital, officials formed The White Pass and Yukon Corporation Limited to revitalize the railroad and modernize freight handling. "We've got to find a way to reduce the number of times we handle each parcel," Brown told his newly recruited young executives. Result: his team invented the all-steel, temperature-controlled container—and the world's first integrated container system was born.

At about the same time, a fleet of modern trucks replaced the old riverboats, the railway was upgraded and dieselized, and freight-handling equipment was introduced. The coastal shipping link between Vancouver and Skagway, handled by independent freighter operators, was taken over by the company's new ocean division, which promptly set about building the world's first specially designed container ship. It was an immediate success, and soon the railroad extended the container concept to its growing truck fleet serving the isolated communities of the North out of Whitehorse.

Rising from secretary of the company to president in 1969, Albert Friesen added more new equipment and pushed the railroad's modernization. But it was the Yukon's rich new mining discoveries that really turned the tide: the ores, for example, from the Anvil lead and zinc mine. To handle the additional traffic created by the mine, in 1969 the railroad spent more than $30 million in rebuilding its route and in constructing new dock facilities.

So the railroad that couldn't be built, and

wouldn't give up, was at last striking pay dirt. "As to the long-term future, we are optimistic," the railroad told its shareholders and employes.

Back at Skagway one evening, I sat entranced as veteran trainmen reminisced. Naturally they like the present-day prosperity and steady pay, the reballasted roadbed and station-to-train radio communication. But they miss one thing—the old steam locomotives. Looking back on his 30 years of railroading, engineer True spoke wistfully:

"Sometimes you couldn't see for steam, so you opened the window and froze to death in the cab. You shoveled on the coal and you came home black as the ace of spades. But I tell you, a lot of the glory went out of railroading when they took off those old Baldwins we used to wheel over White Pass."

# Anvil! Tapping the Yukon's Great Wealth

## By Paul Friggens

Heading back to his base camp in the Yukon bush one July day in 1953, prospector Al Kulan stopped to examine a "rusty" creek bank. Sampling the nearby mineral outcrop, he became excited over signs of an appreciable lead-zinc deposit and promptly optioned his claims to a Toronto mining company. A $1-million exploration showed the ore was low-grade and uneconomic to mine. Undaunted, Kulan pursued his prospecting in the Yukon wilderness 300 miles from the Arctic Circle,

On a visit to the area, I saw the great Anvil mine (named for the Anvil Range) and the "instant" town of Faro which has sprung up in the wilderness. Today, where Al Kulan prospected, hard-hat crews have blasted and excavated a huge open-pit mine more than three quarters of a mile long and a half-mile wide. Nearby, 120-ton, $400,000 trucks feed a mammoth mill, its giant grinders thundering like Niagara as it crushes and pulverizes the raw ore. Then, by flotation process, it separates the lead and zinc sulphide particles. The end product, a heavy black "concentrate," is trucked 240 miles to Whitehorse and transferred to 35-car "unit" trains (operated by the White Pass & Yukon Route) bound for Skagway, Alaska, where oceangoing ore carriers load it for Japan and Germany.

Just how was Anvil's real potential "discovered"? Unlike the thousands of hopefuls who stampeded up the Klondike trails in 1898, a new breed of men uncovered the Anvil deposit, waging a combined ground-air attack with the most advanced techniques of geology, geophysics, geochemistry.

Having located his rusty creek bank, Kulan was hopeful of a major find, but unaware of the $2-billion ore body directly beneath his feet. Desperately in need of exploration capital, he was unable to interest investors while lead and zinc prices remained depressed. One day in 1964, the market looking somewhat brighter, Kulan walked into the Vancouver office of Dr. Aaro E. Aho, a leading geological engineer, who had tramped some 10,000 miles throughout the Yukon and knew the Faro area well. Impressed by Kulan's reports, he agreed to join forces. With another geologist, Gordon Davis, and a Vancouver businessman, Ronald Markham, they teamed to form a small syndicate, later incorporated as Dynasty Explorations Limited. Pooling their private resources, and selling Dynasty stock at 40 cents a share, they raised some $200,000

eventually staking 24 new claims—this time in a swamp. But the 1956 metals market was depressed and exploration money was hard to get. Still undeterred, Kulan and his partners tried core-sampling the claims with a small gasoline-powered "packsack" drill, but gave up when the drill became hopelessly stuck 40 feet down in glacial boulders.

Eight years later, with new partners and capital, Kulan resumed drilling. Just a few feet beyond the first attempt, the drillers uncovered what was to prove one of the greatest mineral treasures in Canadian history: a massive lead-zinc-silver ore body worth, in the ground, about $2 billion!

The huge ore body was formed probably 600 million years ago by low-temperature deposits of iron and lead-zinc minerals into brackish seas. In time, the seas were filled by vast mud sediments which, under stupendous pressure, were metamorphosed into rock. Then great glaciers and rivers eroded away millions of years of deposit, almost down to the ore body, which was left covered with gravel and clay and cloaked by muskeg and forest.

Al Kulan (right) discovered the massive Anvil lead-zinc-silver deposit while prospecting in the Yukon near present-day Faro in 1953. With Kulan near the discovery site in 1965 are (from left) geologists Dr. Aaro E. Aho and Gordon Davis, Kulan's partners, and geophysicist John Brock. The plastic bags contain ore samples—which proved the worth of the find.

to "wildcat" in the Anvil mountain range around Ross River.

Arriving by ski-plane, Dr. Aho's crew set up camp early in 1964, core-drilling the area for ore samples, while a helicopter flew over the region trailing a magnetometer detection device, called the "bird."

Originally invented for submarine detection during World War II and modified for mineral surveys, the detector locates magnetite or iron concentrations, which it records as variations in the earth's magnetic field. By making repeated passes over the ground with the bird, expert crews are able to obtain readings of the size and shape of magnetic anomalies, thus providing an indication of the extent of the mineral find.

Dynasty crews located more than 800 mineral claims by the fall of 1964, but diamond drilling (using a two-inch-diameter tube with a diamond-encrusted cutting edge) yielded no sign of commercial ore. Traveling by dog team, the prospectors staked claims throughout the winter. By early spring, the men were scrambling up freezing slopes, fording icy streams and operations were in full swing again.

With helicopter hire at $100 an hour and monthly drilling costs at $50,000, Dynasty soon exhausted its initial capital. Unable to find Canadian backers, the group at last managed to interest Cyprus Mines, a Los Angeles corporation with global holdings, in a joint 60-40 venture and a $1-million stake.

By summer, extensive airborne surveys, and drilling—at $10 a foot—had yielded no significant discoveries. Summer "breakup" had begun, turning the muskeg into a quagmire and forcing the entire camp to move. "We were desperate," Dr. Aho recalled.

On higher ground 28 miles away the team pitched camp. Their first drill hole went through the overburden to discover 50 feet of massive sulphides—iron pyrite, together with lead and zinc. Unknowingly, they had camped right on top of the fabulous ore body! A second hole proved barren. They drove a third through 175 feet of ore until the drill bit twisted off. The fourth hole hit 75 feet of the highest grade ore of all—with a high lead-zinc content, later confirmed at about nine percent.

Now the joint venture launched a "saturation" exploration over 100 square miles. Two helicopters were ferried in, and a gravel airstrip was bulldozed out of the bush. Using war-surplus equipment and "anything that would float," Al Kulan's "navy" barged vital supplies down the Pelly River. Soon the tent camp was bursting with 117 people, who slept in shifts. Geologists were dropped for several days' surveying; pilots picked them up by spotting their signal fires.

The modern town of Faro stands
where less than two decades
ago there was nothing but wilderness.
Built to house employes of the
Cyprus Anvil Mining Corp., it today
boasts a recreation center, department stores, a beauty salon, a
$750,000 ice rink and a newspaper,
*The Raven.*

In one particularly rich area, crews sank 18 holes
and never missed. "By December 1965," said Dr.
Aho, "the Faro was shaping up as a 40-million-ton
discovery." Word leaked out, triggering the biggest
Yukon staking rush since the Klondike boom—
more than 10,000 claims. (With insufficient development money or negative results, 80 percent of
them lapsed.) At the same time, Dynasty stock,
once 40 cents, soared to $15 and $20 a share on
the Vancouver Stock Exchange.

Now began a task as challenging as the mineral
search itself. The joint exploration venture was
reorganized as Anvil Mining Corp. Ltd., which
later merged with Dynasty to form the Cyprus
Anvil Mining Corp. With Cyprus President Ken
Lieber in overall command, intensive feasibility
studies were begun. Engineers drove a 2,800-foot
tunnel into the ore body to determine the quality
of the ore and how it could best be treated. Studies

covered mine and mill operations, power supplies,
transportation of the ore concentrate, and the building of a new town in the bush.

"Originally, we had planned on 5,000 tons a
day," an Anvil executive recalls, "but after spending
heavily on feasibility studies, we decided the damn
thing just wouldn't fly. 'Build it bigger,' Lieber
ordered, and we re-engineered the whole project
up to 8,000 tons per day." (In 1974 production
would be increased to 10,000 tons a day.)

By mid-1967, with $10 million in risk capital
spent, Lieber and his colleagues were ready to pull
their costly project together. First, Anvil staff traveled to three continents seeking potential buyers.
After lengthy negotiations, two Japanese companies—Mitsui Mining and Smelting Co., Ltd. and
Toho Zinc Co., Ltd.—signed a $250-million con-
tract (since increased to over $300 million) to buy
the bulk of the ore reserves. A West German company, Metallgesellschaft, contracted for the balance.

Next, Anvil looked to its pressing power and
transportation needs. Meeting Arthur Laing, then
Minister of Indian Affairs and Northern Development, at a cocktail party in Whitehorse, Anvil officials told him: "We've got a very fine ore body,
but no roads, no power, no people." Laing met
the group again at 11 o'clock that same evening—
with happy results. In the end, the Canadian government spent more than $20 million to expand
hydro-generating capacity on the Yukon River,
string a 230-mile transmission line from Whitehorse to Faro, improve some 110 miles of road,
and bridge the Pelly River. It also agreed to pay
two thirds of the cost of the mine access road.

Support was soon coming from the private sector. The White Pass & Yukon Route undertook
a modernization program and a consortium headed
by the Toronto-Dominion Bank arranged one of
the largest financings ever undertaken by Canadian

banks for a single project—$42 million for development of the mine, the mill and the town of Faro. In all, more than $100 million would be spent by Anvil, the Canadian government and the White Pass & Yukon before any ore was mined.

Now the colossal construction job began. As giant bulldozers removed millions of yards of glacial overburden, a 600-man camp rushed construction of the complex processing facilities, a reservoir to

At the 1½-square-mile open-pit Anvil mine a drill bores blast holes into rock and a geologist examines ore samples taken from the mine site.

supply six million gallons of water daily, and the Faro townsite. At times, when it hit 50 to 60 below zero, lubrication failed to work on the heavy construction equipment, and brittle metal snapped like straw in the bitter cold.

Then, in the summer of 1969, disaster struck. A forest fire wiped out the partially completed Faro townsite, causing $2 million damage. But, speedily rebuilt, the Yukon community today boasts all the amenities of a modern city.

Right on schedule, the Anvil mine began operations in September 1969. Keeping track of total production by computer, engineers now block out each day's ore removal so as to feed the mill a proper balance of lead and zinc minerals. Removing about three cubic yards of waste for every ton of ore, the electric shovels will eventually have to strip 120 million cubic yards of waste material, posing the question of what Anvil eventually will do about the awesome pit and mountains of overburden. Meanwhile, Anvil is producing average sales of more than $100 million a year, and is opening up a new era of economic development in the Yukon.

As for Kulan and his partners, they scarcely paused to enjoy their rewards. Before his death in 1977, Dr. Aho discovered a massive lead-zinc deposit only 12 miles from Faro worth, in the ground, some $1.5 billion. Ronald Markham went to South Africa in search of diamonds, and Gordon Davis became a director of Cyprus Anvil.

A wealthy man like the rest, Kulan moved his wife and three children to "live it up" in Vancouver. But the bright lights soon paled. So he packed up his family and returned to live amidst the Indian log cabins of Ross River—40 miles from Faro. Al Kulan died in September 1977 at the age of 55. To the end his love of the Faro region never waned. He remained convinced that there lay much of the Yukon's great wealth—mostly untapped.

# Being Fully Alive, *That's* the Thing!

### By W. J. Lederer

**W**hile cross-country skiing at a resort in Vermont I skidded on an icy patch, hurtled over an embankment and spilled, almost upside down, into the deep snow. As I struggled to get upright, I heard a voice shouting from up the trail, "Lie still. Relax."

Down the treacherous path a man was skiing toward me as nimbly as a jack rabbit. He stopped and looked me over. "You're okay," he said, with a slight Norwegian accent. And as his strong hands helped me up, I took a better look at him. He had a tanned, weather-beaten face, twinkling blue eyes. He wore no gloves despite the cold. His cross-country skis were old-fashioned, made from hickory, with ancient bindings.

Back at the ski lodge I learned that my seemingly middle-aged rescuer was Herman Smith-Johannsen—who in 1975 turned 100! I wanted to meet Johannsen to thank him but he'd already checked out, traveling light—carrying his skis and knapsack—on his way to a hundred-mile ski tour in the Laurentian Mountains. A week later I telephoned his home in Piedmont, Que. He was away cutting a new cross-country trail north of Mont-Tremblant in 20-below-zero weather. Could I telephone him at night? "You can't reach him," said the friend who had answered the telephone. "He's camping in the bush." Not until the following winter did I meet this remarkable old man again and find out more about his legendary energy and vitality.

He was born in Oslo in 1875. At 24, he had a degree in engineering from the University of Berlin, and by 1900 he was on trouble-shooting assignments around the world for a U.S. company. One trip brought him to Canada to sell machinery to the Grand Trunk Railway. He liked what he saw and, in 1907, quit his job, set up his own business in Montreal and began a vigorous outdoor life.

Take February 1919, for example, when Johannsen showed up on *skis* at a wild, northern logging outpost in temperatures averaging 25° below zero to show a Quebec lumber company how to haul out its logs. The loggers were aghast. "You can't go into the bush like that," they said, pointing to the skis. "You must use snowshoes." But Johannsen insisted. Every day, he was at a different rendezvous deep in the bush—two or three hours before the snowshoed loggers—with a fire going and a meal cooked. At the end of the week the loggers decided that their company should take full advantage of those "crazy long sticks."

Johannsen was to demonstrate time and again that an experienced cross-country skier could make 50 miles a day over almost any terrain in the northern wilderness and explore places impossible for those traveling on foot, snowshoes, or today, even on snowmobiles.

On his ski trips Johannsen frequently went into the distant Indian country. The Cree Indians, admiring his nimbleness, his ability to slalom at high speeds down the sides of heavily wooded mountains, honored him with the title of *Okumakun Wapoos*—Chief Jack Rabbit. The name stuck, and most Canadians know him today as Jack Rabbit Johannsen.

The stock-market crash of 1929 wiped out the then 54-year-old Herman Johannsen as a well-to-do engineer-merchant, so he took his wife Alice and their three children from Montreal to an inexpensive cottage in Shawbridge, Que. They worked all summer getting ready for the cold. By fall the house was snug, and a six-month supply of firewood had been cut for the wood-burning stove which heated it. There were no jobs then, and no money. Members of the Johannsen family today recall a predominantly cabbage diet for months on end.

"But," says his daughter Peggy, "we had family spirit. We enjoyed working together. Daddy and Mother were so determined that this was an adven-

Jack Rabbit Johannsen and a youngster relax by a campfire in Quebec's Mont-Tremblant Provincial Park. For many years, Jack Rabbit has instructed young persons on how to enjoy the wilderness, how to be self-reliant, how to ski and canoe and how to survive with flint and steel for making fire, and a bit of wire for a rabbit snare.

ture, not a catastrophe, that we managed the whole thing with more fun than most families." In time, because of their father's instruction, Peggy and her brother Bob became Canadian national skiing champions.

"During the Depression," Jack Rabbit recalls, "I had time for the things which enriched my life—being with my family, cross-country skiing, exploring the wilderness, enjoying nature, and teaching these pleasures to others. The Depression had turned out to be a godsend for me. Our children were almost grown. My wife and I liked to ski together (they did so every winter until she died in 1963 at age 80), to canoe, hike, and climb. We knew we could always manage to eat somehow.

I couldn't see any reason for going back into business and wasting my life trying to outsmart competitors in order to get rich. I knew I had to retire so that Alice and I could devote our energies to living. But here's the real secret. Alice and I did not consider solving this-problem or that-problem as chores. No, quite the opposite. Surmounting difficulties is a game. It's fun. Being fully alive, *that's* the important thing!"

Johannsen kept his word. He never did go back into business. Over the years he took occasional free-lance jobs—survey work for railways, trail cutting, inspecting new ski resorts. At 94 he was out cutting a new cross-country trail north of Mont-Tremblant—this after an energetic summer of mountain climbing in Iceland and Greenland!

In the villages of the Laurentian foothills near his home, everyone knows Jack Rabbit. Older people recall how he would ski into the towns in those Depression years saying, "We don't have jobs and we don't have much to eat. But we have lots of free time. Let's use it for our health and enjoyment."

He organized young people's ski clubs in 23 towns. Weekly ski meets became big events. Some competitors had no money to take trains and buses to the ski races. They skied 10 or 12 miles before competing—and the same distance home after dark. But they lacked downhill experience. The problem was how to get up hills quickly so more time could be spent practicing downhill slaloming. Johannsen batted the problem around with his friends. Out of the sessions, Alec Foster of Montreal conceived the idea of a ski lift. With Johannsen's encouragement, he built it in 1932 in Shawbridge—the first ski lift in Canada. It was a jury-rigged affair consisting of an old automobile motor, lines and tackles, and heavy concrete blocks, but it worked. The price to be towed up the hill was five cents.

Rev. Hector Deslauriers was one among many

64

In 1937 Jack Rabbit Johannsen (left) and Gerald Birks, skied into this wilderness near Lake Renard in northern Quebec (the dog pulled supplies on a small sled). Although Jack Rabbit often carried a rifle on such trips, he was—and remains—a staunch opponent of hunting for sport. "A fellow has the right to kill game only if he's hungry," he says.

who noticed the cheering effect of Johannsen's ski meets. He decided he would build a ski trail and a ski jump for Mont-Tremblant. "We had no money, no equipment, no knowledge of ski jumping or how to construct things. So I wrote to Herman Johannsen for advice. Two days later he skied 40 miles and arrived in person.

"The ski jump and trail became village projects. Almost everyone gave volunteer labor. Every weekend was a fiesta. The village got its laughter and confidence back and was able to organize and start other community projects. Chief Jack Rabbit Johannsen had demonstrated how a village could be self-energizing. It was like a miracle."

The electrifying effect of Mont-Tremblant's suc-

cess gave Johannsen another idea. The Laurentian Mountains form one of the best cross-country areas in the world. Tourists would flock there if there were skiing facilities, trails and resorts, he reasoned. Tourism would bring work and money to everyone.

So from 1932 to 1935 Johannsen laid out and cut the famous Maple Leaf Trail. This 80-mile loop went through some of the most beautiful wilderness known to man—its southern part only 40 miles from Montreal, then a city of more than a million people. Johannsen laid out the trail so that the gradings and turns allowed safe, yet spectacular, cross-country skiing. For this feat, the highest peak in the Laurentians (3,150 feet) was named after him. The trail passed by all possible resort locations, was close to farmhouses and within easy skiing distance of railway stations (there were no highways in that area then).

Although Johannsen's Maple Leaf Trail fell into disuse in the 1940s as the area became more developed, it brought a new industry to Quebec. Says Stanley Ferguson, who as a boy helped build the trail, "Herman Johannsen did much more than cut the Maple Leaf Trail—which was a tremendous undertaking. His sense of joy, his generosity, his zest for the outdoors spread to everyone in the Laurentians. Our people had such a good time skiing that they knew how to be hosts to visitors coming for the same pleasures. Today, more than a million tourists come to the Laurentians every year. They owe thanks that they can to Johannsen."

Because young people enjoyed helping Jack Rabbit build trails, they flocked to him for other education in nature. For those girls and boys who could not come to his home, Johannsen would ski from one village to the next to make certain everyone had an opportunity to learn. In his 65th year (1940) he skied a total of 1,258 miles on his teaching rounds. Why did he keep track of the mileage?

Jack Rabbit Johannsen preaches fitness and common sense in the outdoors—this time to a crowd at Val-David, Que., at the start of a ski tour marking Johannsen's 100th birthday, in 1975. Each time he has been offered large sums to teach skiing techniques, he has given the same reply: "What little I know I'll teach you. But why should I be paid for doing something which is fun for me?"

To demonstrate to the Canadian Army that he could still act as a ski instructor!

That same energy and persistence took Johannsen back to visit Norway when he was 93. He had no money. "But why should that stop me," he said to his daughter Alice. "There's always a ship which can use a good sailor." He went to Montreal, to a Norwegian ship, M.S. *Topdalsfjord,* and asked the boatswain for a job as a seaman.

"Bosun," said Johannsen as he tells it today, "I want to work my way to Norway. I've been to sea before, both on deck and in the engine room.

I know about rigging. I can splice wire rope and secure deck cargo. Can I be of any help to you?"

After demonstrating his skill, Johannsen became the bosun's mate. Later, when he disembarked in Oslo, the crew members lined up, shook his hand. One seaman said, "Just having him on board made it a happy and memorable trip. If he ever wants his job back, we would all welcome him."

When I went to Piedmont to see Jack Rabbit one winter day, he was on crutches. Seeing my surprise, he explained, "I slipped on the ice at my daughter's on New Year's Eve and broke my leg.

Just in from the ski trail, Jack
Rabbit throws a log on the fire at
his house at Piedmont, Que.

It's a darn nuisance. How can a fellow ski in this condition?" The doctor had told him he'd have a permanent limp. "Your bones are brittle. Count yourself lucky to get around without a wheelchair."

"I didn't hear what he said," Johannsen said, winking. "I'm a little deaf and my hearing aid was turned off."

At noon we walked the mile to the post office— with Jack Rabbit using a cane instead of his crutches. I offered to drive, but he refused. Patting his leg, he said, "My friend here and I have to learn to walk again before we can ski. And I'm determined to be in shape to ski in Norway next year."

He smiled. "A fellow can do anything if he takes care of himself. Daily exercise is important. Even city people can manage it by walking to their offices, their schools, or stores. Never ride if it is possible to walk. Climb stairs, don't use elevators. Eat only if hungry, never from habit. If you look after your body, your body will look after you."

Two months later I drove north to visit Jack Rabbit again. The snow in Vermont where I live had melted. But as I turned off Route 11 from Montreal to reach Piedmont, I saw snow patches in the wooded hills behind Jack Rabbit's house. It was almost as if these few square miles had received special dispensation from Old Man Winter.

As I drove around the last bend, Jack Rabbit was just coming out of his house. He had his knapsack on his back and he carried his skis. He walked carefully, feeling his way, making certain he did not slip on the thin, crusty snow.

Unnoticed, I stopped the car and watched.

Placing his skis parallel on the snow, he supported himself on his ski poles. He stepped on the skis and secured his boots to the bindings. Gradually he shifted his weight from the poles to his legs. First to his good leg and then to the other. Satisfied that his leg would hold him, Chief Jack

Rabbit Johannsen began gliding slowly forward over the few inches of remaining snow. Eventually he climbed the slope to the woods, glided down to his front door and went inside.

I drove to the house but before I reached the front door, it banged open. There stood a happy vital man. "Welcome! Welcome!" he shouted—and led me to a large map of Norway on the wall next to his Doctor of Laws certificate and a plaque from the Skiing Hall of Fame. "Now here," he said, pointing to an area north of Oslo, "is where I'll ski next Easter." And he did.

# The Zoo That Aims to Be Best of All

By Anker Odum

This rare Siberian tiger is one of 3,500 animals at the Metro Toronto Zoo.

Dense forests rise on either side of the train. Squirrels and jays chatter noisily in the trees while mule deer move quietly through the sun-speckled undergrowth. Excited, the train passengers move from side to side, eager to see as much as possible of the valley's rich fauna. In a clearing, restless, rutting elk bugle aggressively and rub huge, velvet-covered antlers against trees and shrubs. While the air-conditioned train crosses a grassy plain, a herd of bison abruptly breaks into a mini-stampede, then stops just as suddenly, and resumes grazing in peaceful coexistence with a group of pronghorn antelope. High above, like animated snow patches on a mountainside, white Dall's sheep nimbly scale the face of an almost vertical 90-foot cliff.

A gasp ripples through the passengers: lurking like grim shadows in the underbrush, a pack of great gray timber wolves hungrily stalks a herd of white-tailed deer in a nearby clearing. But there is no cause for alarm. Hidden from view, a strong fence separates prey from predator. For, incredibly, these are zoo animals, inhabitants of the Canadian Domain, a part of the Metro Toronto Zoo, 25 miles from Toronto's city hall. Sprawling over 710 acres of the most beautiful, unspoiled countryside within Metro Toronto, this magnificent $40-million zoo is one of the largest in the world, and from its earliest beginnings promised to become one of the finest as well.

Although huge compared to the average zoo, the 410-acre Canadian Domain is only one part of the whole. A few hundred yards away, amid the lushness of an authentic jungle, red-billed ground cuckoos and tree shrews mingle with orang-utans and other exotic birds and beasts from Indo-Malaya. Elsewhere, on an immense plain, shaggy-coated yak oxen from the high Himalayas calmly chew their cuds while a little girl waves her bright red coat vainly, shouting: "Hey, Toro!"

Further on, a crowd of visitors throng three and four deep on the "Polar Walk," admiring the powerful grace of half a dozen huge, cream-colored polar bears.

Bold in concept and design, the zoo is one of the world's most advanced, perhaps the first ever to employ a total zoo-geographic concept. Some 3,500 animals of more than 350 species are grouped according to geographic distribution, in spacious replicas of their natural habitats. Visual barriers have been kept to a minimum.

From a high vantage point in the center, you gaze down on a sparkling stream meandering through a landscape of forests, plains, wooded green hills and slopes dotted with animals of all sizes, shapes and nationalities. Here and there the stream widens into lakes and ponds, peppered with waterfowl and wading birds. High overhead, a skein of Canada geese banks sharply at the sight, and planes in to alight among the captive fowl, thus putting their stamp of approval on the Metro Toronto Zoo as a good place for bird and beast.

This unique park attracted more than three million visitors in its first three years of operation, and it has been praised by zoo experts from around the world. When the famed author and zoologist Gerald Durrell visited the site in 1973 he exclaimed: "I'm overwhelmed. You have all the elements of the finest zoo in the world right here if used properly." Two years later Dr. Theodore Reed, director of the National Zoological Park in Washington, D.C., added: "It is an exciting place, beautifully laid out in a fine setting. Given a few years to mature, it will without doubt become a world leader."

Toronto has had a zoo since 1887. But despite able management by its last curator, Dr. Norman Scollard, the old nine-acre Riverdale Zoo had long been hopelessly antiquated. A $6-million renova-

An electric monorail glides through the 410-acre Canadian Domain, home of such animals as the arctic wolf, plains bison, elk and lynx.

tion was proposed in 1953 but never carried out. Instead, a $100,000 provincial grant permitted improvements, but still left Riverdale far short of ideal. Scollard kept pressing for a new zoo without result. In 1963, however, Hugh Crothers, a prominent Toronto businessman familiar with North American zoos, revisited Riverdale and found it "simply a disgrace."

A man of action, with considerable influence, Crothers promptly contacted then Metro Chairman William Allen, who urged Crothers to form a citizens' committee. Under Crothers' determined leadership, the Metropolitan Toronto Zoological Society was formed on May 26, 1966.

By 1967, the 710-acre Glen Rouge site in Scarborough had been chosen and a master plan was approved by Metro Council in September 1969. Many of its features, including the arrangement of the exhibits in five continental areas, the minimized fencing, and the use of the Rouge River valley for a Canadian Domain with freely roaming animals, came out of lengthy discussions of zoo philosophy held over the years in Scollard's tiny office at the Riverdale Zoo.

Building of the zoo was a joint venture between Metro and the Zoological Society, with Metro putting up $20 million for landscaping and construction, plus $13 million for the Domain ride, while the society agreed to raise the $6 million needed for animal purchases and other facilities. When the Zoological Society launched its fund-raising campaign in December 1972, the public response was enthusiastic. A sponsored 15-mile "Walk for the Animals" with 25,000 marchers, raised $146,000. Toronto schoolchildren collected an astonishing $250,000 for "Project Noah" by organizing bake and rummage sales, bingo games, pet and puppet shows. Within two and a half years every penny of the $6 million had been amassed.

In the Metro Toronto Zoo's "African savannah" are such animals as giraffes and (from left) wildebeest, cheetahs, zebras—and a greater kudu and a rare white rhinoceros, seemingly oblivious to each other.

To fulfill the design concept, some 750,000 cubic yards of earth were shifted to transform 300 acres of flat tableland into hills and valleys, pools and ponds, and 20,000 trees and shrubs were planted to change a part of rural Ontario into an exotic environment.

By autumn 1973, the pavilions were ready for landscaping and planting. Because it is illegal to import soil from abroad and thus difficult to import plants, even vegetation for the tropical pavilions had to be found on this continent. The quest for these plants took Ken Brown, then the zoo's horticulturalist, to Florida where, since there are no restrictions on seeds, Ethiopian and Indo-Malayan plants are grown from seed by local nurserymen.

By late spring 1974, 400 tropical trees, 4,000 tropical shrubs and flowers and 6,000 square feet of tropical sod had been planted. The pavilions awaited their tenants.

In bygone days, animal collectors faced perilous expeditions into unexplored corners of the world; today, says a zoo official, "You can do most of it by phone and mail. The majority of our animals come from other zoos." However, in cases where it is safe for the species, certain animals are still obtained from the wild. To obtain pronghorn antelope for the zoo's Canadian Domain, veterinarian Dr. Kay Mehren, accompanied by overseer Herb Southam and his wife Mable, flew to Brooks, Alta., and ranged the prairie for 11 days.

When they returned to the zoo with their quota of six young pronghorn, one little female tried to jump the holding area's three-foot gate and broke a leg. To mend her thin, soft bones, veterinarians put on a splint and placed the animal in a hammocklike sling to keep the injured leg off the ground. She spent six weeks in this sling and when she was finally released, her legs were weak and deformed from disuse. The vets were trying daily

treatment and physical therapy, without notable success, when Mable Southam offered to nurse her at home. Today the pronghorn runs with the herd in the Canadian Domain, as healthy and agile as her companions.

The zoo opened for business in August 1974. Entering its main cedar gates, the visitor is immediately informed of the design concept. Stylized, color-coded maps of the world's major zoo-geographic zones are flanked by signs pointing to the corresponding pavilions.

The largest structure in the zoo is the African pavilion, covering 60,000 square feet with 40 feet of headroom at its peak. Just inside the entrance, nocturnal animals are kept active during visiting hours by reversing their day and night. When you first walk in, you are likely to bump into other visitors, but as your eyes adjust to the dusk, you begin to discern the dim silhouettes of fellow visitors and catch satisfying glimpses of lively bush babies, strange skunklike zorillas, brush-tailed porcupines, and a shuddering display of flying bats.

Through the luxuriant foliage of an equatorial rain forest, the visitor is offered breathtaking views of African fauna. A rare pygmy hippo dives under the bridge across its pool and emerges with moist snorts on the other side. Colorful DeBrazza's monkeys with olive backs, black arms and tails, bright orange foreheads and distinguished white beards, take turns babysitting their precocious youngsters. But the most popular inhabitants are the lowland gorillas who look like little old men with worried, wrinkled faces, but behave like uninhibited teenagers.

Leaving the rain forest behind, and moving through a 50-acre African savannah, the visitor can observe herds of zebras galloping jubilantly across the plain, while white-tailed gnus lift grotesque, heavy heads against the distant Ontario

73

A regular chore at the zoo: keepers
pin a powerful Dall's sheep to
a soft mat while the animal's hooves
are trimmed.

skyline, emitting their strange, revolverlike snorts, and lion, cheetah, ostrich and giraffe roam spacious paddocks with a freedom denied most zoo animals. On my first excursion I could have sworn a zebra had escaped from its enclosure as it trotted directly toward me across the plain. I was just about to look for a guard when I discovered the restricting wall and moat almost at my feet.

Eurasia and North America share the "Polar Walk," whence a path leads to the North American pavilion. Largely underground, this attractive building houses our smaller birds, mammals and reptiles, including fascinating underwater views of muskrat, otter and beaver and a beautiful Florida everglade setting with deep, quiet pools inhabited by complacent turtles and menacing alligators.

Although the South American and Australian pavilions are yet to come, several animals from these areas are already on display. At the South American site a 35-foot man-made waterfall tumbles into a series of ponds populated by pink flamingos, white-faced whistling ducks, and black-necked swans. In a nearby paddock several capybaras, the world's largest rodent, hop about like overgrown guinea pigs. Australia and New Zealand are represented in a huge walk-through area where kangaroos, wallaroos, and wallabies hop shyly about, while ridiculously tame emus are apt to walk up and peer myopically into your face, often with the result that human and emu perform the classic sidewalk dance before coming to terms over the right-of-way.

74

Animals' meals are carefully planned
by nutritionists, then prepared
daily in the zoo's main kitchen.
Weekly consumption includes one ton
of meat, 1,000 pounds of fruit,
one ton of vegetables—and 4,000
crickets, a favorite of the reptiles.
Right: In the zoo's clinic, a day-old
tiger gets its first check-up.

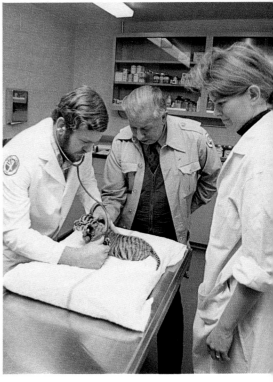

Blending beautifully with the landscape are the service buildings, where a dedicated staff of more than 200 runs the day-to-day operation. In a greenhouse, new generations of plants are grown from seed, to plant new exhibits or replace damaged vegetation. Under the direction of the zoo's nutritionist, a kitchen worthy of the finest hotels prepares what may be the world's most varied daily menu. One specialty is "gorilla fudge," a mouthwatering mixture of soybean oil, wheat germ, honey, orange juice, gelatin and other delights. Originally concocted for primates, this has proven a lifesaver, irresistible to sick animals with fussy appetites. In the zoo's hospital, veterinarians perform operations ranging from mending a giraffe's fractured jaw to cosmetic surgery on a gorilla's heavy squint.

Zoos cost money, however, and despite average annual revenues of more than $2 million, the Metro Toronto Zoo has had its share of deficits. In the fall of 1976 the board of directors, citing lack of funds, voted to close the zoo for the winter.

But letters poured in from Metro citizens, praising the zoo, demanding that it stay open. They could not be ignored. Once again Metro Council decided to pitch in and provide the $225,000 needed to keep the zoo open during the winter and Tommy Thompson, one of the eleven founding members of the Zoological Society, was made interim director. One can only hope that, as the Metro Toronto Zoo moves out of its infancy, it will continue to develop toward its original aim of becoming The World's Greatest Zoo.

# THROUGH
# THE EYES OF
# CANADIANS

**"First I was an explorer,
then I was an artist."**

Robert Flaherty

# The Many Faces of Yousuf Karsh

### By Adrian Waller

**T**he evening before Winston Churchill visited Ottawa in the bleak winter of 1941, Yousuf Karsh, a local photographer, set up his floodlights in a corner of the Speaker's Chamber in the Parliament Buildings. Then 33 and on the brink of fame, Karsh had asked his friend and patron, Prime Minister Mackenzie King, to make the arrangements. "When Mr. Churchill has finished his speech," King said, "I'll bring him directly to you."

After a sleepless night, Karsh hurried to the House of Commons, heard Churchill's historic "Some-chicken-some-neck" speech, then sped across the hall to the Speaker's Chamber. Soon he heard approaching voices and, just as Mackenzie King ushered Churchill in, he turned on his lights.

"What's this? What's this?" Churchill demanded, biting on his cigar. His entourage laughed. Mackenzie King smiled. Karsh performed a respectful bow. "Sir," he said, "I hope to be fortunate enough to make a portrait worthy of this historic occasion."

Churchill's face bristled with anger. "Why was I not told?" he insisted. As all present stared silently at the floor, he said: "All right. You may take *one!*"

Then, as Karsh was about to release the shutter, he was overtaken by a strange boldness. "Forgive me, sir," he said, and he plucked the cigar from Churchill's mouth. *Click.* As Churchill glowered, the picture was taken.

In the darkroom, Churchill's bulldog face appeared through the acid. The darkroom technician confidently pronounced: "This picture is a triumph." It was. Recognized the world over as a symbol of Britain's wartime spirit, it was made a postage stamp by seven countries and became perhaps the most widely published photograph in the history of photography. In two minutes flat, Karsh had made himself world famous. "And I have had no rest ever since," he says.

Later, he was to add to his reputation of taking three-dimensional photographs quickly when, in Ottawa, he caught Gen. Charles de Gaulle's cold, imperious character in just 30 seconds—all the formidable French leader would permit him.

Since those early triumphs, more than 15,000 men and women of achievement have faced his camera, at least half of them household names. Karsh of Ottawa has made the human face his challenge—faces that belong to history, faces worn by political struggle and artistic triumph. Soon he was Karsh of London and New York as well. "I have an insatiable appetite for giants," he once said.

Karsh, in turn, has won praise from even the most perverse of his famous subjects. "You can make a roaring lion stand still," Churchill told him at that historic Ottawa sitting. George Bernard Shaw said: "Come back and photograph me again when I'm 90." And the famous, acerbic U.S. architect Frank Lloyd Wright observed: "Your wonderful portrait makes me the American Voltaire." But perhaps the greatest accolade of all came from Lord Beaverbrook, the domineering newspaper tycoon. "Karsh," he said, "you have immortalized me." Karsh relayed Beaverbrook's verdict some days later to another subject, Lord Tedder, Marshal of the Royal Air Force. "Lord Beaverbrook said I had immortalized him," Karsh said, elated. Tedder replied wryly: "Do you think that was such a good idea?"

Soon there was no question about time allotted to Karsh. John D. Rockefeller, who disliked being photographed, shooed away a time-conscious senior executive, saying "Please go away, I'm having the time of my life visiting with Karsh." Soviet Premier Nikita Khrushchev set aside a whole spring afternoon for Karsh at his country home outside Moscow, and U.S. Chief Justice Charles Evans Hughes sat statuesquely for 45 minutes before intoning: "And now, lettest thou thy servant depart in peace."

Yousuf Karsh: a self-portrait. One critic wrote: "When history reaches out for an understanding of the great men and women of our time, it will use Karsh portraits."

Of this photograph taken of Winston Churchill during World War II, Karsh says: "He stands in my portrait in what has always seemed to me the image of England in those years, defiant and unconquerable."

Soviet Premier Nikita Khrushchev set aside a full afternoon for his 1963 sitting with Karsh. "As I watched Khrushchev's portly figure approaching," Karsh recalls, "I suddenly thought: 'Here is a personality I must photograph in a fur coat.'" Khrushchev agreed. The result: "The face of the eternal peasant, perhaps the collective portrait of a great people, painted like Cromwell, warts and all."

As Karsh prepared to photograph scientist Albert Einstein, he asked: "To what source should we look for the hope of the world's future?" "To ourselves," replied Einstein. Karsh remembers: "He spoke sadly yet serenely, as one who had looked into the universe far past mankind's small affairs. In this humor my camera caught him . . . the portrait of a man beyond hope or despair."

Yousuf Karsh was born of Christian Armenian parents in Mardin, Asiatic Turkey, in 1908. His father shipped furniture, rugs and spices to and from Damascus, but could neither read nor write. Yousuf's mother, on the other hand, was well-read and interpreted the Bible with devotion. So, when her son was stoned going to and from school, during the 1915-18 Turkish massacres of the Armenian minority, she could tell him: "If *you* ever have to cast a stone in self-defense, be sure you miss."

Persecuted and near starvation, the family fled Turkey in 1922 and finally reached the safety of Aleppo in Syria, having lost everything. Three years later, young Yousuf Karsh sailed alone for Canada, to be met in Halifax by George Nakash, his uncle, who was a respected portrait photographer in Sherbrooke, Que.

During the summer vacations, he helped his uncle in the darkroom, mixing chemicals, developing, enlarging and printing. For his 17th birthday, Uncle Nakash gave him a Brownie box camera with which Karsh scored his first photographic success—a $50 first prize in a competition sponsored by Eaton's.

Delighting in Yousuf's growing interest in photography, Uncle Nakash sent him to Boston to study with his friend, John H. Garo, the foremost

When Karsh visited author Ernest Hemingway at his home in Havana, Cuba, he expected to meet a composite image of the writer's tales of ruggedness, physical activity and worldly despair. "Instead I found a man of peculiar gentleness, the shiest man I ever photographed . . . . On developing my negatives, I liked best the portrait printed here, the face of a giant cruelly battered by life but invincible."

portrait photographer of his day. "Garo taught me to trust my own vision, and my own way of seeing," said Karsh. "Boston was my university and my alma mater." Years later it was to Boston's Francis A. Countway Library of Medicine that Karsh presented *Healers of Our Age,* his collection of medical and scientific luminaries such as Albert Schweitzer, Carl Jung, Albert Einstein and Paul Dudley White.

In 1933 Karsh borrowed $150 from a friend and opened his own Ottawa studio at 130 Sparks Street. Times were lean and his secretary often had to lend him money to pay the rent. The studio furniture consisted of orange crates covered with cloth. But through portraits of the Governor-General, the Earl of Bessborough, and Lady Bessborough, his work became well known. Two years later he was commissioned to do government portraiture and was appointed official photographer of the Dominion Drama Festival.

After the Churchill photograph had brought him international renown, Karsh took a two-month trip to England. Among the 60 personalities who faced his camera were George VI and Queen Elizabeth, Princess Elizabeth, Lord Wavell (then Viceroy of India), Clement Attlee, H. G. Wells, Noel Coward, Field Marshal Smuts and Lord Portal, the Royal Air Force chief of staff.

Seventy-five of his portraits were published in 1946 in his first book, *Faces of Destiny,* which drew generous reviews. Three years later, Karsh embarked on a series of portraits with the unifying theme "Men of Peace," among them Pope Pius XII, Richard Strauss, Bertrand Russell and Jean Cocteau. Twenty-six million impressions of his portrait of Pope Pius XII, deep in prayer, were printed for the 1950 Holy Year observance.

For many years Karsh worked in his unpretentious Sparks Street studio in Ottawa, flanked by

a coal company office and a ready-mix concrete firm. Later his studio was moved to the sixth floor of Ottawa's Chateau Laurier Hotel.

Planning a picture is a torture in itself. Karsh is haunted by the possibility that he will not achieve exactly what he wants. Before a major sitting he has been known to pace the floor at night and, oddly, considers himself at his best when tired and taut. "I judge the success of a sitting," he says, "by the number of hours of sleep I lost the night before." Even during a sitting he can be so profoundly affected by the importance of the occasion that he has been known to lose his voice. "But that," he adds, "was before I became experienced."

81

Karsh says of Canadian figure-skater
Karen Magnussen: "She brought to
the photographic session the same
grace, inventiveness and warm
personality which won her a coveted
Olympic silver medal, and, in 1973,
the world championship."

For hours an old man stood before this Karsh portrait of renowned Spanish cellist Pablo Casals, which hung in a New York City museum. Finally, a museum official asked why the elderly visitor lingered so long. "Shh!" the man whispered. "Can't you see I'm listening to the music."

After climbing the stairs to the Paris studio of Jean-Paul Riopelle, Karsh "found this Canadian-born painter to be a very natural, robust fellow. There is a courtly and gallant quality about him—a born gentleman in the guise of a rough-hewn cavalier."

Karsh's experience has sharpened what he calls that special sense, which all photographers must have or cultivate. Karsh explains: "It registers in a fraction of a second the inward power of greatness. There is a brief moment when all that there is in a man's mind and soul and spirit is reflected through his eyes, his hands, his attitude: *this* is the moment to record."

When he is not working, Karsh relaxes at his home, Little Wings, a bird sanctuary on the Rideau River, south of Ottawa. There are no Karsh photographs on the walls, because he also enjoys other art forms, such as painting and sculpture. Nature and music are Karsh's loves, and he frequently rises at 6:30 a.m. to roam the land and listen to the songs of birds.

In his travels, Karsh has photographed such contemporary personalities as the controversial communications guru Marshall McLuhan, Prince Rainier and Princess Grace of Monaco, Prince Charles, and a stunning gallery of women, among them Canadian figure-skating queen Karen Magnussen, artist Georgia O'Keeffe and folksinger Joan Baez. All have been immortalized with an ordinary camera, two modest flood lamps, and the perceptive eyes of a man who says simply: "Look and think before opening the shutter. The heart and mind are the true lens of the camera."

# Gentle Genius
of the Screen

By Lawrence Elliott

At the Montreal headquarters of the National Film Board, an office is guarded by a notice taped to the door, "Please Do Not Clean." Inside, among reels of film, an antique zither, paints, brushes and other clutter, is Norman McLaren, Canada's genius of the screen, *painting* a movie onto a strip of film. As he goes along, frame by frame, he is also producing haunting musical rhythms for it with a series of minute pen strokes on the edge of the film.

The technical achievement of this gentle man with faraway eyes is remarkable enough. But it is the emotional impact of his work that has won him more than 130 film awards. His films have none of the trappings of a conventional picture, rarely any people, never any stars or dialogue. "That would be an intrusion," says the Scots-born film-maker. What they do have is surprise, movement and all the zest of his teeming imagination. When Len Lye, the Australian film pioneer, saw his first McLaren movie, he said, "There I was, looking, when suddenly there came this meat cleaver of a film effect. It split me clean down to the middle of my spine." Picasso said of McLaren's work, "Here, at least, is something new in the art of drawing."

At the 1968 Canadian Film Awards, trail-blazing filmmaker Norman McLaren walks off with an Etrog—the Canadian equivalent of an Oscar—for his film *Pas de Deux* (below), in which he used slow-motion techniques to capture the fluid grace of ballet.

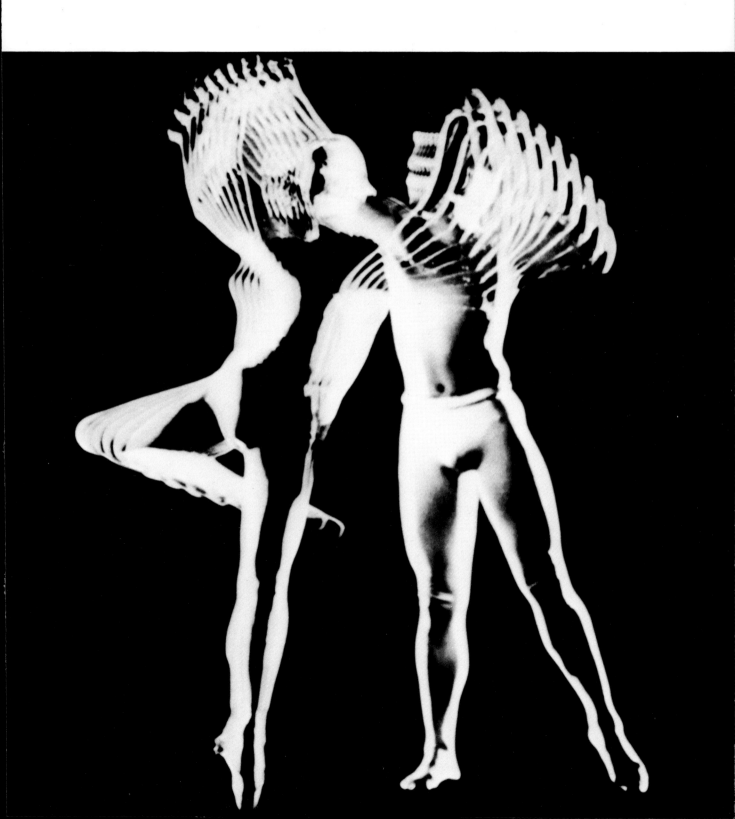

What are these effects? What are McLaren's secrets? Dancing lines, rivers of color, visualized sound, objects and humans stunningly freed from the laws of gravity. In one film, *Blinkity Blank,* his cavorting lines turn into hens whose color-splashed eggs explode and vanish from the screen— but go right on shining in the mind's eye. In another, probing the spirit of music, McLaren uses india ink to draw both image and sound—in the same figures. You *see* the tune, a dot bouncing along to the very rhythms its changing shape creates, a musical note sailing out at you from the screen as it gathers intensity. All this is abstract art of the highest order, but so sprightly are McLaren's dots and loops, so expressive their gyrations, that no one needs to know the first thing either about abstraction or about art to become an instant enthusiast. His award-winning masterpiece, *Fiddle-de-dee,* for example, which lasts about four minutes, and cost exactly $950 (including the 20 percent allocated to the Film Board's overhead), keeps its audiences captivated. "The less money there is, the more imagination there has to be," says the frugal McLaren.

For all the honors and acclaim, McLaren has changed little since he arrived at the Film Board in 1941 with what one producer called "a paper bag full of crazy tricks." He cannot be drawn into argument—no one has ever even heard him raise his voice—and the work of every other filmmaker in the place seems more important to him than his own. A then very junior colleague, Grant Munro (who appears in McLaren's best known film, *Neighbours*), recalled the time he asked McLaren for help with some technical difficulties: "Norman simply dropped his own work in the middle and sat with me under the camera all that day and, though he wasn't feeling well, all through the following night, until the problem was licked.

86

Grant Munro, a colleague and friend, said of Norman McLaren (below): "He is so completely a visual man that had he been born before motion pictures, I think he might have invented them." Munro appeared in *Neighbours* (left), a powerful cry for world peace and one of McLaren's finest films.

Then he went off to the hospital to have his appendix taken out."

In 1960 McLaren was invited to introduce his work at a Montreal film festival. An intensely private man, who is painfully shy, he did so by bowing once, then scooting offstage. In his place, there appeared a seven-minute short called *Opening Speech* in which McLaren himself hilariously struggles to subdue a demoniac microphone that twists, wilts and falls forever out of his reach. Even before the film was over, the assemblage of 2,000 professionals was on its feet to give it—and its creator—a standing ovation.

The son of a house painter, McLaren was already "passionately excited" by the possibilities of film when at 18 he attended classes in design at the Glasgow School of Art. "The trouble was that I had no camera and no prospects of getting one." It wasn't long before the obvious solution occurred to him: make a movie without a camera. From a downtown theater, he begged a worn-out 35 mm. print of a commercial film and painstakingly scrubbed its fading images down the bathtub drain. He was left with 300 feet of clear film on which, using only a brush and colored inks, he painted his first movie, an abstraction of swirling colors. From that moment in 1934, his course was set as a pioneer of cinema art.

After a spell with the film unit of the General Post Office in London, McLaren moved to New York and supported himself by painting pictures. Then, hearing that the Guggenheim Museum might be interested in buying some abstract films, he went home and made three with pen and paintbrush. Lacking sound equipment, McLaren composed a synthetic, hand-drawn sound track for the first time. The three films—*Dots, Loops* and *Scherzo*—each ran about three minutes and took three months of zealous, day and night effort. But with them he exchanged the paraphernalia that stood between him and the image on the screen for a self-imposed discipline so severe that only a bare handful of filmmakers have had the courage to follow his lead.

Most animated films are made by photographing drawings done on large sheets of celluloid. McLaren eliminated this step by working directly on the 35 mm. film. For every second of film that flashed across the screen, he drew 24 pictures roughly three quarters of an inch square—4,320 separate frames for a three-minute movie, each one slightly different from the one before. On this postage-stamp-size "canvas," McLaren was forced to sum up the character and action of his dots and loops with only a few deft lines.

His "orchestra" was a bottle of ink, a pen and some brushes. Like everyone else who has ever made a movie, McLaren observed that every little scratch on the sound edge of the film produced its own unique squawk when it passed under the photoelectric cell of the projector. Everyone else tried to avoid

87

Norman McLaren's *La Poulette Grise* tells the story of a little gray hen that changes color and nests on clouds, the moon and the branches of trees.

McLaren brushes dye and india ink onto clear film during the making of *Fiddle-de-dee* in 1947.

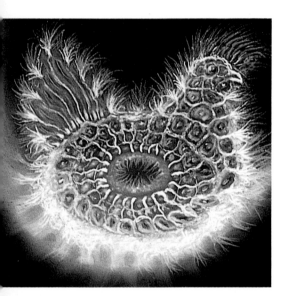

scratching the film. McLaren did it intentionally—then continued his experiment with a series of minutely varying brush strokes on the sound track. "A big, broad stroke went 'Boom!'" he explained, "and a tiny one went 'Hmmm.'" Eventually he would produce a box of cards, each one a picture of a sound wave, which he would photograph onto the sound track to produce vibrations, special percussive effects and, incredibly, music.

When McLaren went to the National Film Board in 1941 (it had been established by an act of Parliament only two years before), the directors were nervous of his originality. Nonetheless they turned him loose to pursue his flights of inspired fantasy. They have never had cause to regret it. With Canada at war, McLaren's first films were fresh evocations of tedious home-front themes: the importance of savings and war bonds, the dangers of idle gossip. One, *Dollar Dance,* dealing with inflation, was still in demand around the world as a painless lesson in economics ten years after the war.

His experiments went on. Intrigued by the processes of art, he tacked a sheet of cardboard to a wall one day and began drawing on it with pastels and chalk. Every 15 minutes or so, he stopped and photographed the drawing on movie film. Three weeks later he had a well-chalked piece of cardboard, and 400 feet of exposed film which recorded the evolving picture in a series of dissolving images. He scored his "moving painting" with an old French-Canadian folk song, *La Poulette Grise* (The Little Gray Hen).

A few more such films and McLaren again abandoned the camera, this time ignoring frame divisions altogether, painting, dyeing and stippling away with abandon on 12-foot sections of clear film. Frustrated at first by the dust that clung to his wet paint, he soon came to enjoy the unique patterns it made. He stomped on the floor to stir up more and even waved the wet strip of film out the window. The result, *Begone Dull Care,* is a color riot, scampering across the screen in antic counterpoise to the frenetic jazz of Oscar Peterson.

In 1949 McLaren was asked by UNESCO to go to China where it was hoped that his stripped-down film technique would be useful in teaching basic health rules to illiterate back-country villagers. There he taught a small group of Chinese artists how to make animated cartoons and to draw pictures and sound track directly on film, imaginatively illustrating the importance of vaccinations and boiled drinking water. "It is a great satisfaction," he reported, "to see 100 or more people at a filming and, next day, to recognize many of the same faces at the clinic."

McLaren had been in China only two months when the communists overran the village where he was living. Eight months later, his work completed, a friend helped him to travel to Peking and arrange for his return home. Out of the emotional strain and his sense of personal involvement in the tragic conflict of men, came *Neighbours,* which has been hailed as the most eloquent plea for peace ever filmed.

Shot entirely in an Ottawa public park and orchestrated with synthetic sound, *Neighbours* starts with two men sitting outdoors, amicably reading their newspapers. A flower springs up between them. Their admiration gives way to greed and they argue over whose property the flower is on. They build fences to enclose it, fight and, in a final paroxysm of violence, destroy their homes, their families, each other and–ironically–the little flower itself. Using yet another McLaren technique–making one picture at a time and moving the actors between each "take"–McLaren gives the film a terrible immediacy. The flower leaps out of the ground full-grown. The houses come crashing down in a single terrifying flash. And the belligerents fly and flail at each other with the savagery of men who have lost control of their passions.

In 1953 McLaren was back at work for UNESCO,

this time in India, training filmworkers for a program in fundamental education. While he was there, in a remote village, a telegram from the Film Board finally caught up with him: "Congratulations. *Neighbours* wins Oscar." Puzzled, McLaren sat down to compose a reply. "I am pleased with your news," he began his letter, unable to see that any of this called for costly telegrams, "but who is Oscar?"

Having said in *Neighbours* what was in his heart about the waste and pain of violence, McLaren never went back to that theme. But he did use live actors and slow-motion techniques to make *Pas de Deux,* generally thought to be his most beautiful film. It is a ballet danced to the thin music of a panpipe and photographed in starkest black and white. By printing the negative in multiple images, each frame reproduced up to eleven times, McLaren captures movement just past, movement yet to come, in a rhapsodic flow of ineffable grace.

In the creative process, day and night and personal life have little meaning for McLaren. There was a time when, lost in his work, he stayed bent over his workbench until 3 a.m., haggard with fatigue–and was back in his tumbled office at ten the next morning. Now his health is no longer robust enough for such extravagance and he tries to keep better hours. But the truth is that even as he listens to the music he loves or experiments with stereoscopic painting, his imagination churns with unborn cinematic imagery. Thus *Spheres,* produced in 1971, was conceived nearly 25 years before, but not until he found the perfect music, a Bach prelude and fugue, did he complete it.

McLaren has become virtually a Canadian natural resource. To movie buffs and professionals in the more than 100 countries where the Film Board sells his movies, he is a legend. For McLaren's work has widened the range of the motion picture by doing something never done before.

# All That's Best in a Reporter

## By David MacDonald

Once while Bruce Hutchison was at his summer camp on Shawnigan Lake, Vancouver Island, and editing the Victoria *Daily Times* by telephone, two visitors came calling. One was an old friend; the other, who'd never met Hutchison, was a Hollywood scriptwriter. Knowing that his host was a famous Canadian author, historian, journalist and political pundit, the scriptwriter was amazed to encounter a wiry, hawk-nosed rustic in plaid shirt and tattered straw hat who greeted his guests on a woodsy trail, led them to a snug cottage under tall Douglas firs, then begged to be excused for a few moments. "One of my colleagues is coming for an important editorial conference," he explained. "There is a crisis in government and I must discuss the stand our paper will take."

The big-city visitors chuckled; this was a funny place for a newspaper conference. But what really astonished them was when the other conferee arrived—by canoe! "I've heard of backwoods editors," the Hollywood man exclaimed, "but this is *ridiculous!*"

Maybe so, but that's precisely how William Bruce Hutchison wanted it. Renowned as an editor-writer and widely regarded as Canada's ablest commentator on national affairs, he has always sequestered himself in the Vancouver Island outback. True, Hutchison makes frequent forays to Ottawa, Washington, London and other world centers, gathering material for his writings. But he has never let business interfere for long with his home pleasures, which are to tend his garden in the Victoria suburb of Saanich and to hole up at his lakeside retreat, 20 miles deep in the up-island bush, communing with nature and reflecting on the human condition. In fact, the Vancouver *Sun* once gave him a sweetheart contract allowing him to function *in absentia*. "If Hutch wants to work in a cave in the Aleutians," said *Sun* publisher Stuart

Keate, "we'll still print whatever he writes. He's that good."

Certainly, Hutchison is one of Canada's most gifted writers. Besides churning out columns and editorials on all the major issues of the past four decades, plus many humorous and satirical pieces, he has produced hundreds of magazine articles and short stories, and more than ten books, including *The Unknown Country*—acclaimed by many critics as the best book ever written about Canada. In doing so, he's won at least 20 major honors. Small wonder that when Britain's Royal Society of the Arts struck a medal in 1961 for the most outstanding journalist in the Commonwealth, the first winner was the sage of Shawnigan Lake.

Hutchison enjoys an equally high rating in Washington. "He's the finest newspaper writer in North America," said a U.S. assistant secretary of state. "To me, he's a combination of Walter Lippmann and Will Rogers, but with more wisdom than either of them."

For all that, Hutchison is agreeably modest. "I'm just a reporter," he says, "an uneducated man who did whatever looked like a good idea at the time." Though famed for his lucid prose and sharp insights into Ottawa, where he has been a confidant of at least four prime ministers, Hutchison prefers a simpler boast—that he has built three cottages with his own hands at Shawnigan Lake. "Your trouble," he was once told by former *Maclean's* editor Arthur Irwin, "is that you can't decide whether to be a whirling dervish or a parsnip."

To keep posted on Canadian affairs, Hutchison reads scores of publications, runs up a staggering long-distance phone bill, takes numerous trips across the country. Unlike many of journalism's thinkers, who merely ruminate on yesterday's headlines, he has always been a hard-digging reporter, carefully cultivating news contacts wherever he goes. "When Bruce comes to Ottawa," said one correspondent, "the politicians phone for appointments with *him*." In Washington, his personal friendships have included such noted insiders as Senator Mike Mansfield, George Ball and Dean Acheson. "The man's amazing," said Richard Murray, a former diplomat at the Canadian embassy. "He'd breeze into the State Department and learn more in 24 hours than all the rest of us did in a year. People *trust* him."

A "mind-writer," he composes his work while puttering in his garden or even drifting off to sleep. Once, after a week in Ottawa, he mentally drafted a series of six articles during a flight to Winnipeg. Then, in the crowded *Free Press* newsroom, Hutchison hammered out 10,000 words of polished prose without stopping. "All our reporters stood around," recalled the publisher of the *Free Press* "and they just gaped."

His finest writing is reserved for what he counts as the most fortunate land on earth. Few have done more to tell Canada's story, or told it to better effect. "Hutchison is the best kind of nationalist," said writer-broadcaster Pierre Berton, "the kind that reminds us of our history and excites us about our own country."

Born in 1901, Hutchison was reared in a succession of small towns in the interior of British Columbia, where his father, an English immigrant, odd-jobbed as a farmer, a real-estate agent and an actor. His mother, from Ontario, was a firm and formidable woman who lived to be 100. In 1918, after the family had moved to Victoria, Bruce called on B. C. Nicholas, editor of the Victoria *Daily Times,* to get help for a high-school debate. Struck by the teen-ager's quick grasp, and sorely short-staffed because of wartime enlistments, the editor hired him as a one-man sports department, at $12 a week. Hutchison was on his way.

From sports he went to police and city hall beats, writing about a rich cast of small-town cops and criminals, bootleggers, tarts, aldermen and assorted oddballs. By the time he was 19, he was covering the British Columbia legislature and forming a strong attachment for politicians. "They're probably more honest than most of us," Hutchison claims, "because they've got to swim in a big, illuminated aquarium." He wrote reams of bright, lively copy, started a hard-hitting column and began moonlighting for magazines and the *Christian Science Monitor.* "I never had any great talent," he says. "I just kept myself very, very busy."

In 1925 Hutchison was assigned to cover a parliamentary session in Ottawa; there, watching the Machiavellian moves of Prime Minister Mackenzie King, he became forever fascinated by the uses and abuses of political power. The same year he married Dorothy McDiarmid, a vivacious Victoria girl whose family owned a summer camp at nearby Shawnigan Lake; in a stand of fir by the water's edge, he built a small cottage for his bride and vowed that they would never move far away from those woods if he could help it.

From then on, while shifting to Vancouver's *Province* and later *The Sun,* Hutchison always contrived to remain a correspondent in Victoria. Offered higher-paid jobs in New York and Boston, he chose to stay put, summering at Shawnigan and raising two children in Saanich. Even when John W. Dafoe later hired him for the faraway Winnipeg *Free Press,* Hutchison refused to be uprooted. "I'll write for you," he told that great Prairie editor, "but I'll never leave home."

He traveled extensively throughout Canada, however, acquiring a deep, almost mystical feeling for the whole broad land. In 1942 he published *The Unknown Country.* That travelogue-*cum*-history text became a best-seller because it beautifully

Bruce Hutchison and his wife, Dorothy, in the garden behind their home near Victoria in 1960. It was a house, wrote Hutchison, "filled with work, merriment and friends."

expressed what most Canadians were only beginning to feel—the stir of pride in their homeland's past and bright hope for its future. "No one knows my country, neither the stranger nor its own sons," Hutchison lyricized. ". . . We have not yet felt the full pulse of its heart, the flex of its muscles, the pattern of its heart. For we are young, my brothers, and full of doubt, and we have listened too long to timid men. But now our time has come and we are ready."

Though an ardent Canadian, Hutchison has always contended that niggling, nagging anti-Americanism "does neither people any good." At the same time, through his work for U.S. publications, he has done much to interpret Canada to others. As Yale University noted in awarding him an honorary degree in 1968, "We sensed the character and quality of our most important neighbor more clearly because of you."

As editor of Victoria's *Daily Times* from 1950 to 1963, Hutchison conducted a running feud with "the reckless and reprehensible funny-money government" of Social Credit Premier W. A. C. Bennett, and helped to jail one of his cabinet ministers (for accepting bribes). He also found time to write five more books, including *Mr. Prime Minister,*

A Washington politician once said of Hutchison: "He is an old-style journalist who learned his business at a time when you were a gentleman first and a journalist second." Here, in 1959, the gentleman-journalist interviews actress Zsa Zsa Gabor at her home in Los Angeles.

a history of Canadian politics through the lives of its first 14 prime ministers. Of the 15th prime minister, he says, "Right or wrong for the country, Trudeau's the most brilliant man I've ever known in politics."

Hutchison has declined to run for the Commons. "I may live off the avails of politics," he concedes, "but I never had the courage to go into public life. Besides, working in Ottawa would keep me away from the woods."

His favorite pastime there, verging on mania, is to chop firewood. Hutchison reckons that the labor is doubly useful, a mindless exercise permitting him to mull over the next day's writing. But he also hoards wood the way some men hoard

money. "It's the only wealth I have," he claims. Cords of fir, cedar and hemlock are cached around his 20-acre property, a five-year supply banked up according to age and type, like so much fine old wine. The oldest are treasured most. When a visitor once gathered an armload of vintage logs for the Hutchison cottage, Hutchison stopped him. "Not those," he cautioned. "My wife will just *burn* them."

All of his wood comes from dead trees or blow-downs, for Hutchison has such a reverence for living things that he can't bear to cut away live branches; the only trail on his land had to be cleared by a friend. Once, when field mice were plaguing his cottage, Hutchison's wife scattered poisoned seed around the kitchen. That night, after she'd gone to bed, he carefully swept it up to protect the tiny creatures.

No couple could have been closer than Bruce and Dot Hutchison. For more than 40 years she shared his life, his travels and his passion for the outdoors. When she was killed in 1969, in an auto accident, it was months before he regained much of his old zest for living and working.

Hutchison takes his work seriously, but not himself. He has a high capacity for amusing self-mockery. When *The Sun* threw a testimonial dinner to mark his 52nd anniversary in journalism—he hadn't bothered to tell anyone about the 50th anniversary—Hutchison was at his self-deprecating best. "I have been seized of only one or two ideas in my life, neither of them original," he declared. "Rubbed together like two sticks, in Boy Scout fashion, they have produced no fire but enough smoke to keep the reader in confusion and me in reasonable comfort."

But it remained for former Prime Minister Lester B. Pearson to set the record straight. "To me," he said, "Bruce Hutchison represents all that is best in an honest reporter."

At a banquet in 1970 commemorating his 52 years in journalism, Bruce Hutchison accepts *Cowichan Lake,* a painting by Brian Travers-Smith. With Hutchison are former Prime Minister Lester B. Pearson and, at right, Stuart Keate, publisher of the Vancouver *Sun,* and J. O. Wilson, then chief justice of the British Columbia Supreme Court. A photograph of Hutchison the woodchopper hangs in the background.

# Trying to Save What's Left

By Robert Collins

The mother grizzly came barreling along the mountain slope, 500 pounds of savage fury with two half-grown cubs at her heels. Unarmed and scared, the two wildlife photographers nevertheless stood their ground. Almost in unison, they shouted, "Stop!"

The grizzlies *did* stop, a mere 15 feet away. The mother stamped her feet and whoofed with rage. "Give her room," murmured Andy Russell to his son, Dick. "Slow and easy!" Carefully Dick moved aside. Grumbling, but glad of the chance to save face, the bear led her family away.

That touch-and-go morning in 1963 still sticks in Andy Russell's memory, though he has since faced dozens of other grizzlies and come away unscathed. "Standing firm isn't hard," he grins. "It's just a matter of planting your feet. You're always scared—but there's a difference between being afraid and being scared."

For decades, Alberta-born Andy Russell was a big-game hunter and one of North America's best-known guides. But in 1960 he laid down his guns to wage a one-man crusade to preserve the wild, free life—including his own. "We were losing our

"You will be good in the mountains," a neighbor once advised the young Andy Russell. "Go and learn what they have to tell you." Russell (foreground, left) did just that, later earning fame as a guide and big-game hunter. Then, in 1960, he traded his guns for pen and camera and began his battle to preserve North America's dwindling wilderness—and such wildlife as the Rocky Mountain bighorn sheep (opposite page) and the mountain goat (below).

wilderness so fast there was no point in carrying on," he says. "I'm trying to help save what's left."

Except for taking meat as needed, Russell now shoots only with cameras. His hunter's lore and stalking skill have enabled him to capture some rare close-ups—of bear cubs suckling their mother, of bighorn rams battling over a ewe, of mountain sheep performing awesome aerial tricks. "These are the ballet dancers of the peaks," he has written of the mountain sheep, "the specialists, the hot-bloods, the wonderfully colorful crag-masters, at home among airy castles . . ."

Russell used a tripod-mounted camera to capture these waterfowl against a Rocky Mountain backdrop. He has received world acclaim for his sensitive photography and eloquent prose. One 80-year-old Englishwoman wrote thanking him "for taking me to the Rockies I have always wanted to see."

With a natural bent for storytelling, he has also written numerous books, including *Grizzly Country, Trails of a Wilderness Wanderer, Horns in the High Country* and *The Rockies.* Requests for lectures pour in from all over North America, and his full-length movie, *Grizzly Country,* has had more than 350 showings.

Russell grew up on his father's ranch in the Alberta foothills. As a teen-ager, Andy left school to run a trapline. Then at 19 he went to work for Bert Riggall, a guide, naturalist, author, photographer and best friend. "In ten years he gave me what boiled down to a university education in botany and science," says Russell.

Nor was that all. Riggall taught his pupil how

to load a packhorse—so well that, years later in competition, Russell and a foreman packed a horse and galloped a 125-yard course in 1:37 minutes. Riggall demonstrated the art of free climbing—a fingerhold here, a toehold there, a fist locked into a crevice to haul oneself up—until Andy could scale a mountain like a fly. Steadily, the young man grew into the complete mountain guide. He became so handy with a gun that he later won the Alberta Provincial Sporting Rifle Championship. Riggall assigned him to the "rough string," 16 horses that had to be broken for other riders—a rare but painful honor. "All summer I never rode a gentle horse. God, how those horses could buck!"

One bright October day, Russell married his

boss' daughter, Kathleen. For their honeymoon, they rode deep into the mountains for a month's sheep hunt, and shot a winter's supply of meat. They were tent-bound for three days in a blizzard. Even with plenty of food, wood and books, it was a good test of marriage. "If either one of us had been shading some opinions about the other," Russell wrote later, "they would have come out during that three-day storm."

Working Riggall's packtrains, and later his own, Russell met such famous people as Bing Crosby and Lord Alexander when he was Governor-General. Russell seemed always on the brink of danger. In British Columbia, Andy and a horse wrangler were trapped during a storm in a stand of dead Douglas firs, which began falling like bombs. The men dived for cover and survived a terrifying half hour. Again, cutting a tree for firewood, Russell stepped back on a log as the tree fell and suddenly was catapulted ten feet in the air toward an open canyon. Miraculously he landed in a small fir growing at the very edge of the abyss, and slid smoothly to the ground.

During those years Russell broadened his acquaintance with grizzlies. He'd seen his first long-clawed track at age five, and at age nine blundered face-to-face with a bear: boy and grizzly fled in opposite directions. Gradually he evolved a theory that many grizzly "charges" begin simply as investigations. The bear, which has poor distance vision, lopes in for a closer look. If the object runs or shoots, curiosity turns into a real charge. "I've researched maybe 50 maulings," Russell says, "and nearly all of them could have been avoided."

He concluded that grizzlies, like dynamite, are explosive but controllable. Over the years he grew increasingly fond of them, watching through binoculars as they played rough-and-tumble games, skidded joyfully down snowy slopes on their rumps,

and pulled practical jokes on other animals. (Once he saw a grizzly pop up in the brush and scare the wits out of two moose, just for the fun of it.)

But, by the late 1950s, Russell could see the species dwindling. He also saw industrial wastes polluting foothill streams, and bulldozers slashing into the wilderness. In 1960 he sold his packtrain business and the next year set out with his oldest sons, Dick and Charlie, on another kind of adventure. For nearly three years they prowled 24,000 miles through western Canada and Alaska by plane, by boat, on horseback and on foot, gathering notes and film for *Grizzly Country,* the book and the movie—revealing in vivid detail the life not only of bears but of all Rocky Mountain wild creatures.

99

Russell himself profited from the experience. "Sometimes I stood and marveled at how I could have lived so long before in wilderness country and learned so little!"

The trio went on more trips to film sheep and goats, growing lean and tough as mountain animals themselves, and running the gantlet of falling rock and snowslides. Yet perhaps Andy's most unnerving moment was the first night he stepped out on the lecture circuit. He swallowed his stage fright by "taking them on a guided tour through the mountains—exactly what I'd been doing for years." While the film rolled, he wove his narrative with a skill nurtured around a thousand campfires: "For two hours that bear and I went like sin at a church wardens' convention"; "I was standin' on the edge of nothin' with my hip pockets hangin' out over eagle country." Russell admits that "telling a story is like selling a horse—appreciation of the product will be higher if you do a bit of currying and brushing." And he savors his own tales as much as his audience, joining in the laughter with a great flash of white teeth.

In magazine articles and newspaper columns, on radio and television, Russell rails angrily at polluting industries and fires a steady barrage of ecological suggestions at government. His most successful lobbying was for Kluane and Nahanni national parks in the Yukon and the Northwest Territories. His efforts, along with those of other conservationists, were rewarded when these superb wilderness areas were set up as national parks in 1972.

Russell does much of his writing at Hawk's Nest, his mountain home perched 4,700 feet above sea level overlooking Waterton Lakes National Park. To the south and west march a regiment of snowclad, sawtooth Rockies; to the east and northeast Alberta's foothills ripple into a blue blur of prairie

On many wilderness trips Andy Russell is accompanied by his eldest sons, Dick and Charlie. Both have profited not only from their father's teachings but also from years in the classroom: Dick (left, silhouetted against a craggy mountain wall) has a Masters degree in zoology; Charlie (photographing a marmot, below) is a graduate of the New York Institute of Photography.

a hundred miles away. Here, without stirring from the stone doorstep one golden spring afternoon, we saw through binoculars two herds of elk, a coyote, a mother bear with two rollicking cubs, and three frisky deer.

Basking in the sunlight, Russell fondly eyed the mountains. "Been away from 'em too damn long," he mused, and his voice gathered excitement as he outlined plans for yet another trip into his beloved high West. "Still some places there I've got to see. Y'know, too many people *talk* about livin' but never *do* it."

101

# "Crazy Old Millie Carr"

### By David MacDonald

To the Indians of Vancouver Island, where she sketched their brooding totem poles on plain wrapping paper, she was known as "Klee Wyck"–the Laughing One–because she always greeted them with a sunny smile. To the stolid burghers of her native Victoria, B.C., she was someone to laugh *at*, an eccentric, despised dauber who traipsed around with a pet Javanese monkey in a baby buggy. But she had the last laugh. By the time her neighbors accepted her as an authentic genius, her sensitive works were so prized in other parts of Canada that hometowners could afford only prints. Today her major works are valued at close to $50,000 each.

Emily Carr was a victim of her times and her environment–and, in a sense, she was a victor over both. In the early 1900s, an era when tidy realism was the vogue in primly provincial cities like Victoria, she dared to be different. So scorned that she felt lucky to get a week's grocery money for one of her paintings, she yet evolved a bold, sweeping style that captured the haunting mystery of deserted Indian villages, the wild grandeur of British Columbia's lush rain forests, the sheer vitality of nature. She went reverently into the deep, quiet woods, depicting them with soaring Gothic grace. "I'm only trying to express something I *feel*," she insisted, "to satisfy myself."

Though hard-tested by discouragement and despair, her career was a heartening triumph of the human spirit. The youngest of nine children of a prosperous Victoria merchant, she was born in 1871 and grew up in a handsome Victorian-style house–the subject of her first known drawing, made at the age of eight. From her father she heard tales of old Indian villages, with weird totems and carved house fronts, to the north of Vancouver Island. "These wild, western things excited me tremendously," she once recalled.

Orphaned at 17, Emily went to San Francisco for six years of study at the San Francisco School of Art (where she was too embarrassed to draw nudes), then returned to teach in the converted barn loft of her family home in Victoria. Traveling on foot, and by packhorse and canoe–almost drowning once–she made frequent trips to remote island settlements like Ucluelet and Alert Bay, painting the bronzed faces and tribal totems of the Indians in a series of mannerly watercolors.

Despite further training in London, nothing distinguished her work until, at the age of 39, Emily made a pilgrimage to Paris. There, at the Académie Colarossi, she fell under the spell of Cézanne and Impressionist forms and colors. She learned to paint in what she called "the despised, adorable, joyous modern way." Two of her newly vibrant landscapes were accepted for the controversial *Salon d'Automne* of 1911, when the painters of Paris were upsetting all of art's oldest conventions.

Home again, Emily showed new power in her painting with more vivid color and far more feeling. Her crumbling old totems stood out like stark, staring symbols of a once-proud culture fast dying in the white man's America. Critics damned them as "barbaric," "grotesque" and–worst of all–"Frenchy." She tried teaching art again but, shocked by her nonconformist techniques, parents withdrew their children from her classes. She took the last of her father's legacy and built a small boarding-house, hoping that the income would let her keep on painting. But it didn't, and she hardly picked up a brush for 15 long, bitter years. To make ends meet she made pottery and hooked rugs for tourists, bred and sold 350 sheep dogs. "Clay and bobtails saved me," she later noted in her diary.

Emily's diaries reveal her as a sensitive, determined, lonely woman pining for a mysterious love of her youth. Though strikingly attractive then (she later became dumpy and dowdy), she never

Emily Carr before her painting, *Sunshine and Tumult*.

Emily Carr was born during a snowstorm in 1871 in this stately redwood house in Victoria. A troublesome child, she often angered her parents (on steps) by clambering on the front fence—and tearing her clothes—or by retiring to the barn (background) to talk to the cows.

married. Fonder of animals than of most people, she made her home into a shelter for dogs, budgies, parrots and squirrels. She had a tame white rat named Susie, Woo the monkey and, once, a young vulture. Whenever she took Woo and Susie shopping in a baby carriage that she very sensibly used to push her groceries, people would gawk and say, "There goes crazy old Millie Carr." Even her roomers snickered. "I was forced to listen with patience," she later wrote, "while my boarders—my bread and butter—jeered at my pictures on my walls before my very nose."

While she was still too poor and discouraged to paint, Marius Barbeau, a Canadian anthropologist, came upon some of her early works in Haida homes. Through the Indians he tracked Emily down in Victoria and bought two of her paintings for $30. "When I first saw Emily Carr's pictures," he said, "I saw that her conception was as big as Canada itself." Then, in 1927, Barbeau arranged to have 26 of her paintings hung at an exhibition of West Coast art at the National Gallery in Ottawa. Eastern critics raved about them. More important, Emily went east to see the show herself

The Carr sisters (clockwise from left): Lizzie, Edith, Clara, Emily and Alice. Staunchly independent, Emily once posted a sign on the gate of a house she shared with Alice that read: "For Miss Alice Carr take the path to the right. For Miss Emily Carr take the gravel path to the left."

So devoted was Emily Carr to her animals that when she fell ill she insisted neighbors care first for them. "What does it matter if I keep monkeys or am fat or thin or stand on my head," she once said. "What's that got to do with *art*?"

and later in Toronto met Lawren Harris and others in the Group of Seven, whose vibrant, monumental Canadian landscapes were then attracting wide notice. After seeing their work, she suddenly felt an exultant urge—to paint again! "Those pictures," she later recalled, "waked something in me that I had thought quite killed."

She began to work again—her style fully matured now, more joyful and relaxed—turning out scores of large, lavish woodland scenes. Everywhere she looked, Emily Carr found beauty. "She could give such dignity to an old gray stump," wrote one of her friends, "that she made it seem almost holy." And that was precisely how she felt about the forest. "Surely the woods are God's tabernacle," she noted in her diary. "We can see Him there."

From then on she attracted good notices at exhibitions in Toronto, Washington, London, Paris and Amsterdam. Even Victoria staged a show of her work—for one day!—and she made a speech to a women's club that included some of her harshest critics. "I tell you," she said pointedly, "it's better to be a street sweeper or a boardinghouse keeper than to lower your standard. These may

Emily Carr did many charcoal sketches (right: Jacob, an Indian boy) but it was bold, colorful landscapes such as *Above the Gravel Pit* (below) and *Wood Interior* (far right) that evoked the brooding beauty of British Columbia, and eventually won Carr fame after years of rejection. "Your pictures have creative life in them," said artist Lawren Harris. "They breathe."

spoil your temper, but they need not dwarf your soul."

Though now a critical success, Emily was still desperately poor. Once, after several canvases were shipped back from a Toronto showing, she noted in her diary, "Took $7.40 to pay express, which leaves me $1.40 to live on for one week." But she was no longer downhearted. As one newspaper reported, "She laughs at life, at idiotic conventions, at people who don't like her pictures."

In Victoria, many still didn't. On one occasion, some of Emily's friends collected $166 to donate her painting, *Kispiox Village,* to the British Columbia government. Duly accepted, it was hung in the Parliament Buildings—on an attic stairway. Later a woods scene was presented to a prominent man on his retirement; he banished it to his basement. (Dusted off and auctioned for $18,000 in 1966, it then resold for $30,000.)

In 1935, after several tradesmen shyly asked to see her paintings, Emily hit upon the idea of con-

verting her studio into a "people's gallery," so that ordinary citizens could inspect the work of various artists. But although Victoria had no galleries, the local Arts and Crafts Society coldly dismissed the idea because "it wasn't pretentious enough." So she sold her boardinghouse and moved into a small cottage. Lacking space, she burned a fortune in old sketches and paintings.

Soon famous art patrons were flocking to her door. Once, while her neighbors gaped, the Governor-General's wife drove up in a swank limousine, calling to pay respects to Millie Carr and to buy a picture. Another time she was visited by Mme. Leopold Stokowski. "You are a very great artist," the conductor's wife told her. "No," Emily answered, weeping at the rare compliment, "I'm just an old fool."

Then, in 1937, she suffered a severe heart attack. Unable to paint for three months, she began writing a book on her years among the Indians. Titled *Klee Wyck,* it won the 1941 Governor-General's Award,

"The Indian people and their Art touched me deeply," wrote Emily Carr. Fearing that West Coast Indian villages and totems were doomed to disappear, she set out to preserve them on canvas. *Kitwancool Totems* (below) typifies the "haunting solemnity" one critic found in her work. Right: Carr painted these canoes at an Indian village at Alert Bay, off the coast of Vancouver Island.

Canada's top prize for literature. Although twice felled by strokes, she managed to complete a second best seller, *The House of All Sorts,* about her boardinghouse, and continued to make sketching trips into her beloved woods, camping in an old wooden caravan and painting as well as ever. In fact, her first and only real financial success came in 1944, just a year before her death, when 57 of 60 paintings were sold at Montreal's big Dominion Gallery. Even the people of Victoria began boasting now about old Millie Carr.

But, despite all the honors heaped upon her, Emily only wanted to paint all she could. At 74, while working on 30 canvases for an exhibition, she was laid up for weeks by another heart attack. Nevertheless she completed her pictures. "She got up dozens of times and painted for just a few minutes until every one was finished," her sister Alice later revealed. "I don't want to trickle out," Emily had written in her diary. "I want to pour till the pail is empty."

# ALL OUR YESTERDAYS

"Faraway comes close
and long ago is now."

Marion Kathleen Henry

# Where the Past Shapes the Future

### By Hartley Steward

When the costume designers for the CBC's lavish television series "Jalna" wanted to know exactly what period dress to select for their characters, they visited the Public Archives of Canada. When Pierre Berton wanted to check the original documents on which he based his best-sellers on the Canadian Pacific Railway (*The National Dream* and *The Last Spike*), he too visited our national archives.

Here, safely housed in a handsome building on Ottawa's Wellington Street, just a ten-minute walk from Parliament Hill, lies the raw material of Canada's history—the precious pieces of paper, parchment, vellum, tapes and pictures that record our past.

Here is an early draft of the British North America Act which finally, on July 1, 1867, secured Canada's bloodless independence.

Here is the 1873 order in council establishing the North West Mounted Police.

Here, in picture and sound recordings, is the surrender of the German 25th Army to the 1st Canadian Corps in Wageningen, Holland, on May 5, 1945, signaling the end for Canada of more than five bitter years of war.

Here is the report of the 1885 treason trial of Louis Riel in Regina, along with letters written by Riel in prison and documents pursuing his appeals in vain all the way to the Privy Council in England. Here also is a copy of Riel's death certificate, signed by A. Jukes, Senior Surgeon, NWMP, confirming "that his death was caused by hanging, his neck being broken."

The Public Archives is one of the most modern, all-encompassing holders of records in the world—"probably the best example on earth of the total archives concept," says Dr. Wilfred I. Smith, the Dominion archivist. At its Wellington Street headquarters, there are some 35 miles of fireproof, corrosion-resistant shelves containing more than 80 million items. Covering 13 acres on 15 levels, the building is open to government officials, scholars, writers, students, amateur genealogists and anyone engaged in serious research.

In addition, the Archives' Records Centre at nearby Tunney's Pasture contains more than a million cubic feet of official government records—many of them routine documents such as letters, contracts and committee meeting transcripts. But the shelves also contain such unusual items as the magnetic tracking tape of Alouette I, Canada's first satellite.

Countless items of this nature are received each year at the center, later to be painstakingly sorted, indexed and filed by historical researchers. Material without historical value is destroyed (only about five percent of government papers are retained), that vital decision lying with the Dominion archivist. "The fate of the records," says Dr. Smith, "rests on a professional and not a political decision."

In addition to its weighty public documents, the Archives often offers poignant human glimpses of Canada past. A letter written in 1933 at the height of the Depression by a Saskatchewan woman asks Prime Minister R. B. Bennett if he would kindly order—and pay for—some long underwear for her husband. She enclosed a completed Eaton's catalogue order form. "My husband will be 64 in December," she wrote, "and has neuritis very bad at times in his arms and shoulders. We have had very little crop for the last three years . . . and my husband is drawing wood on the wagon for 34 miles." Among the papers of Sir John A. Macdonald, Canada's first prime minister, totaling some 272,200 pages, is a handwritten letter to his sister revealing his deep anxiety over the illness of his invalid wife, Isabella.

Among the items that time and events have turned from the commonplace to the significant

At the Public Archives of Canada
painstaking care is taken to preserve
the original and often delicate
material of Canada's past. Here a
worker retouches an 1840 oil
painting of Canadian politician Sir
Allan Napier MacNab.

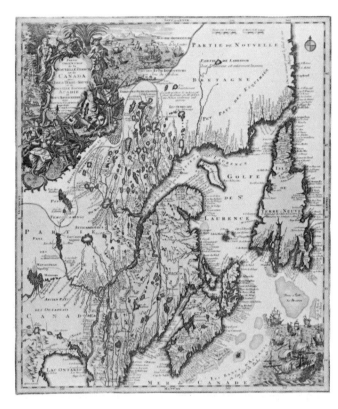

In the Public Archives' National Map Collection (below, left) are more than 750,000 drawings, charts, atlases and maps—including a map (below) of New France drawn by Mathew Seutter in 1750. Left: A technician prepares a map of Ottawa for microfilming.

is an application for a civil air license by W. A. "Billy" Bishop, Canada's greatest World War I air ace and a winner of the Victoria Cross; and a poster, signed by D. Daly, secretary of the Province of Lower Canada, offering a $4,000 reward payable "to whomsoever shall so apprehend Louis Joseph Papineau," wanted for high treason during the Rebellion of 1837.

Of more recent vintage is a tape recording of the 1966 explosion in the House of Commons, when four and a half sticks of dynamite—presumably meant to explode on the floor of the House—prematurely blew up in a nearby men's washroom, killing the would-be bomber. The Archives' Historical Sound Recordings Unit contains more than 30,000 listening hours of discs and tapes.

More than 160,000 visitors and 45,000 letter and telephone inquiries a year flow into the Wellington Street headquarters while the Tunney's Pasture Records Centre averages more than 2,000 requests for information *a day*. Inquiries take a multitude of forms. Hobbyists come in search of pictures of old locomotives or airplanes they are modeling. A veteran may want to recapture memories recorded in the Archives' collection of 750,000 military photographs. Adventure-seekers looking for sunken treasure come to examine early government sessional papers, in which shipwrecks are recorded. Hundreds of Canadians write each year to try to trace their ancestry. An American once wrote, asking: "Do you have any real scalps taken by Indians that I might examine?" The Archives didn't, but it did offer an assortment of drawings and photographs that testified to the reality of the gruesome practice.

Lawyers often make use of the Archives to establish legal precedents. A company involved in a land-ownership battle asked to see early pictures and drawings of a section of Old Quebec City. Examining drawings done before 1860 and photographs taken after that date, they were able to determine the progression of buildings occupying the site and thus the true ownership of the land.

Engineers planning a new garage behind Ottawa's Chateau Laurier Hotel, near the Parliament Buildings, turned to the Archives when they found themselves baffled by soil samples in the area. Pictures of the site over the previous 100 years showed that the soil they had been testing had actually come from excavation work done during the construction of the Rideau Canal.

For the convenience of researchers, the Archives opens three of its six reading rooms 24 hours a day, seven days a week. Researchers can obtain a locker in the Wellington Street building to store their materials, in case they want to make a visit when historians are not on duty to find material.

On a typical day, a Texan named deVilliers examines an 18th-century census return to find out if his great-great-grandmother was really an original Canadian settler from France. A Jamaican studies the history of blacks in Canada by reading reports on the underground railway which transported American slaves to Canada and freedom. A sportswriter listens to a tape of an historic, early hockey game. A Scottish priest examines a book of hymns written in an Indian language by early missionaries to Canada.

While the Public Archives has become a major historical institution, its beginnings were modest. In 1872 Parliament voted $4,000 for the project

and appointed Douglas Brymner, a well-known journalist, as Dominion archivist. Brymner was allotted space in the West Block of the Parliament Buildings. "There I was," Brymner said, "with three empty rooms and very vague instructions."

Brymner had no responsibility for records of the federal government, so he applied himself to the acquisition of private papers and to the copying of documents belonging to the governments of Britain and France. These documents, which could not be brought to Canada, were laboriously copied by hand until as late as 1950, when microfilming made the task so much quicker and cheaper.

Brymner's first major archivistic coup came in 1873. Records of the British military forces which defended Canada from 1759 to 1871, amounting to some 400,000 pieces, were then stored in Halifax. Brymner sailed for London and persuaded the British authorities to allow the records to stay in Canada. These papers tell a fascinating tale of colonial rule and defense. Documents dated 1812 detail the frantic buildup of the British fleet on the Great Lakes to hold off an anticipated assault by the United States in the War of 1812. In the Archives' National Map Collection are Capt. James Cook's charts of the St. Lawrence River, used by General Wolfe to guide his forces against France's General Montcalm.

In 1912 an act of Parliament gave the Archives new importance as the independent custodian of the nation's history. The act made the Archives a separate government department and charged the Dominion archivist with acquiring historical items by gift, by purchase or by copying material "of every kind and description." As well, the Archives was to receive records from government departments.

Today's Archives concerns itself with all aspects of Canadian life, from government to the arts,

113

Once called "Canada's collective memory," the Public Archives is a rich storehouse of the nation's history. Among more than 80 million items here are CPR general manager William Van Horne's telegram to Prime Minister Sir John A. Macdonald announcing the completion of the transcontinental railway in 1885; and a letter from Louis Riel, leader of the 1885 Northwest Rebellion, to Maj. Gen. Frederick Middleton, commander of government forces.

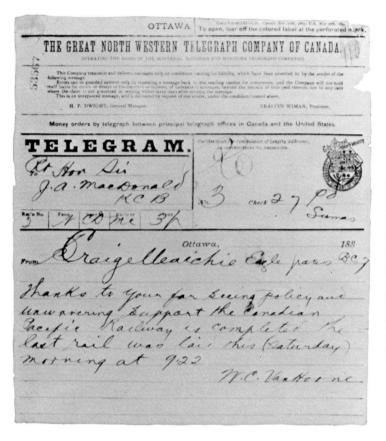

from folklore to heraldry. Through its Systematic National Acquisition Program (SNAP), the Archives is now gathering historical material on hitherto unexplored subjects—science and medicine, sports, ethnic groups, literary figures, business and labor organizations.

As well, the Archives maintains, and keeps open to the public, Laurier House, former residence of Prime Ministers Sir Wilfrid Laurier and Mackenzie King. On display in King's famous third-floor study—"the room from which the nation was governed for 22 years"—is a guest book with the signatures of King George VI, President Franklin D. Roosevelt and Sir Winston Churchill.

In response to the heightened interest in Canadian history, the Archives now mounts traveling and out-of-town exhibits of historical documents and photographs, reproduces documents for use in schools, and duplicates key papers to be put in local archives. In 1969 the National Film Collection was begun—to gather motion pictures of importance to the nation's history.

Left: Stains are removed from a print by soaking it in a bleaching solution. Below: An archives restorer carefully repairs the torn edges of this winter scene of Quebec's Montmorency Falls.

Douglas Brymner would be amazed—and delighted—to see what his "three empty rooms" have become. Documents are at fingertip recall on thousands of reels of microfilm, and a network of regional records centers across Canada answers more than 3,500 requests a day. Almost 75,000 volumes of documents and 20,000 reels of microfilm are circulated each year. To guard against decay or destruction, shelves and buildings are as fireproof as man can make them and delicate documents are laminated in clear plastic and transparent tissue against exposure to corrosive elements in the air.

Shortly before he died, Brymner wrote: "Two or three centuries count for little in the life of a people as regards its development, and particularly those centuries that have witnessed its infancy. These archives, which relate in minute detail the story of that infancy and vicissitudes it underwent, are nevertheless destined to be of the very highest interest to the great people we are yet to be."

Canada's history is taking shape at the Public Archives. Here history is not made by historians, but by the records of the real things done by real people. Here our ancestors can be seen as they truly were—sometimes wicked, sometimes generous, sometimes foolish, sometimes surprisingly wise and farsighted. Here, where the past shapes the future, is distilled the essence of the Canadian experience.

# As Much a Mood As It Is a Race

**By Bill Surface**

It is the 114th running of the Queen's Plate, at Toronto's multitiered Woodbine Race Track in June 1973. Heavily favored La Prévoyante surges around the track's final bend ahead of the 16 other thoroughbreds. Unexpectedly, three colts with combined earnings that wouldn't keep La Prévoyante in oats charge furiously. Showing even greater speed, Royal Chocolate, a reddish-chestnut 23-to-1 long shot, swerves to the outside of the field. Now, lengthening his stride as he's never done before, Royal Chocolate pulls away to a five-and-a-half-length victory—astonishing much of the crowd of 40,137.

In the horseshoe-shaped winner's enclosure, Jack Stafford, the snowy-haired owner, is realizing a lifelong dream. Stepping forward, he receives from Queen Elizabeth a purple leather case containing her 50 guineas (actually gold sovereigns) and the Ontario Jockey Club's $5,000 gold cup topped by a Canadian beaver—both seemingly more prized than the winning purse of $80,697. "We slew them, Your Majesty," says Stafford with a smile.

The lure of the Plate may move some to take uncharacteristic risks. Suspecting that their colt, Sinister Purpose, could reinjure a tendon in his right foreleg, owners and trainer agonized over the drawbacks of running on the rain-soaked course in 1973, but could not bring themselves to scratch him. With less than half a mile to the finish, an unsure step warned the jockey that Sinister Purpose might have "bowed" (ruptured) the tendon. Though in sixth place at the time, the fired-up colt rallied to finish second—then pulled up lame and was unable to race for months.

The Plate's mystique is heightened by the pattern of winning streaks that has characterized its history. While a young man in Galt, Ont., Joseph E. Seagram, founder of the worldwide distillery empire, was so impressed by the inaugural Plate that he

determined to win the race. By importing English broodmares in foal, he entered—and won—the 1891 Plate with a horse known as the "Terror colt"—later named Victorious. Horses carrying Seagram's black and yellow silks then went on to win eight consecutive Plates. By 1935, the Seagram family had won a total of 20. Another frequent winner was industrialist E. P. Taylor, who became honorary chairman of the Ontario Jockey Club. His thoroughbred nursery at Oshawa, Ont., nurtured more than 15 Plate winners.

By the 1973 Plate Day, many fans cheered for the continuation of a unique winning streak by the sons of Victoria Park, fastest Plate winner of all at 2:02 in 1960. Three of Victoria Park's sons won consecutive Plates from 1970-72. But the only son entered in 1973, Albert the Consort, had raced so sparingly that at one time he was a 70-to-1 long shot. Finally given 10-to-1 odds, he finished in fourth place. Asked why he backed "a horse like that," one fan replied: "Plate Day. I don't bet against his old man."

From the outset, the Queen's Plate has aroused fierce passions. Undaunted by the demise of an earlier stake race in Montreal, the Toronto Turf Club petitioned Queen Victoria in 1859 for permission to hold a plate in the manner of Newmarket's town plate, inaugurated by King Charles II in the 1660s. Queen Victoria agreed, giving an annual purse of 50 guineas (the traditional prize for a race since the reign of George I). On June 27, 1860, more than 4,000 residents of Toronto traveled the five miles to Carleton Race Course to see an inaugural Queen's Plate limited to Ontario-born thoroughbreds which had never won a race.

So coveted and hotly contested was the Plate that the placing judges were soon mired in owners' protests about "ringers" and "outsiders." In the fourth Plate, in 1863, Willie Wonder, a seven-year-

116

Horses thunder down the stretch in the 1973 Queen's Plate, won by Royal Chocolate, a 23-to-1 shot. A $5,000 gold cup goes to the owner of the winning horse, smaller replicas to the trainer and the jockey.

old roan, trailed hopelessly throughout the opening heat, then so outdistanced the field in the next two heats that charges were raised that he was not the same horse. After a two-week investigation, the judges announced only that second-placed Touchstone was the official winner.

Two years later, Harry Chappel "of Sandwich, Ont.," saw his horse win consecutive heats, only to be identified as a resident of Detroit and therefore ineligible for the Plate. When the judges declared the winner to be Beacon (which finished second), they found that its jockey had improved his chances by illegally tossing away the lead bars in his saddle. In the match race to decide the winner of the Plate, Nora Criena outran Lady Norfolk by two lengths. But, conditioned by prior shenanigans, the judges waited two months to announce the official winner: inexplicably, Lady Norfolk!

Such controversies served only to heighten the Plate's fame. Politicians lobbied furiously to bring it to their area. Between 1865 and 1882, the Plate was moved to 12 different Ontario sites, including London, Hamilton, St. Catharines, Kingston and Ottawa. In the flag-draped carnival atmosphere of Plate Day, roads were clogged with polished carriages carrying women sporting the latest fashions. Hundreds of men rode atop packed Grand Trunk Railway cars bound for the Plate, and Lake Ontario steamers brought racing enthusiasts from the United States.

By the early 1880s, the Plate sometimes drew so many frontier-town rowdies to the drinking and gambling sections flanking the main grandstand, that the ceremonial hussars had to clear them from the course in order for the race to start. Fearing that its itinerant and controversial image would kill the Plate, its organizers persuaded T. C. Patteson, Toronto's courtly postmaster and financier of the old Toronto *Mail*, to try to stabilize the race. Promising to "put down all nefarious practices with a strong hand," Patteson formed the Ontario Jockey Club to sponsor the race (as it still does) and, in 1883, persuaded Queen Victoria to request that it be permanently run at Woodbine Race Track. With the Queen's daughter, Princess Louise, representing her the same year, the Plate's popularity continued to soar. Such was Plate "fever" that in 1918, when all racing was suspended until the end of World War I, it was held as a nonbetting feature of the Toronto Hunt Club's Red Cross Horse Show.

In 1956, after 73 consecutive years at the repeatedly enlarged old Woodbine, the Plate moved to a new glass and brick Woodbine rising five stories above northwest Toronto's flatland. Other changes, too, have altered the nature of the Plate.

Queen's Plate day: thumb-biting tension, careful study before placing that bet—then the frenzied excitement of the big race.

Gradually, the distance has been brought from the original one mile to the present one-and-a-quarter miles. And in 1944 the rules were amended to permit any Canadian-owned and -foaled thoroughbred to compete. As a result of this increased competition, more and more Plate winners in recent years have become champions elsewhere. For example, Northern Dancer, the cocky bay colt which rallied from last place to win the 1964 Plate, also won the Kentucky Derby and Baltimore's Preakness the same year, while Kennedy Road, the 1971 winner, went on to become one of the leading money winners in the United States.

By now, the Plate is almost as much a mood as it is a race. On and off the track, there are special dinners, breakfasts, a charity ball, a parade of antique carriages and special days enlivened by the colorful pipe and drum bands of the highland regiments.

Two days before the 1973 Plate, for example, Woodbine was a homecoming for horses and horsemen alike. Between races, former winners Victoria Song, Almoner, Jumpin Joseph and Lyford Cay paraded onto the track in their original winning silks. Heavier than during their racing days, they all broke into a gallop at the first inkling of applause. Ears pricked forward. Several old champions so clearly enjoyed their "comeback" that they wanted to race each other.

When it came time to draw the names determining the 1973 post positions, doing the honors was vacationing jockey Ron Turcotte of Grand Falls, N.B., who had just ridden Secretariat to a celebrated

119

Mud-spattered jockey Robin Platts
holds the Queen's Plate trophy
after riding Sound Reason to victory
on Woodbine's waterlogged track
in 1977.

victory in the U.S. Triple Crown (Kentucky Derby,
Preakness and Belmont Stakes). Asked why he
chose a racing holiday after achieving the first triple
crown in 25 years, Turcotte reflected on the irony
that many of Canada's greatest jockeys, including
himself and the legendary Johnny Longden, had
failed to win the Plate. "I've won just about every
major North American race," he said, his grin
widening, "but I'm a Canadian, and the biggest
prize for me is still to win the Plate."

121

# "That Could Be a Whiskey Boat!"

## By Robert Collins

It was about 4 p.m. on November 18, 1922, when the long blast of a whistle, the wail of a ship in distress, rang out along Lake Erie's north shore. Five miles west of the fishing village of Port Rowan, Ont., farmhand Charles LaChapelle looked up from his chores. The steamer, a couple of miles distant, was laboring toward shore through whitecaps ten feet high, a vicious 45-m.p.h. gale at its back.

"That boat's in trouble!" he cried. He and his boss, Charlie Foster, yanked on rubber boots, jumped in a Model T Ford and drove to the edge of the beach. LaChapelle then sprinted ahead to join Stanley Skuce and Lee Beaupre from neighboring farms. "Boys," said Skuce, more by hope than by hunch, "that could be a whiskey boat!"

In Ontario, as in most Canadian provinces in 1922, it was illegal to make or carry liquor for sale *within* the province, except for medicinal purposes. However, it was permissible to *export* spirits by rail or water. Earlier that month, two carloads of Old Crow and Corby's Special Selected—more than a thousand cases and kegs valued at $50,000—went out by train from Corbyville, Ont., to nearby Belleville. There the cargo went aboard *City of Dresden*, a 50-year-old wooden steamer with a crew of six. Officially, the load was bound for Mexico via a port in Michigan.

On Friday, November 17, the *Dresden* was pulling out of Port Maitland, Ont., having moved from Lake Ontario through the Welland Canal into Lake Erie. A storm was rising, and fishing boats were hurrying back to port. But Capt. John Sylvester McQueen, with a deadline to meet, pressed on. By afternoon, a howling gale was blowing as the *Dresden* approached Long Point, a notorious "graveyard" for Lake Erie shipping. In no shape to buck a storm, the ancient *Dresden* hove to in the bay north of Long Point. Then, on Saturday, a northerly wind began to sweep the steamer in to shore. Cap-

tain McQueen pulled out around the Long Point lighthouse while his crew lightened the ship by dumping some whiskey cases stowed on deck.

On shore, a lone Port Rowanite patrolled the beach as duty member of the lighthouse lifesaving crew. Suddenly, like a mirage, a case of Corby's whiskey frolicked in on the waves. The lifesaver stood transfixed. Then came another and another. The lifesaver sprang into action. By night he had rescued and neatly buried 42 cases beside the telephone poles leading to the lighthouse.

Meanwhile, laboring toward Port Burwell 35 miles away, the *Dresden* was in serious trouble. The wind, shifting to the southwest, was again driving her inshore and the hull was leaking so badly that even the fireman would not go below. Ray Sawyer, the engineer, went to the wheelhouse. "We better beach her, skipper," he urged.

Captain McQueen, short and 65 but still an imposing figure in his blue uniform, would have none of it. Sawyer then turned to his friend and ex-schoolmate, 21-year-old Peregrine McQueen, the skipper's son. "*You* tell the old man to beach her," he begged. Peregrine did, and reluctantly his father headed for a cove five miles west of Port Rowan, blowing his distress signal.

But Lake Erie's treacherous undercurrent dragged the ship onto a sandbar several hundred yards from shore. As she began breaking up, the crew lowered a lifeboat. It turned over and was swept away. They dropped a second boat, with no oars or life jackets, and scrambled in. It, too, capsized. In the melee of arms and legs, Peregrine, who couldn't swim, struggled for his life. Although hampered by an artificial leg, Sawyer tried to help, but too late. The young man was lifted on a breaker and vanished in the waves.

Somehow righting the boat, the others drifted helplessly for perhaps an hour. Each time their craft

The fury of a storm on Lake Erie was recorded in this early print of wave-tossed ships off Long Point, a slender, 22-mile-long finger of land near Port Rowan, Ont. Long Point's beaches, marshes and waters are a graveyard for many sailors and for the remnants of wrecked ships—including the hulk of *City of Dresden*, a 165-foot steamer that went down in 1922, setting off a mad scramble for its cargo of whiskey.

neared shore, the waves and undertow threw it back. It was getting dark and colder; ice was forming along the edge of the beach.

Meanwhile, in her farm home not far from the lake, Pearl Rockefeller, wife of a cattle buyer, and her niece Viola Blackenbury, had also heard the distress signal. With her husband Delbert away in town that afternoon, she and her niece hitched a fast horse to the buggy and galloped off to watch the drama unfold. "That boat was being tossed around like a top," Pearl recalled later. "And I saw that those poor men didn't have much chance of getting ashore without help."

What happened after that has been disputed for six decades. Newspapers all over southern Ontario later cited Pearl and Viola as heroines and Ray Sawyer always insisted that the two women pulled the lifeboat in single-handed. But others,

including Charles LaChapelle, claimed that Mrs. Rockefeller "didn't even get out of her buggy." The truth may lie in a letter written by nine Port Rowanites to the Toronto *Globe* a few days after the wreck: "The lifeboat drifted nearly half a mile down the lake with the current, then a line was thrown ashore and some half-dozen or more people, Mrs. Rockefeller included, drew the boat up on the beach so that all but the captain got ashore themselves."

The captain, barely conscious, was carried ashore by Skuce, Beaupre and LaChapelle and tucked into Pearl Rockefeller's buggy. People gave up their own coats to the shivering crew and hustled them to the Rockefeller and Skuce homes.

Back at the beach the stage was set for what *The Simcoe Reformer* later described as "glorious revelry and debauch." The *Dresden*'s hull had disintegrated and her engines had sunk. The beach was literally awash with whiskey—some 6,000 gallons of it. As scores of people surged in with wagons, buggies, cars and wheelbarrows, it was quickly established that Corby's Special Selected was a mellow brand while Old Crow was made of sterner stuff. "When that Old Crow took effect, you were dead all over!" an old-timer marveled years later.

A half-dozen young bank employes sped 35 miles from Aylmer to fill a bag with bottles. Some of the beachcombers buried entire cases in the swamp, marking the site for future reference, whereupon their neighbors frequently shifted the markers and staked out the booty for themselves. Other prohibition-parched citizens simply sat down and guzzled on the spot.

In the carnival atmosphere nearly everyone overlooked the tragedy of the night. On Sunday morning young Peregrine McQueen's body drifted ashore, a deep gash on his forehead indicating that he had been stunned when the second lifeboat capsized.

Although news of the wreck flashed like lightning in some quarters, it was pitifully slow reaching the law in Simcoe, 30 miles away—mainly because the Simcoe telephone line had been cut Saturday night. By the time license inspector Richard Edmonds and two constables arrived, they found little but wreckage and a crisscross of tracks that blotted out any hope of following a trail. Clearly there had been a massive violation of the Temperance Act—but where was the evidence?

All sorts of ingenious hideouts were used—eaves troughs, floorboards, even manure piles. One farmer ploughed a furrow in his field and hastily sowed it with whiskey. Lorne Skuce sank some bottles in the cistern outside his house, prudently skimming off the labels that surfaced every few days.

On Monday afternoon, after a fruitless four-mile search along the beach, the lawmen returned to Simcoe, weary and frustrated. But Inspector Edmonds doggedly continued the search. He questioned the lifesaver on duty at the lighthouse, who readily admitted to "finding a few bottles" which he would gladly turn over to the law. But he had instructed a crony to unearth just one case from the cache along the telephone poles. When he and Edmonds arrived they found a gaping hole and an empty case. "Why, some sonofabitch has stole my whiskey!" raged the lifesaver.

"Ill-gotten gains can do no one any good," remonstrated Edmonds. The Port Rowanite hung his head remorsefully until the inspector was gone. Then he briskly moved the other 41 cases to a safer hideout, later sold them (going rate: $60 a case) and reportedly paid off a mortgage.

By Tuesday whiskey-hunters were arriving from as far away as Simcoe. Chortled the *Reformer*: "Charlie Terhune says water from the bay is selling at five cents a glass." Yet Inspector Edmonds persisted. Within two weeks he had located 22 cases of whiskey in the swamp, charged six Port Rowanites with theft and hailed five of them into court. (The sixth, reported the *Reformer*, was on "an extended leave of absence" but ultimately returned with a lawyer.) Court was promptly adjourned for lack of evidence, the crown attorney complaining that he couldn't get witnesses to testify for the government.

Indeed, Port Rowanites were not about to squeal on their neighbors when fines for illegal possession of liquor could run to $1,000 or three to six months in jail, while unlawful sale could cost the vendor $2,000. And few saw anything wrong in claiming salvage from the sea.

Finally, in a series of comic-opera courtroom scenes, the law and Port Rowan came to grips. Delbert Rockefeller was found with ring marks

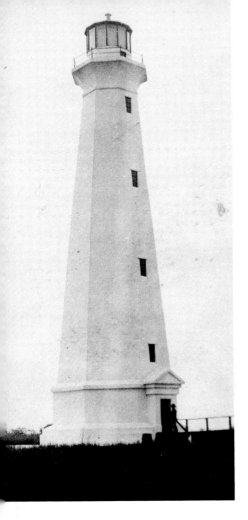

When whiskey from the foundering *City of Dresden* (below) washed ashore, a member of the local life-saving crew wasted no time: within hours he had cached 42 cases of liquor near the Long Point lighthouse (left).

of ten whiskey kegs in his wagon on the Monday after the wreck. "His horses were rarin' in the stables with harness on," police testified. Noncommittal, Rockefeller elected trial by jury.

Two other Port Rowanites were charged with theft of wreckage but refused to admit that they had possessed liquor, even though Richard Edmonds produced a written statement saying one of them had been drinking on the beach. Lee Beaupre testified that the beach was strewn with cases and kegs on Saturday but that they had vanished by Sunday. "The majority of the witnesses were at the scene of the wreck within a few hours of the catastrophe," summed up the *Reformer*, "but remembered little of what took place."

The handful finally convicted, among them Delbert Rockefeller, were fined a grand total of $700. The presiding magistrate fumed that certain Port Rowanites were "a disgrace to the community." But the Port Rowanites quietly swallowed their shame, along with comforting dollops of Old Crow.

Officially, that was the end of it, but the whiskey saga lingered on. Some citizens, upon finishing a keg, sold the empty barrel to a farmer for storing cider. It was said to give cider a remarkable lift. Others, during the following summer, were seen to go into their gardens and dig up an evening's refreshment. Local bootleggers went nearly bankrupt for a year or more.

In the summer of 1923, Captain McQueen and Sawyer returned to salvage the *Dresden*'s engines—and recovered a keg, too. Two years later a farmer's hogs rooted up a bottle in a pigpen. Later still, whiskey was found in a drainage ditch, and in a false ceiling during a fire.

But even now Port Rowanites are loath to mention names in telling the tale of the *Dresden*. Few actually admit to having possessed the spoils. ("Well . . . I guess it's all right to tell you . . . I had a *little* of it," said Charles LaChapelle.) And if any of the spoils have been found recently, marvelously aged after more than half a century, nobody is talking.

Of course, anyone can now get Corby Special Selected at the Port Rowan liquor store. But the legal product somehow just doesn't taste the same.

During the two world wars some 113,000 Canadians were killed in action, most on the battlefields of Europe. By their sacrifice these men helped to shape the destiny of Canada—and of the world. Here are two stories of remembrance: Holland's remarkable tribute to Canada's fallen; and, on page 131, one man's recollection of a young soldier's last letter.

The Canadian war cemetery at Bergen op Zoom in Holland.

# The Message of the Tulips

### By George G. Blackburn

It was a cold, foggy Sunday morning in December. The Canadian war cemetery at Bergen op Zoom in southern Holland lay under a blanket of freshly fallen snow. It was only 8:30, but already there were footprints leading to one of the graves.

What prompted this early-morning pilgrimage to a Canadian soldier's grave? We shall never know. It could have been the anniversary of his death, his birthday, or merely that someone remembered he had died on a morning such as this. Such days seldom pass unnoticed by the more than 2,000 Dutch families who have adopted the graves where Canadian soldiers were buried during World War II.

Back in October 1944, when the weary, rain-soaked Canadians fought their way into Holland, they had no inkling that they were setting the stage for a remarkable expression of affection between two far-flung nations. Fighting on the left of the Allied line, the First Canadian Army had been ordered to clear the Germans from the estuary of the River Scheldt and so open the shipping lanes to the vital port of Antwerp. It was a bitter, bloody battle fought over the flat and sodden *polder* country the Dutch had reclaimed from the sea.

"The countryside was a diabolical ruin of felled trees, craters, wire and mines, with the enemy dug in along every dike bank," wrote war correspondent R. W. Thompson in *The 85 Days*. "There were no fires. There was no rest. Men lived and died and slept always wet and caked with ooze." By December, more than 6,300 Canadians had been killed or wounded; 11,600 more were to follow them before Holland was liberated in May 1945.

During the happy days after the victory in Normandy, the French and Belgians along the liberation routes had made their emotions known with cheering, flowers, fruit and cognac. But the people of the polders were quiet and reserved, and the battle that raged over their ruined villages left them too exhausted for immediate expressions of gratitude.

When peace came, and the happy Dutch took to the streets in celebration, most Canadian troops were deep in northwest Germany. Later, when they returned to Holland to await repatriation, they experienced a warm welcome in Dutch homes. But they were unaware of the special place they had won in Dutch hearts.

The first official gesture of gratitude to Canada was the gift of the finest embassy building in The Hague. Typically, the Dutch made it acceptable by claiming that it was in recognition of necessities supplied by Canada in the first days of liberation. In Holland's impoverished state–the country had suffered material losses of more than $7 billion, including 100,000 homes destroyed and 50,000 damaged–this was a remarkable sacrifice.

Then in September 1946, Holland shipped, as a thank-you gift from her Queen, 20,000 tulip bulbs to bloom in the flower beds of Ottawa. This time, the Dutch were expressing their gratitude to the city which had provided a wartime refuge for their Princess (later Queen) Juliana. The next year another shipment arrived–and the next year, and the next. With more than a million blossoms bursting forth in Ottawa's flower beds each spring, the bulbs are still arriving.

When nations were vying to prove how advanced they were at Expo 67, Holland devoted her pavilion's central theme to telling the world of Canada's role in her liberation, and to back it up distributed a handsome book entitled *Thank you, Canada.*

But 1970, the 25th anniversary of the liberation, was unquestionably the high-water mark of the Dutch people's expression of gratitude. Canadian embassy officials despair of ever completing a final report on all the events honoring Canada that took place throughout Holland. Moreover, Dutch Cana-

127

Princess (later Queen) Juliana holds Princess Margriet following the baby's christening in 1943 at St. Andrew's Presbyterian Church in Ottawa. Looking on is her husband, Prince Bernhard (with hand on railing). Their child was born at Ottawa's Civic Hospital in a room temporarily declared Dutch territory.

dians across Canada arranged their own commemorative projects, setting up a national committee to organize "Operation Thank You Canada."

The planning began in autumn 1969 with a Canada-wide distribution of 150,000 tulip bulbs. Recalling how bulbs were the daily diet for many during the 1944-45 hunger winter, Dutch Canadians bought the "Liberation" bulbs from their homeland and gave them away for planting in parks, local war memorials, and gardens of friends. Next spring the tulips blossomed across Canada—a thank-you message in flaming red (for the blood of the fallen) and orange (Holland's royal color).

To make their Canadian-born children aware of their new country's bond with Holland, the Dutch Canadians had arranged a "walkathon" to raise money for this national thank-you gift. And, as hundreds of children walked 10 to 15 miles to a farm to ask for a potato or a carrot, they acted out the grueling hunger marches made by their parents and grandparents during that terrible starvation winter.

A nationwide competition for a Canadian-Dutch friendship song was organized; two 200-voice choirs from Maastricht and The Hague, and the Royal Netherlands Airforce Band toured Canada; bronze plaques were presented to Canadian regiments which had fought in Holland; a roof garden was erected at a Vancouver veterans' hospital where some Canadians wounded in Holland still lay. And if this were not enough the Dutch Canadians presented two magnificent baroque pipe organs to the National Arts Centre in Ottawa.

Yet, generous as such actions are, none are more poignant and meaningful than the quiet, personal gestures of gratitude made each day by ordinary people in Holland. Busloads of factory workers stop to pay silent tribute at Canadian war cemeteries. Children decorate the graves on special commemorative days. And, through the volunteer work of the Netherlands War Graves Committee, Canadian graves have received regular care by Dutch families who have come to regard the men who lie in them as their own.

Schoolteacher Jan Kroon, a former Dutch Resistance fighter, recalled how one evening in September 1946 he pedaled out to Holten cemetery to update his lists of Canadian war dead whose names were then marked only on temporary wooden crosses. In the cemetery, he saw a young woman alone, weeping before a cross. Kroon introduced himself, and learned that she was a Canadian visiting her husband's grave. They had been married only a few weeks before he was sent to Holland. To pay for her trip to his grave, the woman had sold everything she owned.

Kroon never forgot that meeting. As a result of it and other similar experiences, Herman Götzen, a banker, and then chairman of the war graves committee, decided to organize, in coöperation with the Royal Canadian Legion, low-cost group flights to Holland for relatives of dead Canadian soldiers. The visitors stayed with the Dutch families who had "adopted" their men. More than 1,600 Canadi-

In gratitude to Canada for her wartime liberation of Holland, the Dutch have sent more than a million tulip bulbs to bloom in Ottawa since 1946.

ans made this poignant pilgrimage, many on flights financed largely from funds raised by the Dutch.

What prompts the Dutch to refuse to allow the years to erode a memory and to ensure that future generations will keep it bright? "It's the least we could do—did these Canadians not sacrifice their lives for our freedom?" said Mrs. A. Blom-de Recht, former national director of the war graves committee.

The Dutch who endured the occupation have lingering memories of what the liberation meant to them. One, Dr. Willem Enklaar, will never forget a knock on the door soon after midnight on New Year's Day 1943. His father had just proposed a toast of thanksgiving that the family had survived another year. A Gestapo officer at the door ordered them to follow him, and for the next three months he and his parents were held as hostages under threat of

death if any "incident" occurred to displease the local occupation authorities.

Another, Tjibo Prak, recalls how his father helped people to escape the Gestapo until he himself was put into a concentration camp. Tjibo was once allowed to visit the camp, but his father couldn't speak for crying. When finally released, his nights were haunted by nightmares of young boys ordered to retrieve their caps from among electrified barbed wires where the guards had thrown them.

Such memories keep the gratitude alive, as I discovered when I returned to Holland with my wife, and found that Canadian visitors are still made aware, in countless ways, that they are special.

Near Woensdrecht we visited a farm, the shattered wreck of which I'd used as an artillery observation post in October 1944. Here an appalling

number of my comrades had fallen in the battle to cut off South Beveland.

Sjef Pijnen and his brother Louis were living there when the Canadians attacked Woensdrecht. For several days the farm sat untouched as guns reduced the village to rubble. Then, one afternoon a long line of Canadians crawled out from Woensdrecht into the polders. The Royal Regiment of Canada drove the Germans back to the next dike, but for 16 days the Germans lashed the farm with shells and mortars as they counterattacked.

One night—on "Black Friday," October 13—stretcher-bearing jeeps in a steady stream went up to the Pijnen farmhouse and came back loaded with wounded. The Black Watch of Canada had lost 183 men in trying to take the next dike, and all four company commanders had been wounded.

When the battle moved on, Louis returned to survey his wrecked home. His cows were all dead in the fields. An old driving-horse lay crumpled in his yard. His six workhorses had died in their stalls in his brick barn. Brick dust scattered by the exploding shells had settled on every part of them, freezing their final convulsions of agony in a mold of red clay. His faithful dog Fanny, which I had driven from the farm because she had been maddened by the shelling, had not returned.

Now the farm was restored, neat, and prosperous. All afternoon I explored old memories with Louis, conversing in pidgin Dutch and English, supported by wild pantomime. And for me at least one unanswered question was resolved: what had happened to Fanny, whose screeching had haunted me since the day I had chased her away? As Louis replied, I felt foolish at the depth of my relief: yes, Fanny had recovered and lived to a ripe old age.

The Dutch are not inclined to emotional displays, but now and then their well-disciplined emotions *do* break down when memories are too much to bear. So it was as Louis waved us good-by, tears streaming down his rugged face. In searching for the message of the tulips, I found none more eloquent than these tears. For it is in the silent soil of selflessness that the countless strands of friendship between individuals are being nurtured and are binding two countries in trust and friendship more firmly than a thousand treaties.

# A Battlefield Letter

## By Douglas How

Every Remembrance Day the same scene comes back to my mind. As I hear the tramp of the veterans' feet and the majestic lament of "The Last Post," I see a soldier lying in an Italian field. He is very young, little more than a boy—a private in the West Nova Scotia Regiment. He lies crumpled and alone in the fresh grass of May, and no one has yet come to cover him with the gray blanket they use to cover the dead. He has fallen in the great and bloody battle of 1944 to break the Hitler Line, the last vicious barrier before Rome.

All around this young soldier is the lovely valley of the Liri River, shuddering under the blows of war. Behind lies the great rock where Monte Cassino stood, conquered after months of bitter fighting. To the left, in front of him, stands the city of Pontecorvo where the dead lie thick in the streets and the buildings gape in ruin. To the right is Aquino airport, with the charred hulks of a dozen Canadian tanks caught in the open on a sunny

morning and destroyed in a matter of minutes. Not far ahead lies the ugly apparatus of the Hitler Line itself, a mesh of steel and wire and guns, a thing so terrible that one wonders whether men could ever smash a way through it or even have the courage to try.

Just in front of the boy is a snarl of broken earth, torn asunder by the exploding shell that killed him. His hands stretch out toward it, and in one there is a sheet of paper. I see it, white in the sun, as I come across the field, a war correspondent heading for Pontecorvo. I see it and something makes me reach down and take it.

It is a letter to his mother written shortly before he went into battle. "I am well," the letter says, "and hope you are the same." It says not to worry, and it goes on about little things. No immortal phrases. No eloquent appeal for courage if he should die. No mention of the battle ahead. Just a simple letter from a soldier to his home.

I stand there, reading it, stricken by an overwhelming sense of the loneliness of death in battle. I stand for a long time, wondering why he has it in his hand.

I picture him dying, and knowing he is dying. He takes out the letter he has written home. Perhaps he reads it. Perhaps he only wants to make sure it's seen and posted. Or perhaps, as he dies, he wants to feel some link with the most precious things of all, his home and family. Perhaps he even feels he has just enough strength left to write good-by.

I don't know. I didn't know then, and I don't know now. But every Remembrance Day that scene, and his name, come back to me. I found his name on the little tag soldiers wore around their necks. I found it later in the history of his regiment. It gave just his name and rank—listed, where they belong, under "The Immortal Dead."

131

# The House That Smythe Built

**By Robert Collins**

With a minute left in regulation play, Maple Leaf Gardens was in an uproar. The audacious Montreal Canadiens were leading the hometown Toronto Maple Leafs 2-1. It was the fifth game of the 1951 Stanley Cup final and the Leafs had taken three, all in nerve-wracking overtime. A win would give them the supreme prize of professional hockey. But as the seconds ticked by, the 14,577 screaming Toronto partisans were losing hope.

Then coach Joe Primeau benched his goaltender and sent out six attackers in front of the Leafs' empty net—one of hockey's most daring gambles.

Leafs' center Ted Kennedy stole the face-off. Winger Max Bentley dipsy-doodled the puck through a maze of Canadiens. Leafs' forward Tod Sloan, lurking beside the Montreal goal, batted it in, with just 32 seconds left on the clock.

The teams came out for sudden-death overtime. Two minutes and 50 seconds later, Bill Barilko (who was to die that summer in a plane crash) took a pass and backhanded it in one great diving lunge. As he crashed on his face, his winning goal thwanged into the net, and the ice surface vanished in a blizzard of programs, rubbers and hats.

132

Built by Conn Smythe (below), the Toronto-born hockey coach and manager, Maple Leaf Gardens has become a Canadian landmark since it opened in November 1931.

Maple Leaf players celebrate around the Stanley Cup after defeating the Detroit Red Wings in the 1964 final. Players include Frank Mahovlich (far left) and, from the right of the cup, George Armstrong (10), Bob Pulford and Bob Baun, who played the final game on a broken ankle.

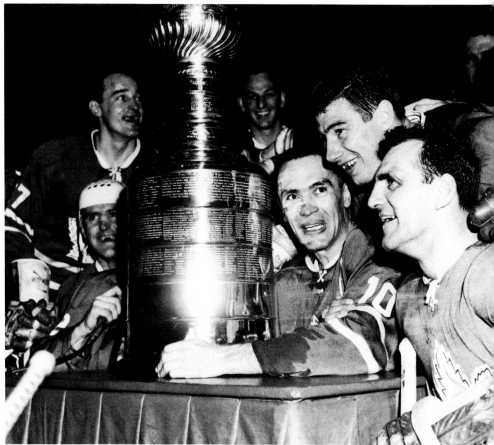

For the more than 80 million people who have gratefully shelled out hard cash to see such action, Maple Leaf Gardens has filled the years with drama and memories. The Gardens has become possibly the most famous building in Canada. A visitor from Saskatoon, reverently eyeing the empty rink one summer, timidly asked a Gardens executive, "Do you mind if I just put my foot on it?" When a Russian atomic energy delegation journeyed to Toronto from Ottawa, they came not to see the elegant city hall but to visit the dowdy brick building on Carlton Street.

It is not just an ice palace, though hockey takes up more than one third of the 250 days a year that something goes on there. Here Winston Churchill spoke; Cassius Clay beat George Chuvalo; Elvis Presley waggled his hips; and John Diefenbaker sang his leadership swan song. Bob Hope, Billy Graham, Jean Harlow, Governor Wallace of Alabama, and the Moscow Circus bears all were here to do their thing.

Risë Stevens, playing *Carmen* in the Gardens with the Metropolitan Opera in the '50s, set a world record for opera attendance with an audience of

133

13,700. Afterward, during the curtain calls, the opera star signaled the houselights up so she, too, could see this famous place. She looked out at a yawning expanse of 13 million cubic feet—big enough to hold two percent of an average prairie grain surplus. Soaring 13 stories from floor to dome, it covers a city block. The inner core now seats more than 16,300 hockey fans (with space for some 100 standees), and about 18,500 for other events. Not one post blocks the patrons' view.

This masterpiece was the creation of Conn Smythe, a leathery little man with burning eyes and a voice like a buzz saw. After World War I, in which he won the Military Cross, Smythe became a hockey coach and manager. In 1926 he and two others scraped together enough money to buy a National Hockey League team, the floundering Toronto St. Pats (which he renamed), and set out to build champions and an arena befitting them.

Smythe's search for land in downtown Toronto was twice foiled. Finally Eaton's offered a corner lot at Church and Carlton streets for $350,000. Smythe grabbed it for $50,000 down, selling Eaton's $25,000 worth of stock in the unbuilt Gardens to boot. Then he stirred up so much public enthusiasm for the arena that, despite the stock-market crash of October 1929, he was able to talk his reluctant board of directors into carrying on. Even so, the Depression frightened many investors and trade unions, and the building might never have risen if a Smythe associate, Frank Selke, had not had the inspired idea to offer the construction workers 20 percent of their pay in Gardens stock. It has handsomely repaid the few who hung onto it. In one 15-year span, a $10,000 investment in Gardens shares multiplied to $65,000.

The Gardens was built in just five months. Among its many remarkable features is the "gondola" for radio commentary, designed by Foster Hewitt, then the Gardens' new radio director. To get into the broadcast booth, perched 56 feet above the ice, Hewitt had to crawl on his hands and knees along a catwalk, 90 feet from ground level, then straight down a marine ladder. Movie actor George Raft almost fainted en route one night and had to be helped back.

Right into the '50s, the only national hockey broadcasts and telecasts were from the Maple Leaf Gardens. "Hockey Night in Canada" became the way millions of families spent a Saturday night. They waited breathlessly for Foster Hewitt's famil-

Canadian George Chuvalo went the full 15 rounds but lost a decision to Cassius Clay in this 1966 heavyweight bout at the Gardens.

iar opener, "Hello Canada, and hockey fans in the United States and Newfoundland..." That voice made Maple Leaf Gardens a byword throughout North America and, during his World War II broadcasts, to Canadian troops overseas in Europe and Asia too.

Conn Smythe built his teams with shrewd trades and careful harvests from his farm system—Harvey "Busher" Jackson, Charlie Conacher, Lorne Chabot, Hap Day, Harold Cotton, and—the prize of them all—Michael Francis "King" Clancy, a talented leprechaun for whom Smythe paid the Ottawa Sen-

ators the then awesome sum of $35,000 and who earned the princely salary of $10,000 a year. Clancy went on to become coach, assistant manager, and vice-president of the team.

The Gardens came to be the heart and soul of Toronto. Always immaculate, it soon attracted every conceivable mass function: political rallies, religious conventions, six-day bike races, ice shows, circuses, wrestling, Scout jamborees, bingo, opera, and folk festivals. The rental policy was liberal. In 1934, Tim Buck—then Canada's leading communist and fresh out of prison—was permitted to stage a rally there, and drew 17,000 people. In 1966 when other North American arenas shunned him, the Gardens took in Cassius Clay for his fight with Chuvalo, at a time when the U.S. draft board dearly wanted Clay too.

Clay's presence enraged the doughty Conn Smythe, a veteran of two world wars. He had already relinquished active management to his son, Stafford, and Stafford's partner, Harold Ballard; now Conn resigned his Gardens directorship over the Clay booking. Stafford and Ballard went ahead anyway, as they had earlier on another issue the elder Smythe opposed: the opening in 1963 of the successful Gardens Hot Stove Club, a private restaurant and bar.

Today, anyone with about $15,000 and an act in good taste can rent the Gardens for a day. Good taste *is* a factor. A closed circuit telecast of the revue *Oh! Calcutta!* was rejected on those grounds, as was a bid from a U.S. rock singer whose act was considered obscene. Big single draws have included the Beatles, the Rolling Stones, Tom Jones, Johnny Cash and Alice Cooper—all running more than 18,000 in attendance.

But hockey is still what the Gardens is all about. Every year 600,000 people attend the games and five million more watch every telecast. The Leafs have rewarded them with 11 Stanley Cups and a succession of stars, from Syl Apps, epitome of the clean-cut all-Canadian athlete, to defenseman Bobby Baun who gave a spectacular exhibition of guts in the 1964 Stanley Cup final. Baun left one game on a stretcher, only to limp back in overtime and score the winning goal. He returned to star in the next and final game. Only then did he reveal that he had been playing on sheer nerve, and a broken ankle.

Behind the visible heroics of every hockey night is the Gardens' staff. They begin arriving by 8 a.m.

on any hockey day: mechanics, electricians, cleaners, concessionaires. By nine some are dusting the seats, sweeping floors, or checking escalators. Two are at their perpetual task of repainting the Gardens' interior, which consumes some 3,000 gallons a year. Others are marshaling the fans' evening snack: $6,500 worth of chips, popcorn, peanuts, cold drinks, candy and coffee.

Down at the ticket wickets a few hopefuls press their noses against the burglarproof glass but, as always, tonight's game was sold out two days ago. The Gardens has had sellout games since 1946, and there's always a long waiting list for season tickets.

Deep in the basement, the building engineer runs an icemaking machine that pipes 30,000 gallons of brine beneath the ice surface, keeping it at 11°C. At game time he sets the Gardens temperature at about 20°C, knowing that those howling fans will generate another seven to 12 degrees of heat.

A man goes up inside the 7½-ton electric timer hanging over center ice, to check the 3,200 light bulbs that blink out penalties, periods and scores. For a half hour, long enough for television crews to "balance" their cameras, they turn on the 78 floodlights, 5,000 watts apiece and more than $3,500 on the nightly hydro bill.

By late afternoon, the Gardens is hushed, glistening, cathedral-like, the ice shimmering like a jewel. The Leafs' empty dressing room is waiting for the gladiators: blue broadloom, blue-and-white walls, blue-and-white sweaters lined up on hooks like ghosts waiting for bodies to inhabit them. The tiny Gardens hospital, crisp and antiseptic, is ready for skate cuts, stick slashes, or a spectator tagged with a flying puck.

By 6:30 p.m. the food vendors and attendants are in position. Usherettes and ushers are instructed

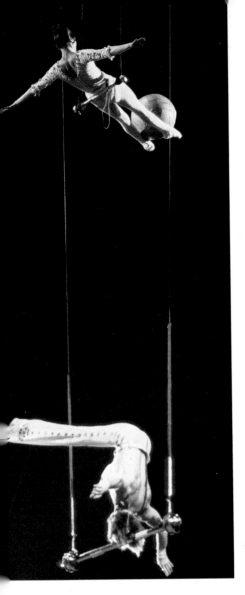

Trapeze artists with the Moscow Circus perform high above the Gardens' floor. For such events the 200-by-85-foot ice surface disappears under plywood boards. For an equestrian event (below) the boards are covered with six inches of clay loam—worth about $10,000.

to be tolerant about noise. Thus, the man who rallies the Leafs every few minutes with off-key blasts from his trumpet is permitted his fun (many fans join him, with stirring cries of "Charge! Charge!"). But the Chicagoan who one night brought in an earsplitting portable siren was urged to desist.

At 7 p.m. the first fans whoop through the turnstiles. On Carlton Street the scalpers prowl: "Awright, awright, who wants two in the blues?" Seats near ice level for a big game might go for $100 apiece.

Foster Hewitt, who calls the radio play-by-play, and his son Bill, who does the telecast, climb to the gondola along the now railed-in catwalk. For the game, father and son have prepared themselves like athletes, with saunas, light exercise and rest. A doctor once told Foster that broadcasting a game expends more energy than playing in one. He stu-

dies the milling players warming up below, absently polishes his spectacles, sets a glass of water on his right, checks with his technician by phone, consults the player list for late changes.

At 8:04 p.m. the arena announcer phones rinkside from his cubicle high in the northwest corner. The referee whistles both teams to attention. As the Canadian and U.S. flags flutter in an electric-fan breeze, a recording of "O Canada" plays. The bell-like voice of Foster Hewitt says "Hello Canada . . ." And for the next two and a half hours, Maple Leaf Gardens belongs to fans across the entire country.

When the final gong sounds, the ushers deftly guide the crowd outdoors, the nets come up, the icing machine goes back to work. The sweepers gather three tons of refuse, dump it down a chute and into an incinerator. And the House That Smythe Built falls quiet again, back in the care of the people who know it and love it best.

137

# The Hockey Final Everyone Was In

**By Foster Hewitt**

The most remarkable comeback in Stanley Cup history began on the afternoon of April 12, 1942, when a grim Hap Day, coach of the Toronto Maple Leafs, sat down with three members of the Leafs' management in a suite of the Detroit Leland Hotel. Something had to be done. Although favored to steamroller the Detroit Red Wings in the Stanley Cup final, the Leafs were down and almost out, confounded by a style of offense utterly new to the National Hockey League. Cleverly handled by their tomato-faced coach and general manager, Jack Adams, the Wings had piled up three straight victories. One more win this very night in Detroit would clinch an astonishing sweep for them.

Later that afternoon, the decision made, Day announced his new plan to the press: Two top players, Gordie Drillon and Bucko McDonald, would be benched for the big game and their replacements would be two young, virtually unknown minor-leaguers. The team was stunned.

In the dressing room that evening, Day gave the Leafs a rousing pep talk, and they took to the ice in a fighting mood. The "shock treatment" didn't look too effective at first. By the middle of the second period, the Wings had taken a 2-0 lead and the Stanley Cup seemed in their grasp. But now the upstart Wings, only half a game away from victory, were themselves in for a surprise.

From the beginning, it had been a series marked by surprises, and Detroit's unexpected success had even sparked an outbreak of Canadian nationalism. In that era, the Saturday night radio broadcasts from the Gardens had built a large following for the Leafs across the country and the prospect of a Detroit win was appalling. The series was far more fiercely played than a final between two of today's NHL clubs, for the simple reason that everyone was in it—players, fans, management, *everyone*.

I don't think there was ever a series in which there was so much tension—or bad blood. Fights in the stands were commonplace. I remember the fifth game in which players from both teams stopped skating to watch dozens of people fighting in the stands. Moreover, Detroit had an excellent center, Don Grosso, who got into more trouble than anyone I ever knew. During one wartime game, a lanky Toronto winger, Hank Goldup, had the puck near the boards. Grosso knocked him over the boards, right into the crowd, who tucked him under their feet and wouldn't let him up. Play went on in Detroit's Olympia Stadium with Hank imprisoned under the seats! Finally, the Leafs realized Hank was missing. When they found him, they went after Grosso, and everybody got in that fight, fans and players of both teams alike.

*That* was the climate of this series. But it also included the most important ingredient of all—great hockey. There was rarely a letup in speed or in good passing plays, and there was remarkable goaltending by Johnny Mowers for Detroit and Turk Broda for Toronto. The Leafs, led by the great Syl Apps, had knocked off the first-place New York Rangers to reach the best-of-seven final, and Detroit had finished fifth during the season.

Nonetheless, most people hadn't reckoned with Jack Adams, who could rouse a team to a frenzy with his own excitement and fiery energy. He was a sharp hockey man, too. It was Adams who devised the now standard tactic of shooting the puck into the defending zone and flooding in after it. The Wings had used this tactic before, but in the series against Toronto they really went all out with it. This was a whole new style of hockey and, partly because of it, the center red line was introduced a year later. But, in 1942, it was legal to fire the puck into the opposing team's zone from your own *blue line*, and the tactic was electrifying.

And so the Wings had the Leafs off balance

The author broadcasts a game from the gondola at Maple Leaf Gardens. Over the years, Foster Hewitt has covered more than 2,000 NHL games and scores of Stanley Cup playoffs. But, he says, "none packed more of the ingredients that go to make a truly outstanding series than the 1942 final."

Bob Goldham (center) and Gaye Stewart raise their sticks to signal what turned out to be the winning goal—by Pete Langelle (8)—in the game that gave Toronto the Stanley Cup in 1942.

from the start. They played a solid hitting game, banging into every blue sweater they could reach. They scored within the first two minutes of the opener in Toronto, hemmed the Leafs into their own end, and just kept thumping them. The final score, 3-2 for the Wings, flattered the Leafs. In the *Toronto Star*, Andy Lytle said: "Wings beat us with a form of lightning attack and constant replenishment of men. Their style is the nearest thing to a 'panzer' movement the NHL has yet seen."

Leafs' manager Conn Smythe, already in uniform as an Army major, was in town especially to see the game and he was clearly upset. "There's never going to be another red shirt knock a blue shirt around," he grated, and instructed the players to meet force with force.

But that didn't bother the Wings in the second game. In fact, they came up with yet another off-putting tactic—they began stalling. First one player

and then another would stop play to adjust equipment or tie a skate. And when Adams changed lines he'd have the players skate slowly from the bench, one at a time. They continued their throw-it-in style, too, and with two goals from Grosso, the Wings won 4-2.

Now the series shifted to Detroit for Game 3 and Game 4. Sensing a victory, the city teemed with hockey interest, and the Detroit newspapers lavished front-page attention on the rejuvenated Wings. The team responded to the roaring din of the fans by defeating the Leafs again, this time by 5-2. The Leafs, it seemed, were all washed up.

With drastic action needed to turn his team around, coach Day benched the Leafs' leading scorer of the past three seasons, Gordie Drillon, and the hardest-hitting defenseman, Bucko McDonald. Still, late in the second period, the Leafs were trailing 2-0 and the Detroit sweep loomed closer.

139

Infuriated by his team's 4-3
loss to Toronto in the fourth game,
Detroit manager Jack Adams attacks
referee Mel Harwood (whose arm
in white is visible at center). Red
Wing Eddie Wares (11) tries to
restrain Adams.

Suddenly, in a minute and twenty-six seconds, the Leafs struck with goals by Bob Davidson and Lorne Carr, and went into the third period on even terms. Again the Wings moved ahead on a goal by Carl Liscombe, and the Olympia was absolute bedlam. But in less than two minutes Apps got the tying goal as the Wings fell into a string of penalties. Now the crowd's mood turned ugly and all manner of debris rained on the ice—hats, rubbers, newspapers, even tomatoes. With less than eight minutes to play, Nick Metz swept in to score for Toronto, and the Leafs hung on to win 4-3.

Wild scenes followed the final whistle. Two irate Wings—Grosso and Eddie Wares—rushed referee Mel Harwood as he tried to leave the ice. While they were pushing and shoving him, Jack Adams arrived at the gate, his round face flaming red and his neck muscles strained taut. He sailed into the referee, hurling punches. More fights broke out

in the crowd. It was a scene that stopped your breath. In the aftermath, Adams was suspended for the balance of the series and Wares and Grosso were fined $100 each by Frank Calder, president of the NHL. For a time, Calder even considered disqualifying the whole Detroit team and turning the Stanley Cup over to the Leafs.

Effective though Detroit's tough style had been in curbing the Leafs, it had also taken a physical toll of the Wings. The fifth game in Toronto was simply no contest. Without Adams to lead them, and in the understandable letdown of losing a heart-breaking game so close to the championship, Detroit was swamped 9-3. For the Wings everything now came down to the sixth game, their last chance to wrap up the series on home ice. Their fans were seething, their emotions fired by the partisan Detroit newspapers.

From the opening face-off they were ready for the game of their lives, crowding the Leafs with stiff checks and shooting the puck in as before. During the first 12 minutes they could have piled up enough goals for an easy victory but for goalie Turk Broda, who did everything but eat the puck in holding them off. The Detroit fans and players were determined to upset him. Once, a fan even threw a fish at him. It went past my face, missed Turk's cage by inches, and skidded all the way to the blue line. Talk about intimidation! But nothing could distract Turk; he shut them out 3-0 and the Leafs tied the series. The crowd went wild.

And so it was back to Maple Leaf Gardens for the final showdown. I can't recall a night when there was more tingling excitement along Carlton Street as the fans streamed under the brightly lit marquee. There had been an all-night lineup for tickets in front of the rink and scalpers were getting $20 even for a $2.50 ticket in the blues. Our listening audience was enormous—something like eight

Toronto goalie Turk Broda blunts a scoring threat by Detroit's Joe Carveth (12) during Game 6, won 3-0 by Toronto. Broda, writes Hewitt, "did everything but eat the puck."

million people, including the Canadian soldiers and airmen stationed in the British Isles. Nearly 17,000 people were jammed into the rink, though seating capacity at the time was only 12,586.

They were in for another thriller. Syd Howe scored for Detroit early in the second period, and the Wings held so tenaciously to that lead that it seemed they might make the goal stand up. As the moments ticked by in the third period, the fans kept urging the Leafs to greater effort, cheering every rush, the noise swelling and then subsiding in a long "Oh-h-h" as an attack missed, then rising again to greet the next one.

When Jimmy Orlando dumped Apps into the boards and was penalized, Hap Day sent out the line of Dave Schriner, Lorne Carr and Billy Taylor. They pressed into the Detroit zone, whipping the puck deftly back and forth so that Schriner was set up at the side of the net; he dumped a short

shot past Mowers to tie the score. Toronto fans let everything loose; the noise was deafening.

The crowd was on its feet again when, just past the period's halfway mark, Pete Langelle, a center from Winnipeg, raced down the ice with Johnny McCreedy. Langelle got loose for an instant in front of the net and snapped a deflection off McCreedy past Mowers to send the Leafs ahead. The roar from the crowd seemed to shake my broadcast gondola. With less than four minutes left in the game, Schriner broke through again and put the icing on the cake with his second goal.

At the final bell, the crowd stood, cheered and showered programs onto the ice. The Leafs had won by 3-1! The din continued as Syl Apps skated to center ice to receive the Stanley Cup. It was an extraordinary scene, the final high moment in a series that had everything—a series that I'll remember as long as I live.

141

# CANADA
# ON STAGE

"This world is but
canvas to our imaginations."

Henry David Thoreau

Karen Kain (below, with Frank Augustyn in *The Rite of Spring*) is nearsighted, has weak ankles and hates rehearsals. But she has technique, talent and ambition—qualities she shares with the Royal Winnipeg Ballet which, despite limited funds, is among the world's great ballet troupes. Both epitomize the pride of Canadian dance, and their dazzling performances have captured the imagination of ballet lovers from Moscow to Moose Jaw. On the following 12 pages are the stories of two of Canada's cultural treasures: a young dancer with unmistakable 'star quality' and the nation's oldest ballet company.

# Not Just a Dancer—a Star

### By Susan Carson

**H**alfway through a dress rehearsal of the National Ballet's production of *The Sleeping Beauty*, the atmosphere was tense. With opening night just 24 hours away, the tempo was off, the lights were too pink and the entrance of Aurora's Friends didn't look quite right.

As the end of Act II approached, Frank Augustyn, immaculate in white tights and gold brocade as Prince Florimund, made his way through the forest to the slumbering castle. For a moment he gazed adoringly at the sleeping Princess Aurora, alias Karen Kain. Then he woke her with a kiss. She rose dreamily, a vision of creamy shoulders, gauzy pink tutu—and red fright wig, owlish glasses and woolly leg warmers!

The ballet master looked on grimly as the company dissolved into nervous laughter. Kain and Augustyn carried on as though he were asking the most beautiful girl in the world to be his bride. The tension was broken and, somehow, everyone felt better. No one else would have dared such a gesture on such a day. But Karen Kain isn't just another dancer. She is a star.

For years the National Ballet of Canada avoided any suggestion of a star system. It had its principal dancers, soloists and *corps de ballet*. Then audiences discovered Karen Kain, Canada's sensational young dancer with the dazzling smile and the long, elegant legs. Soon Clive Barnes of *The New York Times* was calling her "one of the most talented ballerinas in the Western World," and Paris newspapers were rhapsodizing over her "inexhaustible vivacity" and "elegance of line." Rudolf Nureyev has made no secret of his admiration for her as a partner. "She has that special radiance," he says, "which lights up the whole stage. That is what is called 'star quality,' and in her it is unmistakable."

No one is prouder of Karen than her parents, Charles and Winifred Kain, who live in Missis-sauga, Ont. They try to attend two or three of Karen's performances a week during the Toronto season and, whenever possible, her guest appearances abroad. Winifred's proudest moment, she says, was Karen's first appearance with the National Ballet in London, England, in 1972, when she danced Odette/Odile in *Swan Lake.* "People in the audience went outside and pulled up flowers from the gardens, and threw them on stage to Karen. I shall never forget it."

Only 25 when she was honored in 1976 as an officer of the Order of Canada, Karen is internationally recognized. With many years of dancing ahead of her, she may yet become Canada's first homegrown ballet superstar.

Born in Hamilton, Ont., in 1951, Karen was just nine when her mother took her to see the National Ballet perform *Giselle.* The Kains were not ballet lovers; they just believed in exposing their four children to as many of the good things of life as possible. But Karen was entranced and began lessons at a ballet school in Ancaster, Ont., where the Kains then lived. At 11, she auditioned for Betty Oliphant, principal of the National Ballet School, in Toronto. Miss Oliphant took one look at the child and got a funny feeling in the pit of her stomach.

"I've only felt such excitement maybe twice in my life," she says. "I told her mother right away that she was extraordinarily talented. But she really didn't want Karen to do it. Our school was residential and Karen was very close to her family. I kept at it, however, and eventually they agreed."

The years at school weren't easy, for Karen was homesick and disliked the regimentation and discipline. "Yet it would have been cruel," says Winifred Kain, "to take her out. She so obviously wanted to dance." So they gritted their teeth, and made her welcome whenever she came home.

On evenings in Toronto when there
is no performance, Karen Kain
usually returns to her home and prepares supper herself. Then she
puts a load of leotards through the
washing machine, sews ribbons on
some of the hundreds of *pointe* shoes
she will go through in a year,
and collapses into bed well before
midnight.

But there was another problem. The five-foot-six Karen was heavy for a dancer. She was always snacking on forbidden doughnuts and sticky buns from a pastry shop near the school. "I love to eat," says Karen "and there just didn't seem to be an important enough reason to stop."

Then at 18, in her final year, she was given a reason. The National Ballet would be auditioning students in two weeks, Betty Oliphant told her. If Karen wanted a spot, she'd have to lose weight. She went on a crash diet, and qualified.

Her first year in the *corps de ballet* was a disappointment. "I'd do three ballets a night," recalls Karen, "and it was no joy. I was always in trouble for not being in line." Finally, emboldened by having been given a few solo parts, she went to artistic director Celia Franca and begged for something more challenging.

"Learn *Swan Lake*," she was told—a role on which many reputations have foundered. A month later, another dancer injured her back and in January 1971 Karen Kain made her debut at Arizona State University as a slim and nervous Swan Queen. For the critics, it wasn't love at first sight. In those early days, nervousness made her brilliant smile too fixed and she had to work hard to overcome a certain stiffness in her arms, but they noted her great potential and the natural joy expressed in her dancing.

A few months later, Rudolf Nureyev came to the National Ballet to stage his version of *The Sleeping Beauty*. He took one look at Karen, who was scheduled to dance one of the fairy roles, and decided he wanted her for Aurora. Karen was thrilled. Miss Franca was implacable. Impossible, she said. Karen was too young; besides, she was still weak from a recent operation. Nureyev nodded graciously and they returned to work. A few days later he resumed his campaign. Finally, he got his way.

The role of Aurora demands enormous strength and flawless technique. It still terrifies Karen. "It forces me to pull together and do it. Even though I'm glad to dance the role, I feel as if I'm on my way to the guillotine." But Nureyev pushed her mercilessly, shouted, insulted, then got her through her first performance, hissing words of encouragement before rewarding her with champagne and dinner. He remains her friend, adviser and frequent partner, always on the lookout for her. "Whenever he sees a chance for me," says Karen, "he'll push."

Following the success of *The Sleeping Beauty*, Celia Franca played a hunch and sent Karen and

Constant work makes a ballet dancer: Karen Kain pushes herself through a daily grind of 90 minutes of classes and six hours of rehearsals. On stage, it pays off. "When she performs," exulted one critic, "she shines."

fellow Hamiltonian Frank Augustyn to the 1973 Moscow International Ballet competition. It paid off handsomely. They won first prize for the *pas de deux* section and she won the silver medal for women soloists. Moreover, Karen caught the eye of Roland Petit, artistic director of the Ballets de Marseille, who promptly invited her to dance with his company. For the next three years she danced in France as a guest artist, and in the fall of 1976 she was a tough and sexy Carmen in the company's tour of Canada—the first time a Canadian ballerina has been a guest star at home with a foreign troupe.

Perhaps the greatest accolade in her still-blossom-

ing career came in 1977 when Karen was invited, with Frank Augustyn, to make guest appearances in *Giselle* with the Bolshoi Ballet in Moscow. Alexander Grant, artistic director of the National Ballet, who accompanied them to the U.S.S.R., says the Russian dancers were cool to the Canadians until after their first performance. "After all, the Bolshoi has so many dancers, one couldn't help but get the impression that they were wondering who needed these outsiders. But afterward, they were surging with admiration."

Karen's following is as varied as her roles. Two middle-aged ladies from New York, for example,

147

"I'm trying to improve myself all
the time," says Karen Kain. Here she
listens intently to instructions
from Celia Franca, former artistic
director of the National Ballet.

travel regularly to Toronto whenever she is dancing. They send her newsy little letters, hand-knitted leg warmers for class and rehearsal and special pink satin ribbon for her *pointe* shoes, which they buy on annual sorties to London. They are always rewarded with a spot in her dressing room and a smile at curtain call. Earnest young men in jeans and T-shirts push poems through her dressing-room door and older men invite her to dinner.

Karen loves to perform, but hates to rehearse. And for years she has suffered from a painful tendinitis in her ankles. Until she began regular physiotherapy, she often went on stage in dread of the pain. She still has to live with the possibility that her weakened ankles could end her career overnight.

One person who hopes they won't is Frank Augustyn, who often dances with Karen. Their compatibility is obvious on stage, and audiences respond to it almost instinctively. Protective of one another, they often joke about their near-misses. Though they're both nearsighted, only Frank wears contact lenses, and Karen has some difficulty finding him in a blur of fast-moving bodies.

"Once we were doing *The Sleeping Beauty* in Vancouver," she recalls. "I was supposed to come running down the stage and take a flying leap into Frank's arms, landing on my stomach. I misjudged the distance and went sailing over his head. He just managed to catch me by the knees before I landed in the violinist's lap."

They argue frequently, but mildly. One bone of contention, says Frank, is the pre-performance warm-up. "I need a few minutes to myself before a performance and that really annoys her. She's always on stage looking around, wanting to practice all the difficult parts with me once more. I'd rather go through the movements in my head."

In contrast to the gregarious Augustyn, Karen is shy and often reluctant to enter a conversation. To Mary Joliffe, former public relations chief of the National Ballet, she is an enigma. "On stage that girl is sensual and exotic, a creature of deep feelings and fire. I've never been able to figure out how she can be the same sweet girl whose Christmas cards are always a mass of kittens and baby bunny rabbits!"

Is the constant grind of rehearsals and performances worth all the acclaim? Karen admits there are days when the pain and fatigue make her wonder. Yet her face utterly belies what she is saying. It says she'll never give up the ballet.

Her manager agrees: "Above all else, the girl is ambitious. She's got the technique, the talent and something even more precious, something I call bounce-back ability. It'll carry her far."

One February she flew home from Moscow to prepare for the National Ballet's five-week Toronto

Karen Kain and frequent partner Frank Augustyn, who met at the National Ballet School, have developed a rapport that gives their performances a rare tenderness—evident in this scene from *Bluebird Pas de Deux.*

season, which she was to open with *Romeo and Juliet*. But an internal problem, long ignored, finally caught up with her and on opening night she couldn't leave her bed. Her doctor predicted she was out for the season. A week later she bounced onto the stage of the O'Keefe Centre in *La Fille Mal Gardée*, giving one of her most poignant performances as a buoyant, dreaming girl of 16. And as she did, two middle-aged ladies in the front row breathed a sigh of relief; their star was back.

# "Canada's Bolshoi"

### By Martin O'Malley

Clive Barnes of *The New York Times* flew into Winnipeg brooding on the emptiness of the prairie. He had come to report on the Royal Winnipeg Ballet, which was preparing to embark on a tour of Europe and the Soviet Union.

"Why?" Barnes later wrote. "Why here, of all places, should there be a ballet company?"

New York critics are not the only ones puzzled by a ballet company that performs in high-school auditoriums in North Dakota, in dusty Manitoba farm towns, then packs its slippers and tutus and flies to Paris or Moscow or Verona and wins gold medals in stiff international competition. Winnipeggers themselves look on the company as a prairie aberration, as something they don't quite understand, but find completely entrancing.

The success of the Royal Winnipeg Ballet has been so phenomenal that newspapers in Europe refer to it as "Canada's Bolshoi." At the 1968 International Festival of the Dance in Paris it won gold medals for best company and for prima ballerina Christine Hennessy's best female interpretation. Maya Plisetskaya, then prima ballerina of the Bolshoi, was so moved at an opening in Moscow that she shouted "Bravo! Bravo!" from the aisle.

Despite such international fame, the company must live frugally at home. It recovers about 50 percent of its $2-million operating costs at the box office—good for ballet—and each season receives some $500,000 from the Canada Council, about $100,000 from the province of Manitoba and $80,000 from the city of Winnipeg. Until the company moved to more spacious quarters—all under one roof—in 1972, economic realities forced it to rent studios and administrative space in five old buildings in downtown Winnipeg. It had to rehearse and train in a converted bowling alley, and store expensive equipment and costumes on the main floor of a cheap rooming house. Male dancers had to be careful not to hoist the girls too high lest they smash their heads on the ceilings. Dressing rooms were cramped and some feared the floor of the main studio would come crashing down on the wardrobe department.

The dancers themselves have the security of 50 weeks' steady employment, rare for dancers, but a member of the *corps de ballet* earns only $7,500 a year and even a leading principal gets little more than $15,000. Not much when you consider a good ballet dancer requires up to ten years' apprenticeship, and is usually through at 35. Each dancer pays his own living expenses on the road, and the road usually means at least seven weeks in the United States, where they may play as many as 36 cities. Every two or three years the company travels

abroad. In 1972 it spent 12 weeks performing to enthusiastic crowds in Australia and New Zealand, and in 1974 it became the first Canadian ballet company to tour South America.

Not long ago a good turnout for ballet in Winnipeg was about 500 persons in the old, 1,400-seat Playhouse Theatre. Since the company began performing in the larger Manitoba Centennial Concert Hall, the average attendance has climbed to about 1,400—partly because the ballet has begun to attract a younger crowd. It was with this young audience in mind that the company did *Ballet High*, a rock ballet featuring the rock group Lighthouse. The response was so great that the show was held over a week at Toronto's St. Lawrence Centre—the first time in the history of Canadian theater that a dance company was held over because of good box office. And it was one of the rare times that the company actually made money on a tour.

Usually, the harder the ballet works the more it loses. Of some 20 shows in Winnipeg each year, about half sell out, but they still lose money. Yet its losses are a fraction of those suffered by some ballet companies.

Almost every year since 1970 special awards have been presented to persons who have made outstanding contributions to the Royal Winnipeg Ballet. One went to Agnes de Mille, the great American choreographer who has become known as "the fairy godmother of the Royal Winnipeg Ballet." Another was given to R. A. D. Ford, who as Canadian ambassador to Russia assisted the company during its 1968 Russian tour. Still others went to the late critic Nathan Cohen, an enthusiastic supporter of the company through his reviews, and to promoter Sol Hurok, who until he died in 1974 helped to organize the ballet's tours of the United States.

The company's stormy life began in 1938 when

Gweneth Lloyd, an English ballet teacher, came to Winnipeg to open a school with a former pupil, Betty Hey Farrally, as her partner. Shortly after the school opened, they established the Winnipeg Ballet Club and Miss Lloyd began composing works that might appeal to someone who had never seen a ballet. One of her first was *Kilowatt Magic*, a tribute to the development of hydroelectric power in Manitoba. In less than five years she had created 21 ballets. "Ballet is no longer champagne and caviar," she once said, "but beer and skittles for the people."

The club turned professional in 1949 and two years later, with the help of an influential socialite, Lady Tupper, it performed before Princess Elizabeth at Winnipeg's musty old civic auditorium. Emboldened by its progress, in 1953 the company asked for and got permission to call itself the Royal Winnipeg Ballet, thus becoming the first royal ballet in the Commonwealth.

The following year it was out of business. On the morning of June 8, a fire destroyed the company's offices, studios, sets, costumes—everything. And none of it was insured.

It took two years and $60,000 before the company reappeared, and then it was almost killed by dissension among its leaders. For a time it looked like the end of beer-and-skittles ballet in Winnipeg until Arnold Spohr, a former principal dancer, arrived from England and agreed to become the company's artistic director. He is probably the single most influential force behind the company's success. In 1970 Spohr received the Canada Council's $15,000 Molson Prize and an honorary Doctor of Laws degree from the University of Manitoba in recognition of his achievements.

Tall and effervescent, Spohr has shown an enthusiasm for the dance infectious enough to melt the crust off a Philistine. Like Gweneth Lloyd, he wants

Among many firsts for the Royal
Winnipeg Ballet—the company has
mounted more than 50 original
productions—was the troupe's 1977
North American premiere of
Argentinian choreographer Oscar
Araiz' fantasy, *The Unicorn,
the Gorgon and the Manticore.*

Arnold Spohr, Canadian-born artistic director of the company, drills his charges relentlessly. "There is one word I never wish to hear, and I don't allow my dancers to use it," he once said. "That word is *can't*, because you can do anything when you work at it."

ballet to be fun for steelworkers as well as balleto-manes. He leaps and prances around a studio in bright, tight pastel suits and white boots and has been known to bring a sagging class to life by whacking at a tambourine or lunging into an impromptu tarantella.

Spohr revitalized the repertoire, and in 1964 the ballet was invited to the Jacob's Pillow Dance Festival in Massachusetts where it stole the show. "One of the most engaging ballet groups functioning on this side of the Atlantic," said the New York *Herald Tribune*'s Walter Terry. Some reviews were embarrassingly effusive.

"That," said Spohr, "was when we became famous."

Today the Royal Winnipeg Ballet likes to think of itself as innovative and daring. For a company of fewer than 30 dancers, enough to fit in a bus, the repertoire is surprisingly diverse. There is a saloon western (*Les Whoops-de-doo*), a bit of *Swan Lake*, the world's first rock ballet (*Ballet High*), several George Balanchine ballets, ballet to the poetry of Leonard Cohen, the first original full-evening Canadian ballet (*Rose Latulippe*), Oscar Araiz' *Mahler 4*, which the Toronto *Globe and Mail* called "a masterpiece"—and even Agnes de Mille's haunt-

Since the Royal Winnipeg Ballet was formed in 1938, it barely has been able to afford the sets and costumes necessary to stage such productions as *In Quest of the Sun* (below). Yet the company has persevered to become what the *Winnipeg Free Press* once called "Manitoba's best export."

ing *Fall River Legend,* which may be performed in North America by only one other company, the American Ballet Theater.

The company spends more than $55,000 a year on new ballets and has mounted up to five new ballets in a single season, an incredible production for a small operation. Among its most popular works is *The Ecstasy of Rita Joe.* The story of an Indian girl's misfortunes in the city, it was commissioned by the Manitoba Indian Brotherhood. First staged in 1972, the sweeping, $50,000, multimedia affair has folk songs by Ann Mortifee, taped narration by Chief Dan George, and surrealistic, ghostly images flashing on a 30-by-60-foot screen in front of which the company dances. Toward the end, a CBC film takes over briefly, creating a spectacular effect, like a Fellini film.

The pursuit of excellence, and then higher excellence, has always been Spohr's style. Professional dancers hired from other companies must undergo months of adjusting to the special discipline of the Winnipeg company. Even visiting Russians, known for their Spartan indefatigability, are amazed at the rigorousness of the training. There is a definite we-try-harder spirit that hints at masochism.

Vera Volkova, when artistic adviser of the Royal Danish Ballet, gave the dancers special lessons and after each workout the studio thundered with applause, a traditional mark of respect for a great teacher. "It's really strange," said a woman in the front office as the dancers' applause echoed down the corridor. "The harder she works them, the more demands she makes, the louder they applaud."

Beneath the dedication and acclaim, however, is pervasive insecurity, as if the company had listened too long to the query, "Why in Winnipeg?" It is a vague awareness that, yes, the balloon could break. One of these days.

Such insecurity, however, is unwarranted. Agnes

de Mille once told the United States Congress: "One of the best companies in North America is in Winnipeg, in Manitoba if you can believe that, and that is because of the people there."

In *Dance Magazine* Spohr wrote: "Everything that has happened to Winnipeg is organic. Without ever making any great effort in any one direction we have continuously grown, as a good tree grows, our branches never sapping the strength of the trunk." Said an executive of the company: "We don't see ourselves as a Royal Winnipeg Ballet. We see ourselves as Canada's oldest ballet, as a national ballet and one of the nation's treasures."

# Cheek, Charm and Audience Command

By Adrian Waller

More than 20 years have passed since Paul Anka penned his first hit—"Diana," a catchy tune that became a world best-seller—yet the singer is still much in demand on the concert circuit. He travels 300,000 miles annually, playing to packed houses and commanding at least $50,000 a performance.

Just before his 16th birthday—in the early spring of 1957—a determined, tousle-haired boy borrowed $100 from his father, put on dungarees and a red sweat shirt, and headed for New York. His mission: to storm Tin Pan Alley with five songs he had written in the basement of his Ottawa home.

One was a simple, fashionable and bubbly tune that celebrated his crush on 18-year-old Diana Ayoub, who baby-sat his younger brother and sister. It was called "Diana" and, overnight, it launched Paul Anka on the road to become one of the youngest multimillionaire entertainers of his time. Within three months, he had laid siege to the offices of a song publisher, recorded the song—without even a rehearsal—and watched it reach the charts. Then Ed Sullivan asked him to sing it on his television show. Suddenly Paul was swept up in a cyclone of entertainment hysteria.

By 16, he was a star, by 19 a millionaire. Later, with songs like "Lonely Boy" and "Puppy Love," he established himself on the North American nightclub circuit where rock stars of his age rarely trod. His light voice, cheek, charm and audience command, said the New York *Herald Tribune*, made George Jessel look like "a shrinking violet." A New York television producer observed that Anka had the "kind of presence on stage that took Jimmy Durante 60 years to learn."

When "Diana" was eventually heard abroad, it made Anka an international star. In 1958 he embarked on his first grand tour. In Japan, where five of his songs dominated the hit parade, 2,000 intrepid ticket buyers waited in line while a typhoon threatened to level the theater in which Anka was to perform. Japanese enthusiasts gave him ten crates of gifts—dolls, fans and stuffed animals. In Paris a few months later, he attracted nearly 100,000 people to the Olympia theater.

During the next few years Anka was invariably mobbed, at home or abroad, by howling teenagers. French soldiers with automatic weapons lined the orchestra pit during a performance in Algiers, and later took him home in an armored truck to prevent his being engulfed by bobby-soxers. Autograph seekers in Chile stampeded through an airport, breaking furniture and magazine stands. Signing autographs in a Puerto Rico department store, Anka was literally overrun by ecstatic teenagers. He was hastily stuffed into an empty carton, wheeled on a trolley to the elevator, taken to the roof, and plucked away by helicopter.

In those days, Anka sang primarily to publicize his own music. But while many young performers of his era built reputations with one recording and then vanished, the intense, hazel-eyed Anka continued to compose. He wrote "My Way" for Frank Sinatra and "She's a Lady" for Tom Jones, collaborated with Johnny Carson on "Johnny's Theme" for the "Tonight Show," and penned the score for (and appeared in) the movie *The Longest Day*. He even wrote a song called "Girl, You Really Turn Me On" for tennis star Jimmy Connors' singing debut on television. One of Anka's songs, "You're Having My Baby," angered feminists, pro-abortionists and antiabortionists all at once. Meanwhile, "Diana" endures as an all-time favorite. Anka has earned nearly two dozen gold records, each awarded for a sale of more than one million.

Show business was always part of Paul Anka's life. He was born July 30, 1941, in Ottawa, where his parents—both Syrian Canadians—operated the Victoria Tea Shop near the House of Commons, and later, a more elegant restaurant called the Locanda. To Paul's delight, such entertainers as the Platters and Tony Bennett came to eat at the Locanda.

At ten, he discovered he could make people laugh by singing and sobbing like Johnny Ray.

He gave impromptu performances for housewives, paperboys—and, once, a gang of ditchdiggers outside his home, collecting a dime from each workman. At 13, his heart now set on becoming a singer-composer, he formed a trio called the Bobbysoxers with two classmates from Fisher Park High School. Then Paul enthusiastically began grinding out songs.

In 1957, while trying to barge backstage at the Ottawa Auditorium, Paul was confronted by promoter Irvin Feld, who hustled him out. But before leaving, the boy persuaded Feld to take down his name and address. "Some day," he told him, "I'm going to be a star on this show." Later, when Tony Bennett was leaving the stage door in nearby Hull, Que., Paul told him audaciously: "I've been studying your act. *I'm* going into show business."

Sometimes Paul enraged his father by inviting performers to the Locanda for free meals. And when a friend phoned to say that Paul, chaperoned by his mother, had won an amateur talent contest at a local country club, receiving a standing ovation from 300 customers, Mr. Anka was furious. No one had told him about the contest, and his son was in an adults' club until one o'clock in the morning. But when the club agreed to pay Paul $75 for a week's engagement, Mr. and Mrs. Anka sat quietly at a back table and watched their son repeat his triumph. This time, Paul's father was so thrilled that he was brought to tears.

Now Paul was anxious to have his music published. So, shortly after his 15th birthday, he used his earnings to finance a trip to Los Angeles where his uncle worked as a singer. To survive, Paul parked cars and sold candy at a Hollywood theater. When the recorded version of his latest song failed, he earned his return fare by working for a month as a movie usher. Home again, he returned to high school.

The following spring, however, the urge to make a hit record overwhelmed him again and, simultaneously, an Ottawa disc jockey called his father with startling news. "Andrew," he said, "your boy's too big for Canada." Paul borrowed money to go to New York and bulldozed his way into Don Costa's office at ABC-Paramount—demanding to be heard.

"Can you imagine," says Costa, "this 15-year-old kid bouncing into my office and playing five of his own songs? He leaped at the piano like it was a steak dinner and he hadn't eaten for months."

A few days later, while bunking down in a friend's bathtub in a New York hotel, Paul received a phone call. ABC-Paramount would give him a

As a teenage singing sensation, Anka drew crowds wherever he went— from hometown Ottawa (left, at a 1957 concert) to such far-flung places as (clockwise from bottom) the United States, Japan and Belgium.

contract. His first assignment: to complete the lyrics for "Diana." Two weeks later, without rehearsal, he recorded the song that was to shape his career.

Disc jockeys loved "Diana"—and Irvin Feld heard it. Remembering Paul's ambition, he offered him a contract for a tour of more than 90 U.S. cities and towns with the Platters and Fats Domino. When the tour ended, Paul persuaded Feld to become his manager.

Feld's first step was to convince Paul to lose five pounds, get his hair styled and have his nose remodeled. Feld then released "Diana" abroad and arranged six world tours. When Paul returned to Ottawa after his first world tour, about 50 teenage

159

fans burst through the Ankas' front door, poured confetti over Paul's head and shrieked for autographs. "Now that Paul's home," Mrs. Anka sighed, "it's going to be noisy again." By this time, Paul was earning $7,000 a week. His parents gave him $50 pocket money and put the remainder into a fund. By the time he was 19 he was earning $1 million a year. He also headed a vast enterprise built entirely on his talent. So prodigious was his output that he now needed several companies to publish and protect the songs he wrote.

Anka's success, however, had a bitter taste. He discovered that his mother was dying from complications of diabetes. Despite her family's stubborn quest for medical relief, she died when only 39. Of his mother's death, Anka says, "I learned about what we get in this life, and what we lose."

While his future was assured, life was increasingly lonely. "How could I meet girl friends," Anka asks, "when I was in New York one week and Germany the next?" That loneliness ended on Saturday, February 16, 1963, when he put on a dark, two-buttoned suit, and married Egyptian-born Paris model Anne de Zogheb—shattering his adolescent image and breaking the hearts of millions.

By this time the teenagers who had torn his clothes in the '50s were growing up. So in 1968 he began writing new songs, aimed at "older people." He has amply succeeded. In 1976 the U.S. National Association of Recording Merchandisers gave him its Presidential Award, with the following citation: "Through his music he has been an interpreter of the culture of his time, changing as the culture changes, always reflecting in his art the life-style of his generation."

Paul and Anne divide their time between homes in Sun Valley, Idaho, Las Vegas, Nevada, and Carmel, California. Anka spends long hours composing. Inspiration usually arrives between 3 a.m. and 9 a.m., and he keeps a typewriter beside his grand piano so he can work on both lyrics and melody at the same time. When he finishes a song, he sings it into a tape recorder, then sends the cassette off to be scored by a music arranger.

In all, Anka has written more than 400 songs, averaging 20 per year. Many have been recorded by others, not only in English but also in Spanish, Portuguese, Dutch and German. Anka's own recordings have sold more than 30 million copies. By learning to pronounce German, Italian, Spanish and Japanese phonetically, Anka has been able to recycle songs throughout the world—and watch the royalties gush in like a slot-machine jackpot.

Indeed, depending on how hard he wants to work, he can gross $5 million a year. Royalties on songs and recordings comprise about one third of his income. (He gets $20,000 annually from the "Tonight Show" theme alone.) He operates a discotheque in Las Vegas and a restaurant in Sun Valley and owns an airplane leasing company.

Crisscrossing North America, he is piloted in a seven-seat Lear Jet, fitted with telephone and an eight-track tape deck. A sports enthusiast, he is calm, affable and easy to work with. "He's energetic, kind and thoughtful," says music arranger John Harris. "My son," adds Andrew Anka, "has matured into a sensible, stable individual."

As for Paul himself, he remembers his swift rise to fame with gratitude and wonder. "A 15-year-old kid's dream came true," he says, "and it could not have happened without luck." In the days of "Diana," Anka reflects, he was a confused teenager tackling the world single-handedly. Now he's relaxed and happy that he can earn a living from something he really loves: writing songs and singing them.

He does both well. More important, he does them *his* way.

# Mr. New Year

By Adrian Waller

Guy Lombardo and His Royal Canadians

First came the opening strains of "Auld Lang Syne"–then the voice of Guy Lombardo, one of the world's most beloved bandleaders. "Hello," it greeted 60 million people tuning in on radio and on television. "Welcome to our New Year's Eve party."

For nearly half a century, Lombardo and his band, the red-coated Royal Canadians, personified New Year for North Americans. Theirs was one of the longest acts in show business, Lombardo often claimed. The band survived every musical trend since the early 1920s, when ragtime was evolv-

ing into jazz. By rights, it should have fallen victim to capricious public taste over and over again, floundering on the sweeping tides of swing or being thrust out of business by bebop or rock 'n' roll. But it didn't. The Canadian-born Lombardo refused to abandon his slow, strict-tempo music—or to stop working 50 weeks a year.

"Always sweet, but never sticky," composer Irving Berlin said of Lombardo's sound which in time became dubbed "the sweetest music this side of heaven." To which jazzman Paul Whiteman once added: "Yes, and probably the *other* side, too!"

Guy Lombardo (below, in his boat
*Tempo VI*) was an ardent speedboat
enthusiast. In 1946 he captured the
U.S. Gold Cup. Competing for
the cup two years later, his boat overturned at 125 m.p.h. Thrown some
15 feet, Lombardo broke an arm and
was rescued from the water,
unconscious. Undeterred, he carried
on with the sport and won the
prestigious President's Cup on three
successive occasions.

But Lombardo said simply: "My music is for
people in love—or potentially in love." Millions
of the cheek-to-cheek set have glided over waxed
floors to fox-trots, cha-chas, rumbas and waltzes
played in his distinctive style. They have bought
more than 315 million of his records. And they
allowed him to shepherd them amiably from one
year to the next as though that were the *only* way
to go.

Much of Lombardo's success stemmed from his
ability to recognize hit tunes. Down in Tin Pan
Alley they used to say: "If Guy likes your song,
it's in." He is credited with introducing some 500
melodies—more than any other bandleader.

Guy Lombardo was born in London, Ont., in
1902. The eldest son of an Italian immigrant tailor
who insisted that all his children take music lessons,
Guy started violin at the age of nine. Giving his
first public recital at 12, he looked more like Little

Lord Fauntleroy than the weather-beaten roadster
he was destined to become; his mother had dressed
him in a Buster Brown collar, black velvet jacket
and breeches, knee-length socks and a flowing cra-
vat. When a string on his violin broke, he fled
the stage crying, and vowed never to play in public
again.

Papa Lombardo had different ideas. He instilled
so much confidence in his son that, within two
years, Guy formed a five-piece neighborhood
band—including brothers Carmen, who later wrote
such Royal Canadian hits as "Little Coquette,"
"Boo Hoo," and "Sweethearts on Parade," and
Lebert. They played at parties, dances, festivals and
weddings. "Don't forget the melody," Papa advised,
"and choose songs people can sing, hum or whistle."

The advice had its effect. At one early performance Lombardo, still in his teens, detected some
of his musicians improvising like the jazzmen then

springing up all around. "*Play the notes*," he told them. It nearly caused a mutiny. Then later, in a poolroom confrontation, he told them again: "Play the notes, or you don't work! Get that? You don't work!" The rebels surrendered. The band was on its way.

In 1919 Lombardo quit his job as a four-dollar-a-week office boy in a bank, and led his troops to an outdoor pavilion in Grand Bend, Ont., for their first professional engagement. They slept in a tent, received $40 weekly, and—playing afternoons and evenings—barely had time for supper.

In November 1923, after a series of one-night stands throughout Ontario, the Lombardo Brothers Concert Company gambled by taking a day-long bus ride to Cleveland where eventually they were hired by a small nightclub, the Claremont Tent. There Lombardo got the feeling that radio, then in crystal-set infancy, was to be his stepping-stone, and offered to play free for Cleveland stations. "We were playing three different styles then," he recalled. "Hot stuff, like the Chicago bands; big fancy arrangements like Paul Whiteman; and sweet stuff—the way Papa liked it."

Since radio was new, people sat up all night listening. Lombardo asked them to write in, telling him what they thought of his music. One who did was a honey-blonde named Lilliebell Glenn. Two years later they met, and within two months she and Lombardo were married.

Other changes were coming. When the Claremont manager suggested they play "slower and softer," the band had the savvy to listen. They also listened to agent Mike Shea, who told them: "You guys are wonderful! But your band name has no class—no impact." Since bands were often identified with their place of origin—Fred Waring and his Pennsylvanians, the Kansas City Nighthawks—Shea suggested the "Royal Northwest Mounted Canadi-ans," complete with scarlet coats. Lombardo winced. He could imagine audiences shouting "Where's your horse?" Then Shea said: "Hey, how about the Royal Canadians?"

Ready for bigger things, the band accepted a $1,600-a-week offer from the Granada Café, a Chicago club opposite a graveyard. At first audiences were almost nonexistent. Lombardo did, however, have a small following of black musicians who, barred from the premises, would sneak in to hear the band. One was a young jazz trumpeter named Louis Armstrong, and he and Lombardo remained close friends ever after.

Finally a small, struggling radio station agreed to run a wire into the Granada, provided that Lombardo pay the cost and the broadcasts be only 15 minutes. That was hardly time for the band to warm up, but at 9 p.m. on November 16, 1927, Lombardo flicked a switch under the grand piano and said into the microphone: "This is Guy Lombardo, in the Granada Café on the south side of Chicago." The place was empty. "We had to get four waiters and a guy out of the kitchen to clap," he once recalled. At 9:15 the band stopped playing—as scheduled. But then the headwaiter handed Lombardo a message from the radio station: "Keep playing." A few minutes later, Leslie Atlass, the station owner, phoned to ask the Royal Canadians to play until sign-off at 1 a.m.

Around midnight, Lombardo suddenly realized that the Granada was full of couples dancing. "They had heard us on the air and were streaming into the place," he remembered. "There wasn't a vacant seat in the club."

After the show, he telephoned Papa Lombardo long-distance. "Well," he inquired, "did you hear us? How were we?"

"I heard you," Papa answered casually. "You were all right."

"Just all right?" his son persisted. "Weren't we *great*?"

"Look," said Papa, "if it's compliments you want, I'll put your mother on."

Next day, compliments from listeners came in by the hundreds. Wrigley's Chewing Gum wanted to sponsor them, and so did Florsheim Shoes. The following week, a second radio station installed a line into the Granada to pick up the show. So popular did Lombardo's broadcasts become that Bell Telephone once complained: "Everybody in Chicago must be listening to the Lombardo pro-gram—nobody is making calls at that time."

For all that, Lombardo was never very fond of Chicago. One December night in 1927 he ordered an obstreperous gangster off the dance floor for usurping his mike. The gangster was George Maloney. On New Year's Eve, Maloney returned with a girl friend. As the music and the evening mellowed, two rival gangsters started ribbing him about being kicked off the stage by a bandleader. When they insulted his girl friend, Maloney whis-pered to her to go outside and get his gun. He then went to his tormentor's table, tipped it over, and opened fire. The Royal Canadians dived to the floor; when the shooting stopped, two men lay dead before them. And the whole event had been broadcast live! But the show had to go on. Lombardo adjusted his tuxedo, turned to his band and said: "Okay, fellas; let's play the next one."

In October 1929, the Royal Canadians tasted *real* success: they opened in the Grill of New York's Roosevelt Hotel at $2,000 a week. Their premiere on October 3 was crowded; so were all their nights for the next three weeks. Then, on October 24, the stock market crashed. "It was terrible," Lom-bardo recalled. Some nights he played to only four couples in a ballroom that seated 350. "I saw a pan-orama of white tablecloths," he said.

But gradually people began to come back, danc-ing to the rhythm of "I Can't Give You Anything But Love, Baby," and the upswing was for good. The Royal Canadians rode on through the Big Band era of the '30s and '40s. By the '50s, the smooth, low-keyed Lombardo music was being heard over 100 television stations across North America; and Lombardo became a producer of musical spectaculars at the 8,200-seat Marine The-ater at Jones Beach in Long Island, New York.

The Lombardo-Roosevelt Hotel partnership ended in 1963, and the band's New Year's date took place in New York's Grand Central Terminal. Trains were rerouted, and the station was fitted with heaters so that women could wear their ball gowns. Nearly 2,000 persons danced all night and ate box lunches of chicken, caviar and champagne.

Guy Lombardo and his band perform at the 1969 Inaugural Ball of Richard Nixon. A favorite of U.S. presidents, Lombardo played at almost every Inaugural Ball between 1933 and 1977. "And, traveling the long, dusty road," the maestro once said, "it sometimes seems we've played at every engagement party and wedding, too—Canadian *or* American!"

The occasion raised $25,000 for the mentally retarded. Later, the band played in the New Year from the Grand Ballroom of the Waldorf-Astoria Hotel, where patrons paid $100 a ticket.

Lombardo never forgot that the people of London, Ont., gave him his start and he tried to play in his hometown at least once a year. When the city's Thames River overflowed in April 1937, making 5,000 persons homeless, Lombardo called to ask, "Anything I can do?" There was. So at 1:45 a.m. one May night, after the band had driven direct from a Detroit engagement, Lombardo's baton cut through the cheers at Loew's Theater, while at the nearby Capitol a second waiting audience watched a movie. Then Loew's emptied and the Capitol crowd moved over. That night the Red Cross relief fund raised more than $4,000.

Away from the dance halls and the microphones, Lombardo's main interest was boats. He owned a succession of them, each called *Tempo*, and entered the luxury sport of speedboat racing. Music, however, was incontestably his first love. Even in the late 1970s, Guy Lombardo and His Royal Canadians were drawing fans who had first heard the bandleader's soft, sweet style more than 40 years earlier. "When are you going to retire?" they would ask Guy.

"Why *should* I retire," he would reply, "when every other night I meet another auld acquaintance—and every night is like New Year's Eve?"

Lombardo kept working almost until his death in November 1977 at the age of 75. The band he led plays on. "That," says band advisor Saul Richman, "is how Guy would have wanted it."

# They Do It Their Way

## By Robert Collins

By May 1958, most comedians in North America would have given a year's jokebooks to be in Johnny Wayne and Frank Shuster's old soft-shoes. The pair had just emerged from their first appearance on "The Ed Sullivan Show"—then the most coveted television showcase on the continent—to rave reviews. Their 13-minute spoof of Julius Caesar was, said *The New York Times*, a "harbinger of literate slapstick." In bars everywhere, Wayne and Shuster fans were ordering the "martinus" ("Gimme a martinus." "You mean a martini?" "If I want *two*, I'll *order* two!"). And now Sullivan had offered an unprecedented 26-week contract at his top fee of $7,500 a show—on their own terms.

"People down here may try to change your style," he warned. "Resist them. Do it your own way."

"What if *you* try to make us change?" cautioned Shuster.

"If you think I'm wrong, say no," insisted Sullivan. "Do it your way!"

Wayne and Shuster did. Fearing overexposure, they refused the 26-week offer in favor of 16 appearances the first year and they insisted on using their full-length sketches—10 to 20 minutes—although Sullivan restricted most performers to three or four minutes. Then Wayne had a silver medallion engraved: "Do it your way. Ed Sullivan." For 12 years he carried it throughout the twosome's record-breaking 65 appearances on "The Ed Sullivan Show." In times of disagreement he plunked down the medal, grinning wickedly, and the Sullivan crew always gave in.

Today, after more than 30 years in the most precarious kind of show business, Wayne and Shuster are still doing it "their way." Shuster—the gracious, patient straight man—and Wayne—the irrepressible cutup—are as much a Canadian institution as the Mounties or the maple leaf. Their Gulf Oil commercials have won more than 15 awards and U.S. schools have used their recorded spoofs of Shakespeare in English appreciation classes.

Though regarded as one of the top comedy teams in North America, Frank and Johnny have consistently broken the rules of show-business success. They have resisted countless overtures to change their style, get rich quick, "go Hollywood" or appear on Broadway. Shuster says, "We could make a lot more money but we'd rather set our own pace and enjoy life." Adds Wayne, "We have staying power, because we're choosy about what we do."

Thus they rejected the script for Broadway's *A Funny Thing Happened on the Way to the Forum* because "it wasn't right for us" and refused starring roles in another New York play, *The Golden Fleecing*. "If you can guarantee the show will flop we'll take it," Shuster told the astonished producers. "About two weeks in this town is all we could stand!" After their first appearance on "The Ed Sullivan Show," NBC offered them a $600,000 contract for a weekly television comedy show. "We turned it down in seven seconds," says Shuster. "We'd have had no time for our families, our friends, ourselves."

Similarly, they're adamant about staying in Canada. Once a talent agent trying to lure them to the States found Wayne in the swimming pool of his comfortable home in Toronto. "Tell me," urged the comedian, "are you gonna get me some kind of TV job so I can buy a house with a pool?"

On stage or off, Wayne and Shuster fare is a mixture of slapstick, pantomime, visual tricks, sheer corn and sometimes ingenious twists on classic situations: the meek little man whose blundering brother-in-law happens to be Superman (he keeps bursting in through the window, and when you want a quart of milk he brings back the whole refrigerator), and the bumbling German U-boat commander who has sunk 32 ships (all German), but can't be fired because he's Hitler's nephew.

"We believe," says Johnny Wayne (left), "in the Gilbert and Sullivan phrase 'innocent merriment.'" Here Wayne and Shuster create a little of that merriment in "Cinderfella," a skit they wrote for a 1977 CBC television special.

Rarely do Wayne and Shuster miss a chance for a gag: on the road to Dunkirk in 1944 they masquerade as Germans (Wayne parodies Hitler). During the war the duo penned *Invasion Review*, a show they presented to troops in Canada and Europe. "Doing that show for men from every province gave us our first real sense of Canada," says Wayne.

Such a potpourri doesn't always please the critics. It was, said one commentator, best suited to "someone who is simultaneously watching TV, giving a party and washing the car. They hardly demand undivided attention." But critic Bob Blackburn perhaps summed it up best when he wrote: "Often you'll find a flash of almost brilliant wit snuggled up beside a line which would be banal even for 'Comedy Crackers.' I suppose they are trying to be all things to all men."

"We don't try to please the critics," says their CBC executive producer, Leonard Starmer. "Our duty is to a big audience, including children. Anyway, contemporary comedy of any decade is faddish. Traditional comedy is timeless."

Weaned on the humor of such old masters as Chaplin, Laurel and Hardy, the Marx Brothers and Jack Benny, Wayne and Shuster are content to be classified as traditionalists. In the 1920s Shuster's father owned and operated a silent-movie theater in Niagara Falls. His mother sold tickets, so young Frank sat in the projection booth every night, learning to read from the subtitles. Wayne was one of seven children of a Toronto clothing manufacturer who wrote Hebrew poetry in his spare time.

The two met at Toronto's Harbord Collegiate. After producing a Boy Scout play that netted $40 for their troop, they starred as writers, singers and actors in Harbord's annual revue. They kept right on at the University of Toronto, producing college shows and developing a commercial radio program, "Wife Preservers"—household hints mixed with humor—that paid them each $12.50 a week. Amid all this they got B.A.s, majoring in English. "What I like about you, Wayne," said Claude Bissell, then an English lecturer and later president of the University of Toronto, "is you don't let your studies interfere with your education!"

Even World War II couldn't keep them off stage.

They enlisted as infantrymen but were soon writing the music, book and lyrics for a show called *Invasion Review*. It played to troops all over Canada and Britain, and for a while after D-Day they presented five shows a day from a cave in France.

They came home to start families and to enter the business of professional comedy. ("I know he's a very funny boy," Shuster's father-in-law told his daughter, "but what does he do for a *living*?")

Their first radio show was a humorous look at servicemen's rehabilitation problems. By 1947 they had a regular CBC program—and were doing it *their* way. The CBC saw no need for studio audiences, but Wayne and Shuster had seen how audience response was buoying up U.S. radio comedians. After their second performance in an empty studio they threatened to quit unless the CBC provided a live audience and enough studio microphones to pick up the laughter. They got both.

Soon NBC offered them the summer replacement spot for "The Life of Riley" radio show. Fine, said the Canadians, but why do it in New York? NBC was puzzled: didn't *everybody* want to work

Wayne and Shuster made 65 appearances on "The Ed Sullivan Show" and three times hosted the program. Sullivan (center) once said: "They knew exactly what they were doing and what they wanted from orchestra, cast and staging. They are real pros."

in New York? But Toronto's facilities proved satisfactory and the U.S. network show was produced in Canada.

In 1950 Wayne and Shuster were guest stars on a U.S. television show sponsored by Toni Home Permanents. The company promptly offered them their own show, but though television hadn't yet come to Canada, Wayne and Shuster refused. Toni's president then offered them vice-presidencies in charge of the company's entire U.S. television programming. They politely heard him out, sitting on a quiet Toronto lawn, then turned him down. "Why should we leave all this," said Wayne with a wave of an arm, "to spend our lives on airplanes?"

Starting regular CBC television work in 1954, they began honing their style, quickening their pace and building a cast of characters: The Brown Pumpernickel (like the Scarlet Pimpernel, he helps the downtrodden, but the trademark he leaves is a loaf of bread); Professor Waynegartner, a nutty old scientist with runaway white hair (the professor's rocket ship has a crew of 120. Shuster: "That's a large crew!" Professor: "Too large. The first time we flew it, some of us had to go by train."); and Tex Rorschach, Frontier Psychiatrist ("Your husband's problem iss all in his mind, he can valk if he vants to. Good-by, Mrs. Sitting Bull.").

There were contemporary twists on classics: in "The Picture of Dorian Wayne," a glutton gorges himself on food and stays thin, while his portrait grows fat. And there were the Shakespearean spoofs. In "The Elsinore Kid," a horse-opera Hamlet swaggers into a bar: "Gimme a shot of whiskey and don't cut the liquor. I want the uncuttest kind of all!" In the Julius Caesar skit, a line uttered by Caesar's nagging widow—"If I told him once, I told him a thousand times. I said 'Julie, don't go!'"—became an international "in" phrase.

In 1957, millions of British viewers watched them

perform in "Chelsea at Nine." Critics were enthusiastic, actor Charles Laughton said it was "bloody good" and Granada TV offered them a 13-week show. As usual, they refused. "You can't do a weekly show and keep up standards." A few months later, after a guest appearance on "The Rosemary Clooney Show," they turned down an NBC invitation to take over *that* series. "What *do* you guys want?" demanded a frustrated agent. They wanted what Ed Sullivan finally gave them: major U.S. network appearances on their own terms, with freedom to live and continue working in Canada.

Now the industry courted Wayne and Shuster harder than ever. There was a guest spot on "The Dinah Shore Show," another on "The Red Skelton Show" and records for Columbia. The St. Louis Municipal Opera wanted them for a musical comedy. Such comedians as Jack E. Leonard, Jack Carter and Ernie Kovacs visited rehearsals, to kibitz and accord the respect of fellow professionals.

Wayne and Shuster loved it, but gratefully hurried home after every performance. Then as now, they saved time for their families—Shuster has two

During more than three decades together, Wayne and Shuster have assumed countless guises to get laughs. As Tex Rorschach, Frontier Psychiatrist, Johnny Wayne (top, with notebook) analyzes his partner, and (far left) portrays scatterbrained Professor Waynegartner. Often drawing on Shakespeare for comedic inspiration, the pair has spoofed such plays as "Hamlet" (below, with Carol Robinson) and—in perhaps their most famous sketch—"Julius Caesar" (bottom).

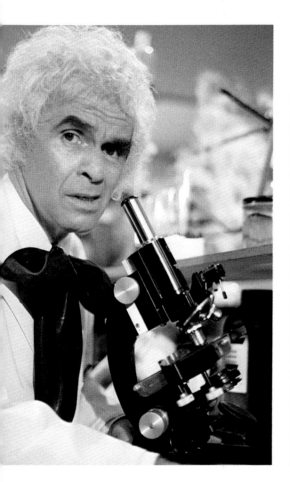

children; Wayne, three—who generally accompanied them on New York or Hollywood assignments. "We embarrass the show-biz crowd because we still have the wives we started with," chuckles Shuster. "Once at a party Groucho Marx told us, 'How dare you flaunt your own wives at a Hollywood gathering! Do you want to undermine the social structure?'"

Unlike most comics, they continue to write most of their material. Ideas come from all around them. Antismoking campaigns inspired a routine about the smoking addict who phones for help from Ciga-

rettes Anonymous; they send over a drunk to sit up with him. Once, riding an aircraft economy class with his wife, Wayne began to fantasize about the "orgy" going on in first class: "They're eating *turkey* up there . . . hey, *they've got wine!* I guess *I'll* go back and pump a glass of water from the well . . . hey, there's a girl in a bathing suit, they must have a *pool* up there . . ." From this came a skit which helped win the Silver Rose of Montreux for the second-best television variety show in the world.

They work at one or the other's home, taking turns at the typewriter and acting out material

until the lines are right. Once a scream issued from Wayne's study. "It's all right," a Wayne child told a startled friend. "It's just Daddy, writing."

The show then goes into a week and a half of rehearsal, during which the two argue vehemently, still polishing the script. "I'm really a bad-tempered guy," says Wayne. "I don't know how Shuster puts up with me." Shuster, always patient, shows his annoyance only with the occasional sarcastic plea, "Will *somebody* please tell my partner . . ."

"It's all for the good of the show, and nobody takes it seriously," says actor Paul Kligman, who worked with them for a quarter-century with nothing more binding than a handshake. "Johnny is really a genius. And few people realize that, behind the straight-man routine, Frank is a highly talented actor."

After hundreds of hours of work from the germ of an idea, the show goes into the studio for taping. "We give it our best shot, always," Wayne says simply. "We owe the people our best possible."

Because they are uncommonly versatile, the death of "The Ed Sullivan Show" in 1970 caused scarcely a ripple in their careers. They have produced and narrated a filmed series on great comedians of our time. They have collaborated on a script satirizing Canadian politics, appeared on educational television and hosted on the CBC a British series on Gilbert and Sullivan. "We're experimenting," Wayne says. "The biggest danger in our business is in getting complacent."

Some years ago Shuster was sitting with their New York manager, who was again trying to lure them to the United States. For ten minutes he wheedled and cajoled to no avail. Finally the agent snapped in frustration, "You know, Frank, there's more to life than happiness!"

Judging by the laughter it got, that line may show up some day in a Wayne and Shuster skit.

171

# THE FACE
# OF A NATION

"Have you loved this land
 For what it is—For its wealth,
 Its freedom,
 Its northern wind,
 And above all,
 For its people?"

Paul Call

# The North

Sprawling more than one and
a half million square miles
across the top of Canada, yet
home to fewer than 60,000
persons, the North (the Yukon
and the Northwest Territories)
is inhospitable, sometimes
forbidding, virtually untouched.
But it is a special place,
say those who know it, a land
of untold wealth and haunting
beauty which, once seen,
invites return.

Like lonely sentinels, Inukshuks stand as reminders of a time when only Inuit and Indian inhabited this harsh but lovely land. Built in the rough shape of humans, these figures of rock were used by Inuit as landmarks and to locate caribou migration routes.

The midnight sun glows over Echo Bay in the Northwest Territories. From April to October throughout much of the North the sun shines for more than 20 hours a day, warming the air to a comfortable 15°C (60°F) and making it possible for Inuit children such as these to play at midnight. Some Inuit cling to old ways, living in shifting hunting camps and subsisting on fish and

caribou, seal, hare and ptarmigan. Most, however, inhabit permanent settlements, buy food at a co-op or a trading store and enjoy the amenities of a modern world—radios, refrigerators, prefabricated housing. With modernization has come opportunity. Less than two decades ago, some 15 percent of Inuit children attended school; now almost 95 percent do.

Running 600 miles north from Grimshaw, Alta., to Fort Simpson, N.W.T., the Mackenzie Highway has opened thousands of square miles of wilderness. It winds through dense forests, past shallow, ice-gouged lakes and—here—across miles of virtually treeless tundra. The highway will eventually stretch more than 1,300 miles to Tuktoyaktuk on the Arctic Ocean.

With its hospital, airport, newspaper and office buildings, bustling Yellowknife is a symbol of modern northern development. Only 320 miles south of the Arctic Circle, the capital of the Northwest Territories sprang up when gold was discovered nearby in 1934.

A worker near Dawson, Y.T., pulls a boulder from a sluice box in which he hopes to find gold. Production of gold here is a fraction of what it was during the Klondike gold rush of the 1890s—down from more than $20 million a year at the turn of the century to less than $2 million by the mid-60s. But dreams of striking it rich are still strong in the North, and new bonanzas are being discovered. Minerals, particularly zinc, asbestos and lead, form the mainstay of the economy: their annual production is worth some $350 million.

Drinking in Dawson today can be impassive and regulated, but the echoes of long-ago, foot-stomping revelry seem to linger around venerable buildings and board sidewalks. During the gold rush this was a rude and boisterous place where a whirl with a dance-hall girl cost $1, champagne went for $60 a bottle, and $2,000 in gold dust could ride on the turn of a card.

Erected in 1946, this three-story log "skyscraper" stands in Whitehorse, the Yukon's capital and largest city.

The spirit of adventure still permeates the North: the spell of the wild and the urge to be independent remain compelling forces. This is a land of sweeping vistas (left: the Rackla range of the Richardson Mountains), a place, someone once wrote, that conveys a "sensation of tranquility." Those who leave behind car and motor home—in much of the North there is little choice—can raft down unspoiled rivers, tramp where trails are few or camp with only wildlife for neighbors, discovering a way of life that has no counterpart elsewhere.

# British Columbia

Unspoiled and magnificent,
British Columbia rises from the
Pacific Ocean in a confusion of
islands, bays and fjords, then
climbs to a panorama of craggy
mountain peaks. In this land
of wild extremes are some of
Canada's wettest, driest, hottest
and coldest places; here too
are alpine meadows, emerald
lakes, deep canyons and mighty
rivers. But always the
mountains.

12,972-foot Mount Robson

Symbols of tribal pride, these faces stare from totem poles at Kispiox. Towering up to 80 feet, such poles commemorate past events, honor supernatural ancestors, ridicule rival tribesmen and—occasionally—depict the artists themselves.

185

Downtown Vancouver (top) is mir-
rored in a quiet corner of the city's
great harbor. Nearby is Chinatown,
the second largest Chinese community in North America. Vancouver,
Canada's third biggest city, was
named for the British explorer Capt.
George Vancouver, who visited the
area in 1792 and wrote of its "innu-
merable pleasing landscapes." Many
such landscapes are in 1,000-acre Stanley Park (right), a wooded retreat
with more than 30 miles of hiking
trails, lush gardens, rolling lawns, an
aquarium and a zoo. The park is still
as a Vancouver mayor described it in
1888–a place to "spend some time
amid the beauties of nature, away
from the busy haunts of men."

186

Indian fishermen use long poles to spear salmon in the Bulkley River. In summer and autumn, Pacific salmon leave the ocean to spawn in more than 1,300 rivers and streams along the British Columbia coast.

The one that got away probably *was* that big. *Everything* seems big in British Columbia—glaciers, mountains, lakes, rivers, waterfalls—for it is a province of superlatives, a place whose stunning geography attracts tourists from around the world.

The moon rises over a stand of Douglas fir, typical of British Columbia's great forests (more than 60 percent of the province is wooded). Since the first sawmill was built in Victoria in 1848, forestry has grown into a $600-million-a-year industry.

On the doorstep of the Pacific, British Columbia's 4,400-mile coastline is a spectacular, often rugged, magnet for sailors, beachcombers—and anyone else who loves the sea. In Pacific Rim National Park, clam diggers probe the sand of seven-and-a-half-mile Long Beach. A showcase of West Coast beauty, the 250-square-mile park features wave-pounded headlands, dense forests and teeming marine life—seals and sea lions, whales and starfish.

Like his sure-footed counterpart, the mountain goat, a climber tackles a cliff face in Yoho National Park, on the west slope of the Rockies. Yoho is a Cree Indian word signifying awe and wonder, a fitting reaction to what one observer called "the terrible majesties of the Canadian Rockies." Thousands of miles of hiking and climbing routes of varying difficulty offer virtually limitless opportunities to explore this mountain world of breathtaking beauty.

# Alberta

Drawing on a wealth of natural resources, Alberta is Canada's fastest growing province. It contains some 90 percent of the nation's known oil and natural gas deposits and 50 percent of its coal. The Athabasca tar sands alone account for three fifths of the *world's* known oil reserves. Alberta has come of age— and looks to a dynamic future.

Group of Seven artist A. Y. Jackson called the Red Deer Badlands, near Brooks, Alta., the "most paintable valley in western Canada." An eerie expanse of gullied canyons, terraced cliffs and natural stone pillars called hoodoos, it is also a burial ground for the dinosaurs that roamed here some 135 million years ago.

Alberta is cattle country, with more than 60,000 farms and ranches occupying some 20 percent of the land. The province has four and a half million head of cattle and supplies 40 percent of Canada's red meat.

A Doukhobor woman near Arrowhead exults in the bounty of a rich land. Development started with the completion of the Canadian Pacific Railway in 1885. Soon, thousands of homesteaders were streaming in from Europe, eastern Canada and the United States to settle the fertile grasslands.

At the Calgary Stampede—"the biggest outdoor show on earth"—a cowboy puts on the brakes but the steer has other ideas. Each July, Calgary is thronged by those who come to enter—or just watch—such events as bronco busting and calf roping. When the spurs are hung up for the year, Calgary resumes its interest in minerals: some 450 companies here are involved in the oil industry.

Not to be outdone by Calgary's Stampede, Edmonton stages "Klondike Days," a summer celebration that recalls the days when Alberta's capital was a supply base for the gold rush of 1898. People dress in Victorian finery, and bars and lounges become "saloons." There is bathtub racing through the streets, panning for gold in a specially prepared stream and a beard-growing contest. An industrial center, Edmonton boasts an opera, a university, a subway, and a football team whose youngest supporters bundle up on chill afternoons to cheer their Eskimos.

195

# Saskatchewan

Saskatchewan is more—much more—than vast fields of wheat punctuated by grain elevators. True, this is Canada's greatest wheat-growing area, but a second look reveals a province of exhilarating surprises. Named for the river the Indians called "Swift-flowing," Saskatchewan has rolling hills, wooded ravines, marshes, sand dunes, eerie badlands, and sparkling lakes and rivers which offer trophy-size fish and challenging canoeing.

The setting sun over Waskesui Lake tints a northern sky in 1,496-square-mile Prince Albert National Park. Also in the park is the log cabin where Grey Owl, the world-famous woodsman, author and conservationist, spent the last seven years of his life. Lean and dark-skinned, he encouraged the belief that he was an Indian. Only after his death in 1938 was he found to have been English-born. Grey Owl established a beaver colony in the park and spent much of his life crusading against the wanton killing of animals for sport.

Newly born Canada geese nestle among shells and unhatched eggs in Regina's Wascana Waterfowl Park, near the Saskatchewan Legislative Building. The marshy shore of Wascana Lake attracts such birds as the mallard, whistling swan and blue-winged teal.

198

An east-European-style church reflects the ethnic diversity of a province which was once the domain of Indians and a few fur traders. Settlers flooded in after the completion of the CPR in 1885–Ukrainians, Mennonites, Britons, Germans, Scandinavians, Americans whose own West was filling up, and farm lads from Ontario and the Maritimes.

Treeless prairie there is, but the Saskatchewan landscape also offers striking contrasts, ranging from eroded clay hills (called dobbies) that dot badlands south of Killdeer . . . to rippled dunes that sprawl like a northern Sahara across 4,000 square miles . . . to the lush green of the Cypress Hills, whose 4,810-foot summit is the highest point between Labrador and the Rockies.

# Manitoba

Manitoba is a broadly painted canvas of grass, grain, rolling parkland and lake-dappled forest. Its capital of Winnipeg is populous and sophisticated, but nonetheless dwarfed by the big-sky country surrounding it. Even the man-made channel (below), which diverts Red River floods around the city, seems to have become part of the natural landscape.

Winter lashes a lonely homestead, uncaring that the occupants have long since gone. A farmer who has stayed takes no chances with frostbite in temperatures that often dip to 40 below. And a four-year-old finds that, yes, the lake is frozen very hard.

A replica of the paddle-wheelers that plied the Red River a century ago cruises near Winnipeg. The Red was, for many years, a major Manitoba artery. Pierre de La Vérendrye explored it in the 1730s, opening the way for generations of fur traders. And Scottish crofters sailed down it from Hudson Bay in 1812, to settle on its fertile banks.

A train trip deep into northern Manitoba winds through desolate country where prevailing winds often let branches of the few hardy trees grow in one direction only. Near Churchill, Canada's northernmost deep-sea port and the route's terminus, wind and water have shaped limestone into gently undulating "benches."

Topped by the statue of the "Golden Boy," the Manitoba Legislature is a Winnipeg landmark. Pierre de La Vérendrye built Fort Rouge at the junction of the Red and Assiniboine rivers in 1738. Today, Winnipeg is Canada's fourth largest city. Here is the legendary corner of Portage and Main, said to be the coldest, windiest spot in the country. But here too is small-town warmth and friendliness in a cosmopolitan setting of theaters, a planetarium, a symphony orchestra, big-league hockey and football teams, and the largest French-speaking community outside Quebec.

206

# Ontario

Here is felt the pulse of a nation, for Ontario is Canada's commercial heartland, the seat of the country's government and home to a third of her people. Of striking diversity, it embraces such geographical extremes as Polar Bear Provincial Park on Hudson Bay, and Lake Erie's southerly Point Pelee, a narrow peninsula at the same latitude as northern California. From rugged wilderness to verdant farm country to the great industrial cities of the south, Ontario is a dynamic province of many moods.

Toronto residents skate under the arches near their ultramodern city hall ... shop at Kensington market, where the babble of German, Portuguese, Italian and Chinese is a sign of the city's multinational blend ... and mingle with birds in one of more than 300 parks, where signs *urge* visitors to walk on the grass. Roughly one in three Ontarians lives in a city appropriately named after the Huron

Indian word for "a place of meeting." It is the hub of Canada's densest manufacturing region, home of one of the world's busiest stock exchanges and center of a rich agricultural hinterland which supplies many of the city's needs. Toronto has been called the "most civilized city in North America." It offers such attractions as the Ontario Science Centre, the Toronto Symphony Orchestra and the Royal Ontario Museum (which houses one of the Western world's largest collections of Chinese art).

In a blaze of scarlet, the Changing of the Guard lends pageantry to Parliament Hill. The 301-foot Peace Tower (below), whose carillon is audible for miles, dominates the Hill and its Gothic buildings.

Skaters take a turn on the world's longest rink, a four-and-a-half mile stretch of the Rideau Canal. The 125-mile system, which links Ottawa and Kingston, was completed in 1832 by British engineers under Col. John By. He gave his name to the small lumbering community that developed where the canal meets the Ottawa River, and Bytown later became Ottawa.

Canada Day festivities in the capital showcase a colorful variety of peoples and costumes—elements of the Canadian mosaic. Clockwise from top are Ukrainian musicians plucking banduras, a Chinese dancer with feathery fans, a Lithuanian girl, an Israeli couple, and members of an Armenian troupe stepping to the strains of traditional folk music.

Living a frugal farm life, Mennonites near Elmira have withdrawn from the mainstream of modern Canada. They refuse to take oaths or to use force, usually abstain from alcohol and tobacco—and still rely on the horse for transportation.

Wheat sluices into the hold of a ship at Thunder Bay, one of Canada's largest ports. Thunder Bay's grain elevators can hold some 106 million bushels, and most Prairie grain bound for markets in the east and overseas funnels through the port. Left: A young hockey player, perhaps with dreams of making it to the big leagues, heads for the nearest ice in Hornepayne.

# Quebec

Since 1535, when Jacques Cartier sailed the broad St. Lawrence River to where Montreal now stands, Quebec has embraced a culture distinctly French. Yet even by the time of the Battle of the Plains of Abraham little more than two centuries later, French Canadians were proudly different from Frenchmen, tempering the customs of France with a spirit of adventure and independence that still survives. Today Canada's biggest province is steeped in an atmosphere of old-world charm, of stone homes and quaint churches. But it is also vibrantly modern, a place whose people—and arts—celebrate the blossoming of a unique society.

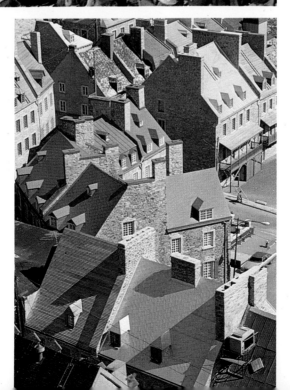

Austere under a dusting of snow, St. Joseph's Oratory in Montreal is a symbol of religious faith. On the site of this world-renowned Catholic shrine Brother André (Alfred Bessette, 1845-1937), whose beatification is being considered by Rome, preached that devotion to St. Joseph would relieve the suffering of the sick and crippled. Many have left the oratory apparently cured, discarding wheelchairs, canes and crutches in the Votive Chapel. Montreal's celebrated *joie de vivre* is exemplified by a juggler-clown in Dominion Square, and by sidewalk cafés such as the Maison Cartier, which lend European flavor to tree-lined streets. The city cherishes its past yet keeps pace with the present: the soaring Canadian Imperial Bank of Commerce building is typical of the downtown area.

Dufferin Terrace, a boardwalk over-looking the St. Lawrence River, runs atop fortifications that make Quebec North America's only walled city. Founded in 1608 by Samuel de Champlain, the provincial capital is Canada's oldest city, a living museum of narrow streets and historic buildings. During the Quebec Winter Carnival, held each February, the city brims with gaiety. There are parades, ice

A ship glides through the St. Lawrence Seaway near Montreal. Almost two thirds of Canada's foreign trade passes through the St. Lawrence River system, an intricate series of inland locks and channels that links the Great Lakes and the Atlantic Ocean.

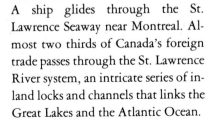

sculptures, street celebrations and the crowning of a carnival queen. A highlight of the two-week event is a race across the frozen St. Lawrence.

219

Horses graze in fields cleared from dense forest in the Laurentian Mountains, north of Montreal. These hills are believed to be among the oldest in the world. Laced with myriad lakes—many unnamed—they are the basis of a thriving ski industry.

Quebecers at work: smelting copper . . . collecting sap for maple syrup and sugar . . . unloading the day's catch in the Gaspé . . . fashioning elegant ceramics . . . crafting a graceful birchbark canoe.

# New Brunswick

Skyscrapers are few and wilderness is never far away in New Brunswick, where the pace of life is unhurried and the land uncrowded. More than 700 miles of coastline rims nearly three quarters of the roughly rectangular province. Inland, New Brunswick is dominated by countless lakes and by the forests which cloak four fifths of its area. The province's 124,000 French-speaking Acadians, many descended from French colonists who settled here in the 1600s, make up more than 35 percent of the population.

Fishing is a vital part of New Brunswick life, and ruddy-faced fishermen in hip boots are a common sight in coastal villages. At a plant run by Connors Bros. Limited in Blacks Harbour, women work in part of the Commonwealth's largest sardine and herring canning operation.

Kissin' bridges they called them, for reasons that made covered bridges a traditional favorite of courting couples. New Brunswick boasts more than 100 such spans, but the granddaddy of them all is this one, at Hartland. Measuring 1,282 feet, it is the longest covered bridge in the world.

Time seems to stand still at King's Landing Historical Settlement. The old-time community of 60 buildings—with staff in period clothing—was created near Prince William to show what life was like along the Saint John River between 1790 and 1870. Many of those who originally settled this area were Loyalists, staunch supporters of Britain who fled the United States after the American Revolution of 1775-83.

225

Baked, boiled, creamed, fried or mashed—New Brunswick potatoes land on many a Canadian dinner plate. Children from potato-growing areas traditionally cut short summer vacations and return to school in late August. Then, in autumn, they abandon classrooms to help harvest the province's largest farm crop.

"Miles and miles they extend, level and grassy, and dim," wrote Charles G. D. Roberts of the Tantramar marshes near Sackville. Separated from the sea by old Acadian dykes and dotted with hay barns, this 80-square-mile expanse of fertility has been dubbed the "world's biggest hayfield."

# Nova Scotia

McLeod, MacPherson, Robertson, McLean...all are common names in a province with its own tartan and the Cross of St. Andrew on its flag. Certainly the Scots are not alone—there are plenty of Doucets and Boutiliers, of Wamboldts and Zwickers and others—but Nova Scotia *means* New Scotland, a land that greets visitors with Gaelic signs saying *Cìad Mile Failte* (100,000 Welcomes) and that owes much of its atmosphere to the 50,000 Highlanders who have flocked here since the late 1700s. None of the province's 800,000 inhabitants live more than 35 miles from salt water, and seafaring has long been a Nova Scotia way of life.

Square-riggers and schooners poured from Nova Scotia dockyards in the 1800s giving the province a mercantile armada as well as a huge fishing fleet. Among the greatest of these ships were *William D. Lawrence,* the enormous cargo carrier; *Lightning,* whose record of 436 miles in 24 hours has never been equaled by a windjammer; and *Bluenose,* whose form graces the 10-cent piece. The great days of sail are past, but shipbuilders and sailmakers still ply their trades in such Nova Scotia ports as Lunenburg (below, and top right) and Clark's Harbour (bottom).

In an underground world of darkness and danger, these miners in a colliery at Glace Bay, Cape Breton Island, are sometimes guided only by feeble headlamps. Coal, the chief product of Nova Scotia's mineral industry, was first mined at nearby Port Morien in 1720; full-scale production began in the 1850s.

High-rise buildings overlook Halifax Harbour, site of North America's largest naval dockyards, begun in 1759 under the supervision of Capt. James Cook. Near the harbor is the Old Town Clock, a parting gift from Prince Edward (later Duke of Kent), a punctual martinet who was the city's military commander from 1794 to 1800. The clock, built in London, was erected in 1803.

Begun by the French in 1720, Fortress Louisbourg was so expensive to build that Louis XV, in Paris, said he expected to see its turrets rising over the horizon. An army of New England volunteers, helped by the British, took Louisbourg in 1745 – only to see it returned to the French in 1748. A decade later the British recaptured the fort, later reducing it to rubble. But Louisbourg has risen anew: old streets and cellars have been unearthed, and buildings have been reconstructed with the tools, techniques and materials of 250 years ago.

Festivals reflect Nova Scotia's Scottish traditions. Highland games are featured, and there is much skirling of bagpipes and dancing of the Highland fling. Every July young and old vie for honors at the Glendale Fiddle Festival (below) on Cape Breton Island.

# Prince Edward Island

The Indians, who knew Prince Edward Island well, called it Abegweit, meaning "cradled on the waves." Fringed with sandy beaches, Canada's smallest province (only 140 miles long, never more than 40 wide) is also the nation's birthplace: at Charlottetown in 1864 the Fathers of Confederation first agreed on the principles of unity for British North America.

A farmer relaxes after a long day in the fields. It often seems that Prince Edward Island—sometimes called The Million-Acre Farm—is nothing *but* farms. Agriculture is the province's leading industry and potatoes are the chief crop. (Refugees from Irish potato famines in the early 1800s were among early settlers here.)

Perhaps training for the big-time harness races at Charlottetown and Summerside, horse and driver kick up dirt on a tranquil road near Clyde River. There are many such rural byways in Prince Edward Island: author Lucy Maud Montgomery called the province "the last refuge for fairies and the old gods."

237

Along the north coast of the Island are countless fleets of fishing boats. Some take visitors into the Gulf of St. Lawrence after cod, herring, mackerel and tuna. In waters near Malpeque (bottom) are found the tasty oysters which have made the town world famous.

Long poles fitted with baskets are used to gather Irish moss, a seaweed that washes up on Prince Edward Island beaches. The province produces some 45 percent of the world supply; on a good day one man can harvest up to 1,000 pounds. Irish moss is used to make a thickener and stabilizer for puddings, ice cream, toothpaste and cosmetics.

Carved by relentless waves, headlands
in Prince Edward Island National
Park display the sandstone base that
gives the province its rich, red soil.

# Newfoundland

Fishing dories bob on an
Atlantic tide. Swarms of birds
wheel past rocky cliffs.
Spectacular mountains give
way to coastal plains, and
granite walls flank glacial lakes
(left: Western Brook Pond)
or plunge to the sea. Part island
(Newfoundland), and part
mainland (Labrador), Canada's
youngest province is populated
by a hardy folk whose age-old
struggle to eke out a living has
bred a sturdy independence.

One of Newfoundland's oldest settlements, St. John's bears the unmistakable stamp of the past. Sections of the Old Town have changed little since being rebuilt after a fire swept Newfoundland's capital in 1892. The city today has modern suburbs and shopping centers—but also colorful jumbles of Victorian buildings, and houses perched on cliffs near the harbor entrance.

A Nascapi Indian tills his garden in Northwest River, Labrador. Less than three decades ago the Nascapi faced extinction from starvation and disease—until Oblate missionaries improved their nutrition and introduced health services. Northwest River Nascapi now live in wooden houses, receive care at a nearby hospital and attend church and school in the English and Indian languages.

Some 900 small outports, such as this one on the Strait of Belle Isle, dot Newfoundland's 6,000 miles of coastline. Change has come slowly to these villages, whose often fanciful names—Tickle Cove, Heart's Content, Ireland's Eye, Joe Batt's Arm—liven the provincial map. Until the early 50s, many such communities lacked electricity and were accessible only by boat.

Churning through a sea of timber, a powerful tug hauls a log boom to the Bowaters newsprint mill, one of the world's largest, at Corner Brook. The pulp and paper industry accounts for some $100 million of Newfoundland's annual exports, giving a vital boost to local economies—and to the many fishermen who supplement their earnings with part-time logging.

"Oh! this is the place where the fishermen gather," runs the first line of "The Squid Jiggin' Ground," a rousing Newfoundland sea shanty. As they have for centuries, the province's fishermen put to sea to reap the bounty of the deep: "king cod," tuna up to 800 pounds, lobsters that sell locally for as little as a dollar apiece and, of course, squid (bottom), which is used as bait. In quiet communities such as Bonavista (below), one of Newfoundland's oldest communities, fishermen rise as early as 4 a.m. during the summer fishing season and are still on the docks until late at night when the last fish is packed in salt.

# THE CHALLENGE

"Fire is the test of gold;
adversity, of strong men."

Lucius Annaeus Seneca

# After a Life of Storm, a State of Grace

## By Harold Horwood

One summer day in 1972 a parade of official limousines purred through Gravenhurst, Ont., and pulled up outside a modest two-story frame house. Doors opened, and out stepped the Canadian trade minister and the foreign trade minister of the People's Republic of China. Followed by a group of Chinese, they entered the home of the local United Church minister and filed slowly through the house. The Chinese visitors, reported Toronto's *Globe and Mail*, "walked from room to room with near-reverence. Questions were asked in hushed voices. It was a visit to a shrine."

The "shrine" is the birthplace of one of communist China's most famous heroes: Pai-ch'iu-en (a transliteration of his surname, which also happens to mean "White-Seek-Grace"). Canadians know him as Henry Norman Bethune—the stocky, cocky, passionate, crusading doctor with piercing blue-green eyes and pugnacious charm who died in 1939 as a frontline surgeon with Mao Tse-tung's guerrilla army. A controversial figure throughout his stormy career—he became a communist three years before he died at 49—Bethune was nevertheless unknown to most Canadians a generation after the war. Only since Ottawa and Peking established diplomatic relations and Chinese delegations began asking to see the places where he lived and worked, has interest in this extraordinary Canadian been revived.

Bethune's achievements were impressive. He was a pioneer in thoracic surgery in Canada and became a world authority in this specialty. He designed or improved numerous surgical instruments, notably a pneumothorax machine and the Bethune rib shears. And, in the Spanish Civil War, he organized the world's first mobile blood clinic.

But it was in China that Bethune found both fame and fulfillment. Joining Mao's embattled Eighth Route Army in 1938, he went into action with Chinese guerrillas fighting behind Japanese lines. He set up hospitals in caves, temples and huts. Stories of his heroic deeds spread rapidly—how he gave his own blood to a wounded guerrilla, then, without pausing, completed the operation that saved the man's life; how he performed surgery under the guns of the advancing Japanese; and how on several occasions he got out of temporary hospitals only minutes before they were captured. His very presence inspired Mao's men with hope, and with confidence that they would not die of neglected wounds. Soldiers went into battle shouting, "Attack! Bethune is with us!"

Ironically, the man China reveres was born on March 3, 1890, into a family of Christian clergymen. His father was the Presbyterian pastor in Gravenhurst. The Bethunes had once been French aristocrats, and Norman never forgot it. Ancestors on both sides of his family had held high positions in church and state, and he grew up with a sense of destiny and dreams of greatness. Stubbornly self-willed and rebellious, he quarreled often with his evangelist parents, and once his exasperated father pushed his face into the ground and made him eat dirt to teach him humility.

The humility didn't take. Instead, Bethune became a lifelong rebel, feuding with everyone in authority—be it the medical establishment, the Republican government in Spain, or the Communist party in Canada. Even to those who knew him best, Bethune was a riddle. His friend Hazen Sise said that Bethune "was an uncomfortable person to have around. He fairly bristled with challenges and had no qualms about expressing them." Yet Sise also spoke of his "extraordinary vividness and charm. He radiated an energy and enthusiasm that was contagious—you came alive in his presence."

When World War I broke out, Bethune was in medical school in Toronto. He enlisted immediately, went to France, was wounded and discharged,

248

This marble statue of Norman Bethune stands near the Canadian doctor's tomb in the Chinese town of Shih-chia-chuang. Bethune, who died in 1939 while serving as a surgeon with Mao Tse-tung's Eighth Route Army, is today glorified as a folk hero in China. He was an example, wrote Mao, of "utter devotion to others without any thought of self."

诺尔曼·白求恩

and resumed his studies. Graduated in 1916, he reenlisted as a surgeon lieutenant in the Royal Navy. After the war he interned in London hospitals but, needing other outlets for his boundless energy and money for his high living, he bought and sold art objects at a handsome profit. In his flat he held court, entertaining writers, artists and doctors with nightly sessions of drink and debate.

Here he met Frances Penney, the shy and delicate daughter of a prominent Edinburgh family to whom during the next 20 years he was married and divorced twice, and whom he might have married a third time had not fate intervened. "It was love at first sound," said Norman, referring to her soft Scottish lilt. Bethune became a Fellow of the Royal College of Surgeons in 1922, and the following year they were married. "Now I can make your life a misery," he said. "But I'll never bore you—it's a promise."

With the help of a modest legacy from Frances' uncle, the newlyweds set off for Europe and a giddy year of domestic strife, partying, skiing—and medical studies in Paris, Vienna and Berlin. One strange incident occurred. Out on a walk, the couple came to the edge of a deep ravine. Though there was no need to cross, Bethune suddenly said: "I would sooner see you dead than funk that." Frances jumped the gap, then fled to their hotel. Norman begged her forgiveness, and later said: "Always look at me through half-closed eyes."

Finally broke, the Bethunes sailed for Canada, then settled in Detroit, where Norman opened an office in the red-light district and earned his living largely by swapping services for food and furniture. Discovered by a prominent doctor who admired his deftness with a scalpel, he quickly rose to social and financial success. But although they moved to fashionable quarters, Bethune continued to work in the slums and treat the poor.

249

Norman Bethune was as unpredictable as he was brilliant. In 1912 he dropped out of a science course at the University of Toronto to join the staff (below; Bethune is fourth from left) of Frontier College, a school for immigrant workers on the shore of Georgian Bay. In exchange for room and board, Bethune worked by day as an axman in the college logging camp; at night he ran the school reading room.

At 36, when Bethune was on his way to affluent middle age, his health and his stormy marriage collapsed simultaneously. Frances went home to Scotland while Norman went to the famous Trudeau Sanatorium at Saranac Lake, New York, for treatment of tuberculosis. There he insisted that his lung be collapsed—then an experimental operation. When told of the dangers, he theatrically bared his chest and cried: "Gentlemen, I welcome the risk!" Bethune somewhat exaggerated his condition—he had only a partial pneumothorax—but he was a romantic who delighted in pretending

he had escaped from the jaws of death by a self-created miracle.

Bethune recovered quickly and became a fanatical apostle of pneumothorax, believing he had found a mission to lead the fight against tuberculosis with the weapon of chest surgery. At his insistence Frances returned and remarried him. The reunion lasted only a year before they decided to divorce a second time.

In 1932 Bethune was appointed head of the newly opened chest surgery department at the Hôpital du Sacré-Cœur in Montreal. But, although he was now an internationally known teacher of chest surgery, his life was turning in another direction. The Depression was at its depth, and the suffering of the poor appalled him. "One incident in particular altered his life—an eviction in Montreal in which he saw a man killed in a tussle with the police," said a friend, Sam Maltin. In the suburb of Verdun, he opened a free clinic for the unemployed and provided a free art school for poor children in his big Montreal apartment.

In August 1935 Bethune met leading Russian doctors at the International Congress of Physiological Scientists in Leningrad. A tour of hospitals followed, and he came home deeply impressed with Russian state medicine. With the help of friends, he set up the Montreal Group for the Security of the People's Health which presented detailed proposals for a system of state medical care and a compulsory health service—ideas far ahead of their time in Canada. But he refused an invitation from the Canadian Communist party to become chairman of The Friends of the Soviet Union. "What stands in the way of my acceptance?" he replied. "My strong feeling of individualism—the right of a man to walk alone, if that's his nature."

In July 1936 war erupted in Spain, and Nazi Germany and Italy sent aid to the forces seeking to depose the communist-influenced Republican government. Bethune and Hazen Sise went to Spain to join the Republicans. On a quick tour of the front, Bethune discovered most deaths were from bleeding and shock. Blood transfusion was needed, right behind the lines. But transfusion was still experimental, confined to well-equipped hospitals. Storage was difficult, transportation impossible; shipping agitation caused whole blood to spoil. Sise suggested a simple solution: fill containers to the top, seal them, and agitation would be greatly reduced. It worked.

Strong willed and dedicated to his work, Bethune made life miserable for his wife, Frances Penney. Their first marriage in 1923 ended in divorce four years later. They remarried, then divorced again—for good—in 1933.

Spanish officials considered Bethune's ideas impractical, but finally he won them over, went to London, outfitted a station wagon, and rushed back to Spain. Eventually his mobile blood bank unit was serving 100 casualty stations. En route to the Mediterranean front one day, he encountered a long column of refugees retreating under fire from tanks and planes. Joining the rescue effort, Bethune helped to bring some of the 40,000 survivors into the port of Almería, only to see them come under another bombing assault. Many of those killed and maimed were children. Bethune

251

returned to Madrid swearing to fight ever harder against "the fascist barbarians."

His profound love for children—his own marriage was childless—was outraged in Spain. "In Madrid," Sise recalled, "we had a house in a wealthy sector full of Fifth Columnists where we enjoyed immunity from fascist bombing. But there was some sniping from the rooftops. One day we returned to find a little girl lying dead on our sofa wrapped in my coat. A bullet had creased her face and entered her chest. Beth picked up the child's body and stormed about the room in a wild passion of anger and grief such as I'd never seen before."

In the spring of 1937 the Republicans defeated an offensive to capture Madrid. Bethune rushed off to Canada to raise money. Since the Republicans had the support of a wide range of political viewpoints, he was hailed as a hero. "The streets in Montreal were full of cheering people," Maltin recalled. "Those with no money gave things like streetcar tickets. When I told Bethune this, you could see his face change—'This is my reward.'" That summer he publicly announced he was a communist.

The Madrid victory was illusory and eventually Franco's fascists won the war. Meanwhile, Bethune's thoughts turned to China, now invaded by the Japanese. The communists wanted to keep him in Canada, where he was their main drawing card. "But Bethune had no use for party discipline," Maltin said. "He was a man unto himself."

Bethune sailed for Hong Kong in January 1938. In China he traveled north by train, by mule and on foot, narrowly escaped capture by the Japanese, and finally met Mao Tse-tung in the cave city of Yenan. With Mao's consent, Bethune set out for the encircled Manchurian border region of Chin-ch'a-chi.

There were several qualified doctors at Mao's Yenan headquarters but in the Japanese-encircled

pockets of resistance where Bethune performed his miracles, he was usually the only one. He trained young guerrillas to do surgery, wrote three textbooks, set up a medical college and nursing school, and worked with a flame of energy that his co-workers could scarcely believe.

During a battle at Chi-hui in April 1939 he stood at the operating table for 69 hours without sleep, and performed 115 operations. When a wall was demolished by Japanese shellfire, he went right on working amid the rubble. He lived on millet, rice and eggs, went barefoot or in rope sandals, improvised surgical instruments from knives, wire and bits of metal. He became skeleton-thin. His hair turned white. "I have operated all day and am tired," he wrote to Sise in August 1938. "Ten cases: five, very serious. But I don't think I have been so happy for a long time. I am doing what I want to do."

In 1936 war broke out in Spain as forces supported by Nazi Germany and Italy rebelled against the democratically elected Republican government. For Norman Bethune, who joined the Republicans, the conflict was an opportunity to save lives. Driving toward the Mediterranean front one day, he met streams of refugees (below) fleeing from the enemy-occupied port of Malaga. Most were exhausted and hungry; many had been injured by enemy fire. Appalled at their suffering, Bethune helped the refugees into his ambulance (left) and evacuated load after load to the coastal town of Almería.

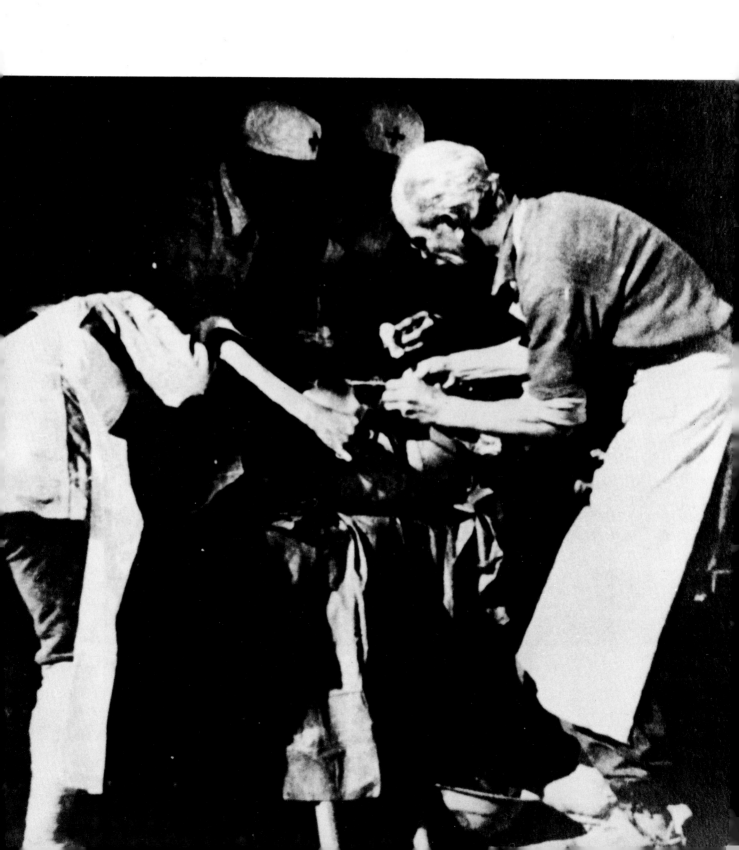

With Mao's Eighth Route Army, which he joined in 1938, Norman Bethune was a tireless worker—often spending 12 hours at a stretch at the operating table (opposite page). Constantly traveling to keep pace with Mao's guerrilla troops, Bethune slept in huts and caves, and lived on a peasant's diet of millet, rice, eggs and tea (below). Right: When not tending to patients or training assistants to do surgery, Bethune spent much of his time at the typewriter. He wrote three medical textbooks, numerous reports to General Nieh (his commander) and letters to North America begging for financial assistance.

The Chinese, frightened at the way he drove himself, tried every trick to make him rest, but he refused. Once General Nieh, his commander, ordered him to bed. Grudgingly he lay down, then suddenly got up, snatched a cigarette from the general's lips, threw it to the ground, and yelled: "In respect to medical matters, I will not take orders— even from you!" Then he stomped off angrily to his operating room.

On October 28, 1939, while operating without gloves—there were none—Bethune cut his finger and contracted septicemia. The poison spread through his body. On November 13 he died in a peasant hut surrounded by heartbroken comrades.

Norman Bethune was buried in the village of Chu-ch'eng in northern China, where the peasants raised a marble memorial to him. After the war his body was moved to the Martyrs' Tombs in Shih-chia-chuang. Heroic statues of him were erected. Schools and hospitals were named after him. His image appeared on Chinese posters and stamps.

By the 1970s, in an era of détente and expanding Sino-Canadian relations, the Bethune legend was helping to bridge the gap between his native land and the country where, at one of the crucial moments of history, he fulfilled his dreams of high destiny. Always driven, he also found something like personal salvation. "All the Chinese who knew him testify that he achieved serenity," said Sise. "After a lifetime of storm and doubt, he died in a state of grace." And honor was finally his at home where, in 1972, the Canadian government took the rare step of designating Dr. Norman Bethune as a person "of national historic significance."

# "I Can Ski Again!"

By Diane Alder

Following a plane crash in 1969, John Gow lost a leg below the knee and half a foot—and his days as a ski instructor seemed finished. Yet artificial limbs—and a fierce determination to overcome his disability—have enabled Gow to return to the slopes.

The weather was typical of early spring—a high overcast and moderate winds—as John Gow and his close friend, pilot Bernie Royle, took off from Golden, B.C., after lunch that April day in 1969. By coincidence, their Cessna 140 bore the call letters CF-GOW.

They were flying among the white, 9,000-foot peaks of the rugged Selkirk Mountains, near the Alberta-British Columbia border. An experienced ski instructor, licensed mountain guide and staff member at the Sunshine Village ski resort in Banff, Alta., Gow was on the lookout for suitable terrain for helicopter skiing parties. Now, ten miles west of Golden, they swung left to follow Gorman Creek. As the plane turned, Gow felt a sledgehammer jolt. Hit by a massive downdraft, the plane dropped suddenly and banked hard to the right. Gow looked out the window. The trees were rushing up at a tremendous rate and he knew they were going to crash. The last thing he remembered before impact was the aircraft plunging through treetops.

When he recovered consciousness, he found himself lying in the snow 100 feet downhill from the plane. The Cessna was a wreck, its roof torn off, the left wing lodged in the treetops, the right wing—the one with his name on it—ominously crumpled beneath the fuselage. Gow took quick inventory. His scalp and face were badly gashed from being hurled through the windshield. His teeth had punctured the skin below the lip, and one cheek was slashed open. But although he'd been concussed, no bones seemed to be broken.

Dazed, he climbed up to the mangled plane. Royle's crumpled form lay five feet away. Gow felt for a pulse: there was none. His friend of five years was dead.

From the wreckage, Gow retrieved a heavy parka, and managed to set up two aircraft seats in the snow before losing consciousness again. When he came to—almost 24 hours later, he figured afterward—he struggled to assess his position. The radio was dead, and he could find no flares. The heavy timber had closed in over the aircraft, making it almost invisible to search planes. Weakened as he was, his hopes were slim if he stayed in the cold of the 5,000-foot-high valley. He decided to walk out. (This is not the recommended procedure, Gow admitted later. "The best thing to do is make some sort of shelter at the crash site, get a fire going, and stay warm until rescue arrives.")

Scratching "Gone to Golden" on the dashboard of the plane, Gow tied rags around the top of his boots to keep the snow out, then set out down the steep slope, a blanket from the wreckage around his shoulders. He knew these mountains well. If he could make it to a logging road he guessed to be about a mile away, he might be able to walk to a house trailer he remembered was ten miles down the road.

Soon the snow was waist-deep and filled his boots. Battered and bloody, he thought of returning to the wreckage, but 100 yards back up the steep slope seemed more formidable than 12 or 14 miles downhill. He tried making snowshoes out of boughs and the rags around his boots; his feet simply slipped off into the deep snow. Sometimes he could make only 20 feet before falling and losing consciousness again. Once he heard a helicopter pass nearby, and his spirits soared momentarily. But it never came into view, and he fell back to his painful slogging. In his light-headed state, the memory of his dead friend strong, the thought of his own death no longer seemed frightening.

At Gorman Creek, he crawled cautiously across a snowbridge on his belly, knowing that if he fell into its icy waters, death from exposure was certain. After three hours of agonized endeavor, he reached the logging road—his route to safety. At the edge of the unplowed road he tripped and fell. Too exhausted and dazed to move, he lay there all that second night without removing his wet, snow-filled boots.

An inch of snow fell that night. In the morning he set off doggedly down the road. *I'll die if I don't keep moving*, he thought repeatedly. For the first mile or so the going was easier. But as the day grew warmer, his feet started breaking through the crust, and with each step he sank to his knees. He forced himself to turn off his mind and keep putting one foot in front of the other. Though water was plentiful from the streams that were opening up, he had eaten nothing since the crash; the few shoots he had picked near tree bases tasted too bad to swallow and he abandoned them. Exhausted and demoralized, he dropped the blanket he had been wearing around his shoulders.

The soft snow limited him to only about one mile during the third, pain-filled day and another on the fourth day. Much of the time he spent collapsed on snow-free patches beneath the trees—drifting from sleep to unconsciousness. Aware of the danger of frozen limbs and gangrene, at night he would take off his wet socks and boots and wrap his feet in a sweater. But by now they were so swollen he could barely pull his boots on again.

On the morning of the fifth day Gow awoke early, shivering uncontrollably in the bitter cold. The temperature had dropped to about ten degrees above zero, but it brought him one advantage; the snow would now be firmly frozen and capable of sustaining his weight. Feeling no pain in his numbed feet, he set off down the road. Weakened after five days without food, his mind kept wandering back to his warm, comfortable room at Sunshine Village. But he knew that he must now be close to the house trailer and that one way or another, the end was near.

John Gow has done much to give
other amputees the confidence to try
skiing. At Sunshine Village (below),
a ski resort at Banff, Alta., he
helps to run a rehabilitation program
for such disabled skiers as Dan
Hiebert (foreground, with Gow), who
lost a leg in a farming mishap.

About 11 a.m., he rounded a bend—and suddenly
saw a figure walking toward him. Terrified that
it was not real, or that it would go away, he yelled
feebly. And as the man approached, Gow collapsed
on the snow-covered road.

Emil Czillinger Horvath, a forestry engineer with
Selkirk Spruce Mills, was checking the road to see
if it could be plowed for logging, when he saw
Gow stagger around the bend. His truck was a
quarter mile away on the final plowed section of
the road: he would run and get help. But, though
his body rebelled, Gow's determination remained.
Leaning on Horvath's shoulder, he staggered and
limped the rest of the way to the truck. Within
an hour he was in hospital in Golden.

John Gow was to spend the next 100 days in
a hospital bed, first in Golden, then in Calgary.
His own love of life and unfaltering will had helped
him to survive four unbearable days and nights

in that snowy wilderness. But now his courage
would again be challenged. His ordeal had only
begun.

In the hospital, he was treated for shock and
loss of blood, then the gashes in his chin, scalp
and cheek were sewn up. His swollen feet were
badly frostbitten, and he knew he would lose several
toes. But the gangrene had, in fact, spread much
further; one leg would have to be amputated below
the knee, possibly both. As the doctors gently told
him the news, the dazed sense of unreality he had
felt after the crash returned. *Without my legs, how
can I ski? How can I climb mountains? At 22, my whole
way of life is gone*, he thought.

The amputations were carried out in stages over
four weeks. Ten times he went into the operating
theater as the surgeons, stage by stage, removed
the right leg, up to seven inches below the knee.
The left foot was amputated at the instep. With

Not content only with recreational skiing, Gow entered the 1974 World Championships for Handicapped Skiers. The results are around his neck—four gold medals.

each operation, Gow's pain and anxiety increased. How much more of his right leg would he lose? Would the knee joint be workable? How would he use what remained of his left foot?

Drugs helped to ease the severe pain after each operation—and to dull his mind to his new predicament. But, lying in bed week after week waiting for his stumps to heal, Gow was plagued with new fears. He had never known anyone with an artificial limb. Would he ever be able to walk properly—let alone ski, or climb?

Yet little by little his determination began to flow back, and his thoughts crystallized. His livelihood, indeed his happiness, he knew, still depended on the mountains. For four years at Sunshine Village he had taught people to ski and climb, and the last winter he had worked in the office with the area manager. *I have to go back*, he decided. *Since I was already working in the office, it won't seem as if I'm being put there because I'm a cripple.*

Ninety days after the crash, a plaster cast was made of his right stump. Then one Friday afternoon, Dave Roberts, owner of the Calgary Artificial Limb Factory, came to the hospital with an artificial limb of fiber glass and plastic that was strapped to the knee. Wangling a weekend pass, Gow left that evening for High Horizons, his summer climbing camp 30 miles southwest of Banff—with strict instructions that the leg was to be used only for getting in and out of cars. But the prosthesis felt fine, so that weekend in the privacy of his room he practiced for hour after hour with his crutches. And on Monday he astonished the doctors by walking 200 feet down the hospital corridor. A week later Gow left hospital for good.

His left foot had not yet healed, so for four months he walked on his heel, progressing from crutches to a cane, and finally jettisoning the cane. Because of the unusual nature of this amputation,

260

and the stress put on the foot by an active Gow, Roberts had to develop a prosthesis of special design—a plastic shell, like a sock, that laced on.

To be able to walk again was heartening. But by now it was November and, back at Sunshine, Gow could see the snow already deep on Mount Brewster. Outside the office window, the crowded Wa Wa T-bar was a bitter reminder of his disability. The thought hit him: *But why not?* On impulse, he borrowed skis and boots, donned a friend's toque, goggles and ski jacket to avoid being recognized, and went out. Still without a prosthesis for his left foot, he stuffed what was left of his foot into the boot, buckled it as tightly as he could, and headed gingerly for the rope tow.

At the top, he hesitated, took a breath and kicked off. Cautiously, awkwardly as any beginner, he tried a turn. It worked. He tried another, and another, each time feeling an electric thrill deeper than any in his 18 years of skiing. *I can ski again!* he exulted. When he reached the bottom, tears of joy were streaming down his face.

All that winter, Gow worked at relearning to ski. Circulation problems in his left foot gave him excruciating pain whenever the weather was cold. Moreover, until a sturdy enough prosthesis was developed for his left foot, he had little turning power in one direction: his stump would twist inside the boot.

One day, skiing down Strawberry run, he took a terrific spill. Looking back uphill, he saw his right ski with the boot still in the binding—and inside it his broken right prosthesis, sock and all!

Perseverance paid off. When John Gow is out skiing the runs at Sunshine, only the best of skiers can keep up with him. He carves graceful arcs through powder snow, beats down hard-packed moguls, split jumps off cornices, and flies down the open runs at breathtaking speeds. He maintains

his senior instructor's rating and is executive vice-president at Sunshine.

John is equally at home climbing the bare rocky pinnacles of his beloved mountains. Summers are spent at High Horizons, teaching young people the skills of climbing in the high Rockies and sharing with them his love of the mountains. "Rock climbing is no great problem with artificial feet, if you have confidence and good boots," he says. Walking through uneven terrain is tiring and requires constant vigilance; on loose scree slopes he generally uses a cane.

Sunshine already had a program for handicapped skiers. With Jerry Johnston, then Sunshine's ski school director, Gow helped to expand the program to include amputees, polio victims, paraplegics and the blind. Among them are above-the-knee single amputees, who compensate for the lost limb by using a pair of crutches with curved ski tips as outriggers, for balance.

In 1974 Gow traveled to the French Alps to take part in the World Championships for Handicapped Skiers. With courses set to standards identical to those for regular international ski competitions, he took the slopes at speeds approaching 60 m.p.h., and won the gold medal for his category in every event he entered—downhill, slalom, giant slalom, and combined.

"I never consider myself handicapped," says Gow —who wears out one or two prostheses a year. (Most people have to replace theirs perhaps once in ten years.) "When you walk into the office Monday morning and say you spent the weekend skiing, people soon stop thinking of you as disabled."

Adds Dave Roberts at the Artificial Limb Factory: "His determination, his spirit are an inspiration to amputees in Canada and around the world. He has proved that, even with a handicap, you can still reach for the top."

# The Guinea Pigs' Lost Weekend

By George Ronald

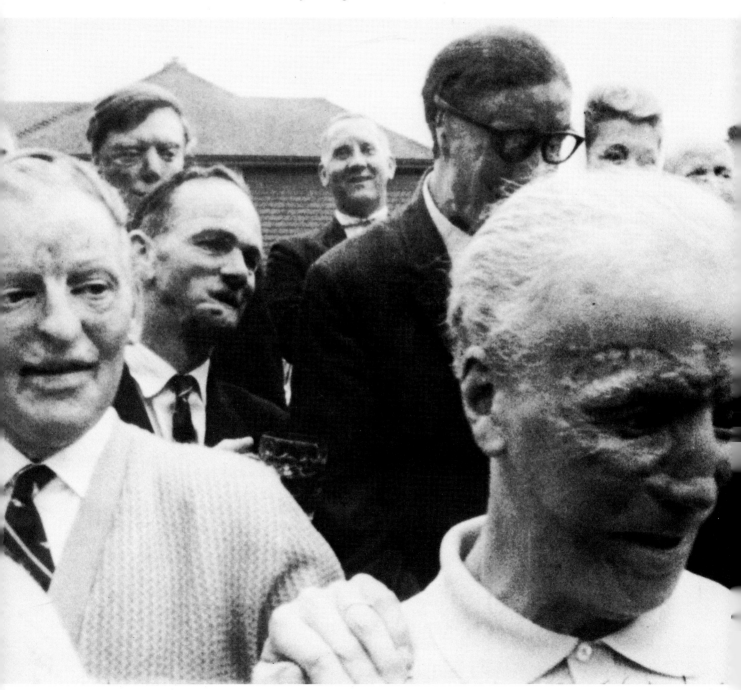

They are the Guinea Pigs, former World War II airmen whose crippled and burned bodies were reconstructed by plastic surgery in the Queen Victoria Hospital in the English village of East Grinstead. Each September, many Pigs return to the village for their "Lost Weekend," a boisterous and boozy celebration— and a chance to recall old times with comrades from as far afield as Canada, Australia, Israel and Russia.

One Friday evening every September scores of scarred and mutilated men down the first pint of their annual "Lost Weekend" in Ye Olde Felbridge Hotel in East Grinstead, a Sussex town 30 miles south of London, England. They are members of an organization called the Guinea Pig Club—Allied airmen badly maimed and disfigured in World War II. What do the club's 600 members have in common? In Ward III of East Grinstead's Queen Victoria Hospital—and in its Canadian wing—they became patients of two remarkable plastic surgeons, Britain's Sir Archibald McIndoe and an RCAF wing commander named Ross Tilley.

There is nothing somber about the Guinea Pigs. Walking among them, you quickly forget that most have faces reconstructed by surgery: manufactured jaws, artificial noses, rebuilt eyelids. Yet their gatherings are loud, full of laughter and high spirits. "I hope," said Prince Philip, the Pigs' president, in one Lost Weekend message, "that it is lost pleasurably." It invariably is, for that is the Guinea Pig way.

Most of the club's 170 Canadians have never been back for a Lost Weekend and probably never will—except in spirit. Yet the link with East Grinstead is gloriously strong: an Alberta businessman often would sign his letters "Stanley G. Reynolds, Guinea Pig."

All the Pigs have found useful places in society. Reynolds escaped from a flaming Mosquito night fighter, was patched up by Tilley and returned to flying: he went on to run a thriving machinery business and a pioneer museum in Wetaskiwin, Alta. Ken Allison, hit by flak over Normandy, passed out from loss of blood and crashed his Typhoon into half a dozen parked aircraft. Tilley pulled him through and he became vice-president of a trust company in Montreal.

Paul Warren, an air traffic controller, was wireless air gunner in a Halifax bomber that came down near the English coast. Third-degree burns to face and hands sent him to East Grinstead for 12 operations. His "date" on his first wheelchair trip away from the hospital was Nurse Patricia Brennan, who pushed him a mile to see a movie. She became Mrs. Warren.

As the Pigs jest during their Lost Weekends, so they laughed and joked almost four decades ago in Ward III and in the 50-bed Canadian wing that Ross Tilley ran. They were very young then, mostly between 19 and 25, and were fine physical specimens until a few horrible moments brought grotesque disfigurement. Like boys too proud to show their real emotions, they often tried to hide pain and depression behind horseplay.

One Pig remembers how, regaining consciousness in Ward III after his Halifax bomber crashed on the Sussex coast, he couldn't believe he was in a hospital: "Crippled Pigs were folding newspapers into darts and flying them round the ward, and a group on crutches were singing at a piano."

Self-pity was never tolerated. Gordon Frederick was brought to East Grinstead after his Hampden torpedo bomber crashed into a gasoline dump in November 1941. He was badly burned about both eyes and nose, and skin was hanging from his fingertips like inside-out gloves. Five days after his arrival at East Grinstead, Frederick's clothes were brought to him and he was bundled out to a concert in town.

"My arms in slings, my hands in bandages the size of boxing gloves, my face covered with gentian violet, I was a shocking sight," he says. But Frederick *enjoyed* that concert. More important, he'd seen and been seen, and had discovered that most people didn't stare.

The Guinea Pig saga began one Sunday morning in July 1941. Five scarred Battle of Britain pilots

Many fliers who escaped from their flaming aircraft were horribly maimed by the "airman's burn"—a flash burn of face and hands. Those sent to East Grinstead came under the care of two brilliant surgeons, Archibald McIndoe and Ross Tilley. Rebuilding faces and limbs from damaged flesh and shattered bone, the innovative doctors gave new hope to men who had feared they would never again lead normal lives. To sooth healing tissue and painlessly wash away bandages, the doctors pioneered the use of saline baths (left, opposite page). Far right: Ross Tilley examines one of countless skin grafts performed at East Grinstead.

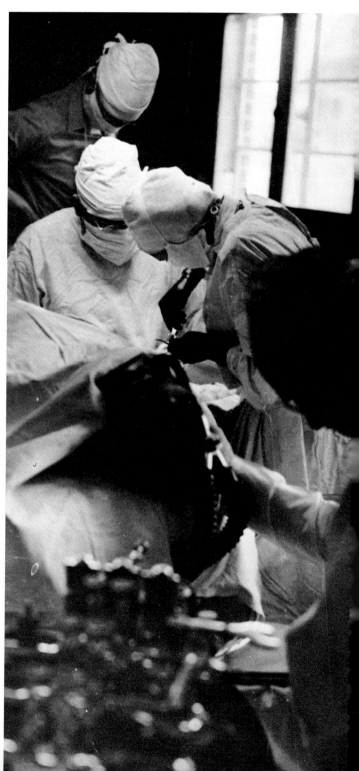

had one bottle of sherry and only two good hands to uncork it. They got to discussing Archibald McIndoe's skill as a surgeon.

"Nobody has ever redesigned men the way Archie's redesigning us," said one.

"That's true," said another, laughing. "We're just the Boss's guinea pigs." That did it. Six months later the club was formed and its officers chosen with the gentle self-mockery characteristic of the Pigs. Peter Weeks was selected as treasurer because he couldn't abscond with the funds: he was too badly crippled to move. With a similarly sardonic touch, Henry Standen was picked to write and edit *Guinea Pig*, the club magazine. He'd lost an eye, much of his face and most of his fingers.

The Pigs were from 16 nations. More than half were Britons. The next biggest group were the 170 Canadians. There was a Russian Guinea Pig, a Greek, a Norwegian, an Argentinian. Though

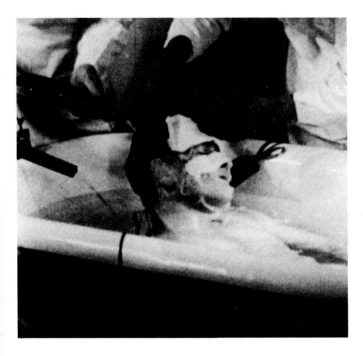

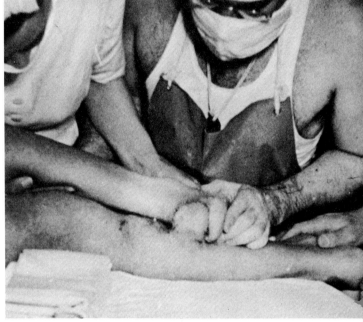

most members now live in Britain, others are spread around the world from Fiji to the West Indies.

The first key man behind the Pigs was Archie McIndoe. A New Zealander, he won a fellowship to the Mayo Clinic in Rochester, Minnesota, then went to London to concentrate on the infant specialty called plastic surgery. He was appointed consultant to the RAF in 1939. The following year, airmen badly burned in the Battle of Britain began streaming to East Grinstead. There were countless problems with this new technique, and experimentation was necessary. The Pigs submitted with quiet courage to the long and painful ordeal of skin grafts and surgery.

McIndoe observed that the burns of airmen saved from the sea healed faster and responded more readily to treatment than those of men shot down on land. The difference, he decided, lay in the effect of salt water, so saline baths were introduced.

Guinea Pig Tom Gleave explained: "At my first hospital I was given the traditional tannic acid treatment. This formed a hard crust on my raw, burned flesh. But parts of my body were already infected, causing festering and reopening wounds. It was agony. The bandages used to stick and could not be removed without causing indescribable torture.

"I'll never forget the soothing sensation of my first saltwater bath at East Grinstead. It washed the bandages and the tannic acid away gently, easily. Over and over again I whispered 'Wonderful! Wonderful!'" Saline treatment pioneered by McIndoe and the Ward III Guinea Pigs is now universal practice for serious burns.

Ross Tilley reached East Grinstead early in 1942. He was born in Bowmanville, Ont., studied medicine at the University of Toronto and specialized in plastic surgery. An RCAF reservist, he went

After the war, Archibald McIndoe (left) was knighted and later became the first New Zealander appointed vice-president of the Royal College of Surgeons. When he died in 1960, aged 59, the Guinea Pigs lost what one of them called "the joystick of our ship." Ross Tilley (right), awarded the OBE, pioneered a plastic surgery service at Queen's University in 1948 and later entered private practice in Toronto.

active at the outbreak of war and two years later became principal RCAF medical officer overseas. Then, with more and more Canadian airmen suffering severe burns and crash injuries, he was sent to the Queen Victoria Hospital. He worked closely with McIndoe, operating on all Canadian patients (and many others), then moved into his own command when the RCAF wing was opened in July 1944. When he left in 1945, some 835 operations had been performed there.

The colorful, outspoken McIndoe and the retiring, enigmatic Tilley were not merely brilliant surgeons. They were great humanitarians who knew the importance of mending a man's spirit as well as healing his body. They insisted that Guinea Pigs be treated like "ordinary" men, doing away with "hospital blues," the uniform with the red rag of a tie that made them look like clowns. And they urged them to go to movies, visit pubs, date girls and "live a little."

Tilley objects to talk of "miracles" in the Queen Victoria's operating rooms. "It was plain, straightforward surgery," he says. Nonetheless, McIndoe and he would fill out a shattered cheekbone with bone from the hip, make new cheeks and mouths with flesh from the chest or stomach. Bringing down a triangular flap from the forehead, they would sculpt it into a new nose; they would fashion the delicate tissue from the inner side of the upper arms into eyelids.

Everett Ferguson, who became an advertising executive, had his smashed nose rebuilt by Tilley with hip bone. Next, Tilley "did a flap" for Ferguson's badly burned right hand, attaching it to his stomach for six weeks and then cutting into the refurbished stump to make fingers and a thumb.

Perhaps nobody reached East Grinstead with lower morale than W. E. "Bill" Martin, another Canadian. Snatched from a blazing Blenheim bomber that crash-landed in Malta in October 1941, Martin came to with bandages from his fingertips to the top of his head and straps holding his numerous fractures in place. Attempts at skin grafts had made his condition worse.

Martin's evacuation to Alexandria was delayed for three agonizing months by incessant German air raids. It took another three months to get around the Cape of Good Hope to England.

By the time he reached Britain he'd lost the will to live. "I thought I was a freak," he says. "I was belligerent. I couldn't say a civil word to anybody." The RAF doctors asked McIndoe to see him.

"He told me there was nothing they could do to repair the damage to my chest and lungs," says Martin. "I would have to remain deformed. But they could remove the scar tissue on my nose and straighten it up, re-form my lips and remove the heavy scar tissue from my hands so I could have full use of my fingers."

There is no sadness or self-pity among the Guinea Pigs as they gather for their "Lost Weekend" at Ye Olde Felbridge Hotel in East Grinstead. That there isn't, is a tribute to their courage and to the dedication of McIndoe and Tilley, who believed that rebuilding a man's confidence was as crucial as rebuilding his features. "My job," McIndoe once said, "isn't simply to do a piece of fancy surgery on a man's face. What's behind that face is more important than what the face looks like."

Martin didn't believe McIndoe but, told there was a fine Canadian surgeon at East Grinstead, he reluctantly agreed to be moved. "I didn't hesitate to tell the 'Wingco' what I thought of plastic surgeons after my experiences in Malta. But Tilley assured me they'd attempt no graft until the infection had been cleared up."

With the first graft on his hands, Martin realized what a craftsman Tilley was. "I'll never forget his look of anxiety as he cut away the bandages—and the smile when he saw the graft had taken perfectly. The smile said, Look, Bill, look what you and I have done!"

The "airman's burn" of World War II was a flash burn of the face and hands caused by intense dry heat. "Men exposed to this heat for more than a few seconds," says Tilley, "were beyond treatment. The job of restoring the hands and faces of those who *did* survive sometimes took more than five years and from five to 40 operations."

Not all Guinea Pigs were wounded in battle. Robert T. Lloyd, a retired tobacco company executive, was training on Wellingtons in April 1943 when he had a bicycle accident en route to his aircraft. RAF doctors said all the bone and teeth on the right side of his face—and his right eye—would have to be removed immediately. Lloyd refused. Told by the RAF of their problem Canadian, Tilley stood by at East Grinstead with dental surgeons and eye specialists. Operating within the hour, he saved Lloyd's eye. Like many of the Pigs, Lloyd returned to action. Of the Pigs who went back to flying, 41 died, including 16 Canadians.

Every Guinea Pig reunion includes a toast to the memory of McIndoe, the beloved "Boss" who died in 1960. It reaches its climax after dinner when the whole crowd breaks into the club anthem (to the tune of "The Church's One Foundation"):

We are McIndoe's army,
We are his Guinea Pigs . . .

And on it goes until they reach the rollicking finale:

We've had some mad Australians,
Some French, some Czechs, some Poles;
We've even had some Yankees—
God bless their bloody souls.
While, as for the Canadians—
Ah! That's a different thing—
They couldn't stand our accent
And built a separate wing.

It's blasé and a bit boozy, this Lost Weekend of the Guinea Pigs. But it's much more than a big party. It's exciting proof that a man's spirit can be unconquerable, no matter what happens to his body.

"It's incredible," says Ross Tilley, "that these men came back to live normal lives after what they went through. They're superb."

# "Everybody to the Corvée!"

### By Louise Cousineau

It was just past noon on September 6, 1972, when the cry went up. "Glendale's on fire!" Mayor Adrien Ouellette, a high school English teacher, was on his way back to class when he heard the news and headed for the Glendale factory at the south end of town. But although volunteer firemen were at the site in minutes, they were unable to stop the blaze; the factory burned to the ground.

Glendale (Quebec) Ltd. and its $1.2 million yearly payroll were vital to the 4,400 people of Saint-Joseph-de-Beauce, 42 miles south of Quebec. Glendale mattered not only to its own 238 employes but also to scores of men and women in plants that made parts for Glendale mobile homes.

For general manager Pierre Ypperciel it was a personal disaster. He had made Glendale a going concern in only three years. Now he would have to start afresh. Five hours after the fire broke out, he and his office staff were settling into an office loaned by a neighbor, Grondin Transport. Soon technician Nicolas Jacques was hard at work on plans for rebuilding.

But construction workers were scarce that September. It would take at least six months to rebuild. Too long. Six months would mean the loss of current orders and an uphill struggle to regain the company's place in the mobile-home market (they then produced 900 units a year).

Adrien Ouellette had an idea: why not let the Glendale workers rebuild the plant themselves? It was against Quebec law to hire unqualified workers on construction jobs, but Ypperciel asked the provincial Ministry of Labor to make an exception. The Glendale workers knew plenty about construction–didn't they assemble mobile homes?

But when the ministry was approached, it was firm: there could be no exceptions. The Glendale workers could not qualify as construction workers under the law. There seemed no loophole.

The future looked bleak for Saint-Joseph-de-Beauce. Then a committee headed by Mayor Ouellette found a happy answer in the past: *la corvée!* "The peasant's unpaid work for the seigneur," says the dictionary. It had been a common form of "taxation" in New France, but with the disappearance of the seigneurial system the word took on new significance. It no longer concerns seigneurs and peasants; it means work done "for free" in aid of a neighbor stricken by bad luck. People of Beauce County hold frequent corvées–to replace a house destroyed by fire or a barn struck by lightning.

Several days after the fire, workers gathered at the plant. Gilles Grondin, president of the union local, urged his members to join in. "Our union," he said, "has always favored open dealings with the company. We have shown that we can work together for a common goal: let us go back to work."

That Sunday, Curé Fernand Doyon announced the plan to rebuild the Glendale plant. "Everybody to the corvée!" he urged from the pulpit and, as the tradition demanded, his parishioners set off for the corvée after mass. Thomas-Jacques Groleau, director of the Saint-Joseph-de-Beauce welfare service, was relieved of regular duties to work full time as corvée chief. He had no trouble getting volunteers. "I phoned the mayors and other community leaders of neighboring municipalities. They replied immediately: 'How many hands do you need? When?'"

Groleau smiled. "I'd been told I'd never get the people of Saint-Georges to work here! Well, I accepted the challenge–and they came. Saint-Georges was our traditional rival. The corvée brought us friendly enemies together."

Groleau's volunteer teams worked under a local contractor and specialized workers with labor ministry permits. By day, the work was usually done

Smoke billows from the Glendale
factory in Saint-Joseph-de-Beauce,
Que., on September 6, 1972. Firemen
fought to save the building
but the blaze ran out of control and
Glendale was destroyed.

by Glendale employes and local farmers. After 5 p.m. and on weekends workers came from throughout the community.

The first nail had been hammered home by the town's Robert Cliche, then associate chief justice of the Provincial Court. "If we're going to have any trouble with the law," said Judge Cliche, "it might as well be me who is accused." Another celebrated nail-hammerer was Governor-General Roland Michener, who did his stint, then ate with the workers.

Representatives of The Construction Industry Commission and a labor union showed up to remind the workers that technically they were violating the law. But there was no precedent in Quebec law for a case against the people of a corvée. The work went on.

One morning old-timer Thomas Majoric Lessard, the town's former blacksmith, walked in carrying a bag and a swan-neck lamp. "I am going to sharpen compass saws," he said. Three days later, all the teeth of all the saws were cutting to perfection. Emile Petit, a retired agronomist, busied himself picking up nails around the site to guard against tire punctures. Mayor Ouellette worked after school hours and on weekends. Ypperciel spent each day on the phone, ordering materials and pushing for immediate delivery, then at 4 each afternoon he too went to the corvée.

The women of Saint-Joseph-de-Beauce played a big part in the corvée's success. At the outset, Mme Adalbert Lessard rounded up members of the Women Farmers' Circle to cook pork and beans and asked for volunteer servers. "I drove from house to house, picking up pork and beans. The car smelled good!" said Mme Thérèse Lambert. "Our meals didn't cost much, and on Tuesdays I went to collect from the farmers. They gave vegetables, chickens, quarters of beef. Grocers and bakers helped and the abattoir at Vallée-Jonction gave 70 pounds of beef for *bœuf bourguignon*."

The task of feeding meals and snacks to 100 to 150 persons a day bothered no one: the Beauce is a county of big families and big family reunions. "I don't remember the faces," said Madame Lambert, who served at table, "but I surely remember the hands." The blistered hands, for instance, of notary Guy Mercier, more accustomed to drawing up deeds than using a hammer.

For Madame Lambert, mother of 11 children, the corvée was a glowing experience, "a blessing in disguise. It gave us a chance to pull together, to help one another." For Thomas-Jacques Groleau, it was an eye-opener. "I had thought there might be three stages," he said. "First a period of wild enthusiasm, then a week at a slower pace, and finally a resumption of the original pace. But there was never any letup at all."

The figures tell the story. The factory was rebuilt in 21 days. The corvée produced 22,500 hours of unpaid work by 3,250 persons. Two metal and wood buildings, one 600 feet long, the other 300 feet long, were erected in record time. The new factory (87,000 square feet) was bigger than the old one (69,000 square feet).

The official opening took place on Sunday, October 1, with 1,500 spectators. Mass was celebrated at an altar at one end of the rebuilt factory and Curé Doyon compared the parish feat to a resurrection. "This great gathering is for us like an Easter morning," he said, "a day of joy and fraternity." At the offertory, ten men and women offered objects symbolic of their work: hammers and saws, pots and pans, ledgers and journals.

Pierre Ypperciel, applauded as he rose to speak, said that in token of its thanks, Glendale would donate $30,000 to a municipal fund for an arena in Saint-Joseph-de-Beauce, and announced creation

Doctors, lawyers, teachers, newspapermen, laborers—almost *everyone* in Saint-Joseph-de-Beauce pitched in to help rebuild the Glendale factory. Within a month the task was complete (below, right). Then on October 1, 1972, a fine autumn day, 1,500 persons jammed the rebuilt factory for the official opening. Bottom: As a gesture of thanks to the community, Glendale general manager Pierre Ypperciel (center) presents a cheque for $30,000—for a Saint-Joseph-de-Beauce arena fund—to Mayor Adrien Ouellette (right). To the left is Robert Cliche, then associate chief justice of the Quebec Provincial Court.

of a Glendale foundation to provide scholarships for students attending the local high school. The factory opened its doors the next day. On October 12, the first mobile home came off the assembly line—36 days after the factory's destruction.

The people of Saint-Joseph-de-Beauce—and of the 15 municipalities that helped—talk with pride about their corvée. For the facts are clear: Beauce people love their good corner of the land and see no attraction in an exodus to big centers. And Beaucerons, like so many people in a world ever more bureaucratic, seek to *do* something about their own destiny, to deal with problems in their own way. They had made no gift to Glendale. "Nobody felt exploited. It was a question of helping a prosperous industry keep going," said Groleau. "We rolled up our sleeves and got the job done."

Six months later, on April 16, 1973, Mayor Adrien Ouellette was called to Ottawa to receive the Order of Canada—the highest Canadian civilian decoration—in recognition of his "exceptional devotion to his fellow citizens." Back home, Ouellette declared: "Deep down, at that ceremony, I was really only a messenger. This medal belongs to every one of us."

271

# The Quebec Town That Disappeared

### By Joseph P. Blank

The dogs of Saint-Jean-Vianney were the first to recognize the signs of disaster that night in 1971. Eleven-year-old Marcel Riverin had never seen his pet in such a frantic state—scurrying about, barking, yelping. Mrs. Jacques Tremblay's toy Pomeranian was also unusually nervous. "He yapped to go out and yapped to come in," she recalled. "Finally I slapped him."

Laval Blackburn followed his father's dog outside and watched him dash around in circles, sniffing the ground. Blackburn was baffled. He returned to the television (most of the men that night were totally absorbed in the Stanley Cup hockey play-off between Montreal and Chicago). But the dog's commotion drowned out the announcer's voice. Still, no one in town realized what the dogs were trying to say.

Saint-Jean-Vianney was a well-kept, suburblike community of 1,308, located 135 miles north of Quebec City. Once farmland, the town had bloomed with houses in the last decade. Most of the men worked as skilled laborers or technicians at the nearby Alcan plant or the Price paper mill. Their homes were impeccably maintained, and both husbands and wives spent much of their leisure time making improvements. It was a young town, and a proud one. "A good place in which to live and raise children," Harold Simard remarked later.

No one knew—and the knowledge probably would not have disturbed anyone—that the town had been built on the site of a gigantic landslide that occurred some 500 years ago. That slide didn't pour down the side of a mountain. It happened on relatively flat land. Beneath the crust of topsoil, the earth in this part of Quebec is generally composed of clay with pockets of sand. The particular quality of this clay, which runs about 100 feet deep, frequently causes slides. When the sand pockets become oversaturated with moisture, the pressure against the clay causes it to break down and simply flow away.

Several things occurred in Saint-Jean-Vianney before the disaster that might, collectively, have represented a warning. A few cracks appeared in the asphalt of two streets. Two driveways settled about five inches. One man painted the exposed portion of his house foundation; the following spring the earth around the foundation settled about eight inches and neighbors kidded him about the unpainted margin. And sometimes the power pole outside the house of Gilles Bourgeois swayed when there was no wind.

On the night of April 23, many residents heard a loud thump that seemed to come from under their houses. People checked their basements and peered out windows, but could detect nothing. On the following day Pitre Blackburn drove out to the far eastern corner of his farm to work. At that location stood a 40-foot hill that blocked Saint-Jean-Vianney's view of the big town of Chicoutimi, six miles away. "When I drove around the hill I saw that the back half of it had disappeared," Blackburn said. "In its place was a great hole, a V-shaped thing, maybe 80 feet deep, 200 feet wide and 500 feet long. Many people from town came to look at it."

A week later Mrs. Robert Paquette (not her real name) was visiting her neighbor, Mrs. Patrick Gagnon. "I don't know what's happening around here," she complained. "I hear water flowing under our house, but my husband tells me I'm crazy."

Since the rains had been heavy during April, and an abrupt rise in temperature was producing a fast thaw, Mrs. Gagnon thought it might just be a natural spring phenomenon. No one realized that all the rain was not running off, that it was seeping slowly into the soil, and slowly liquefying the substratum of clay.

This house, mired in a river of liquefied clay, was one of 38 that plunged into a canyon formed when heavy rains undermined the Quebec town of Saint-Jean-Vianney in 1971.

Told by rescue authorities to collect their belongings and leave Saint-Jean-Vianney, families salvaged what they could. Many lost everything.

The clay began moving on Tuesday evening, May 4, a gray, rainy day. At 10:45, Mrs. Paul Laval (not her real name) telephoned her close friend, Marcelline Fillion, six houses away. "Something strange is going on," she announced. "The Blackburn hill is no longer there. I can see the lights of Chicoutimi." Then she hung up.

Mrs. Fillion turned to her husband and said, "It's getting scary around here." He nodded absently, his eyes riveted to the television screen. A few minutes later the lights flashed out and the screen went black. "A car must have hit a power pole," he remarked.

Fillion told his wife to light candles and went outside to investigate. He heard shouting on the east edge of town. In the street he could make out a bus, headlights burning, angled into a hole. Beyond that he could see only a void where the Laval house had stood. He ran back inside. "Marcelline!" he shouted, "the Laval house is gone! Get our boy. We must leave. NOW!" It was too late.

The slide had begun at or near the Blackburn hill and swiftly moved westward toward the homes on the east side of town. The earth simply dissolved to a depth of nearly 100 feet; in the canyon thus formed, a river of liquefied clay—sometimes as deep as 60 feet—flowed at 16 m.p.h. toward the Saguenay River, two miles away. At its widest, the canyon was a half mile across, and it extended for approximately one mile.

When the slide reached the Laval house, everything—house, car, tricycles—plunged like a fast-moving elevator into the river of clay. Laval, his wife and three young children found themselves on a large cake of slippery clay. Waves of melted clay battered them. The children disappeared one by one. Then Mrs. Laval went down. Laval himself was smashed against the roots of a standing tree. He grabbed them and pulled himself to solid ground. Stripped of all clothing, shocked, dazed and unbelieving, he staggered along the edge of the crater until the police found him and rushed him to a hospital.

Next door to the Lavals, Robert Paquette was in his basement when the lights went out. He walked to the street to find out about the trouble. His wife and five children remained in the house.

He heard excited voices up the street, so he

No one heeded Saint-Jean-Vianney's dogs, whose frantic behavior heralded impending disaster. This puppy awaits his owner—who perhaps never came.

quickly walked about 200 feet to join the group. As he reached them, Patrick Gagnon gasped, "Look!" Paquette turned toward his house. He saw it swivel a little, tilt, then slide from sight. He began running toward the hole, but Gagnon grabbed him. "I don't understand," Paquette sobbed. "I don't understand."

Huguette Couture lived next to the Paquettes. About 11 that evening she heard a cracking noise and felt the house shake. Alone with her three children (her husband worked the 4 p.m.-to-midnight shift at the aluminum plant), she was terrified. From the kitchen window she saw a nearby house, lights still on, disappear from view. She ran to pick up three-year-old Benoit, screaming to her girls, "Let's get out! It's the end of the world!"

She jerked open the front door, but saw only blackness. The concrete steps had disappeared. She ran back to the kitchen door. It was jammed. She flung open the window. Martine, 13, clambered out. She shoved her younger daughter, 11-year-old Kathleen, through the window just as a five-foot crack opened alongside the house. The girl fell into it, then scrambled out. The house moved and Martine yelled, "The foundation is going! The hole is getting bigger!"

Mrs. Couture pressed the boy to her breast, sat on the window and fell backward into the hole. Holding the boy with one arm, she raised the other for help. Martine, with a strength beyond herself, pulled her mother and brother out of the hole. As they raced to safety, little Benoit, who was facing the rear in his mother's arms, said, "Mommy, our house has melted."

Jules Girard, who operated a bus service for employes at the aluminum plant, was driving his bus across a crack in the road when the front end of the vehicle sank into the earth. Through his windshield he saw the whole road ahead sinking.

275

"This town meant tranquillity, fresh air and quiet," said one homeless survivor. "Now all that is gone." Uprooted by the landslide, families were evacuated to hastily established tent and trailer camps in outlying communities.

"Everybody out the back door!" he shouted. "Quick!"

The last man out, Girard fell into a hole and clawed his way up. He and several passengers ran up the street, throwing stones at houses and yelling warnings. When he looked back, he could see only the red roof lights of his bus. For a few seconds he watched in horror as a car came racing down Harvey Street on the far side of the crater. Then the headlights disappeared into the hole.

As the alarm spread, Georges Vatcher grabbed his high-powered battery lantern and cautiously approached the crater. Several men joined him. "The beam of light showed only the edge of the hole," he said. "It couldn't penetrate enough to show the size or depth. I heard screams for help from below. There was a muffled, liquidy, sucking noise from the hole. Then the cries grew fainter and stopped, as if they were coming from a boat moving down the river."

Throughout the east side of town the slide caused panic, shock and disbelief. People didn't know which way to run or drive. In fleeing their homes, several women took only their wigs. An 18-year-old girl couldn't make up her mind what was most precious to her, so she grabbed a worn doll from her childhood. One man, leaving his sinking house, told his wife, "I forgot to lock the door." "You can do it later," she answered.

By midnight the sliding had stopped. Thirty-one men, women and children had perished; 38 houses had disappeared from the town. The surrounding communities and the Quebec government reacted quickly to the emergency. A relief mission was established in nearby Kenogami (now a part of Jonquière), and the government began moving 131 mobile homes into the area.

Six days after the slide Mrs. Jacques Tremblay and her family climbed down into the crater to look at their house. It was one of the last to sink. Except for the foundation, the house was intact. The glassware was unbroken. The little turtle still crawled around in its bowl. Mrs. Tremblay spent two hours in the house that she knew the government would have to burn. She dusted about, made up the beds and wept.

Twenty-three days after the slide the Quebec government declared Saint-Jean-Vianney unsafe for habitation. Before the year was out, the area was evacuated.

The survivors examined several sites for a new community. Ninety percent of them chose a tract of land in Arvida (also now a part of Jonquière), donated by Alcan. At a cost of $8.25 million to the Quebec and federal governments, homes destroyed by the slide were replaced and undamaged ones moved to the new community.

Private contributions flowed in from across Canada and around the world–$100 from Whitehorse in the Yukon, $73,000 from the diocese of Chicoutimi, $28 from a Japanese employe in the Canadian embassy in Tokyo, $50 from inmates of the St. Vincent de Paul penitentiary in Montreal. The $850,000 collected enabled families to replace all their lost household effects.

Saint-Jean-Vianney is now empty and desolate. Weeds and wild undergrowth camouflage the house foundations. The enormous crater grows shallower year by year as the rains carry earth into it. The name of the town, deleted from atlases and road maps, lives on only in the memories of those who resided there.

What happened seemed unreal to most families on that terrible night and it is even more unreal today. "Sometimes it all seems like a dream," said Leo Bourgeois, who lost his son, his daughter-in-law and his grandchild. "I find myself asking, 'Did the earth really open up and swallow those people?'"

# First to Sail Around the World — Alone

### By Pierre Berton

**M**ay 6, 1896. The sun burnishes the sky and the sea is limitless. In all the vast circle of the South Pacific, there is only a single moving speck, a sloop barely 36 feet long, aptly named *Spray.* Her decks are empty. No one is at the helm. She will remain alone and unobserved in the immensity of the ocean for 72 days, until she reaches Samoa, 5,700 miles as the gull flies from her last stop. And this is only a small part of a remarkable odyssey.

Aboard *Spray,* Joshua Slocum sits hidden in his book-lined cabin, totally alone, as he has been since he departed Yarmouth, N.S., the previous July. He is reading his way through his library, especially the stories of Robert Louis Stevenson and Mark Twain. Occasionally he pokes about in his galley, or digs out his sextant to check his longitude.

At 52 he is one of the most experienced saltwater men of his age, but also an anachronism—a committed sailor in a world that has done with sail. But Slocum, the out-of-work sea captain, doesn't care. Too old to learn new tricks, he has embarked on an adventure no one else has dared: sailing by himself around the world. Forty-six thousand miles. Three full years. Another lifetime.

For what else is left for Slocum? He has stacked salt cod out of Kamchatka, gunpowder from Shanghai to Taiwan, sugar from the Philippines, timber out of Brazil. He has broken three mutinies, and survived storms, hidden reefs and the explosion of Krakatoa in the East Indies, which killed 36,000 persons in August 1883—but not Joshua Slocum, who sailed past the smoking volcanic island as it was erupting.

He has made fortunes. His race to catch the crack mail schooner out of Honolulu brought him a $5,000 sack of gold. But he has also lost everything. The lovely barque *Aquidneck,* with its stateroom's parquetry floor, paneled walls and blue and gold scrollwork, was battered to pieces off the coast of Brazil with a full cargo of timber, leaving Slocum a pauper.

Since the age of 16, Slocum's whole existence has revolved around salt water. All seven of his children were born at sea or in foreign ports. The wife who bore them, the marvelous Virginia, sailed with him on every voyage, from their first honeymoon trip out of Sydney, Australia, to that last voyage aboard *Aquidneck.* When a mutineer stabbed Slocum's first officer aboard *Northern Light* in 1882, Virginia covered her husband, a revolver in each hand, as he subdued the crew. Her death at 34 was a terrible blow. His 24-year-old cousin, Hettie, whom he married a year and a half later, could not take her place. After one remarkable 5,500-mile voyage together, from Brazil to the Carolinas, they sailed together no more.

So here he is, alone as he prefers to be—Joshua Slocum, born in 1844 in Nova Scotia's Annapolis County, into the age of clipper ships: a seaman at 16, second mate at 18, master of his own ship at 25, king of the ocean at 37, washed up at 50. Joshua Slocum, master mariner, stubbornly refusing to come to any accommodation with steam power or iron hulls, instead picking up odd jobs on Boston harbor boats and dreaming of the great days of canvas, hating his work, until one day a load of coal half buries him. In that moment, he can stand it no more. He determines to return to the sea.

*Spring, 1893.* In a pasture at Fairhaven, Massachusetts, the hulk of an ancient oyster sloop lies rotting in a field. Slocum can have her; her owner is a friend. Like a sculptor gazing on a lump of Carrara marble, Slocum sees a new ship hidden somewhere in the old. He will keep her name, *Spray,* but little else. He cuts new timbers to replace old, and the new ship takes form: 36 feet, 9 inches overall; nine tons net; rigged as a sloop—a big craft for a lone man to handle. She has no engine, no power windlass, few navigational aids save a compass, some charts, a sextant and taffrail logs. But there's a secret to her, which even Slocum doesn't yet know. He has hit upon a perfectly balanced vessel that, ballasted with cement, will be almost impossible to capsize. He has worked on her for 13 months, supporting himself with odd jobs, and she has cost him exactly $553.62.

Though *Spray* claims Boston as her home port, Slocum's voyage will really begin at Yarmouth. He has come back to Nova Scotia to spend six weeks in the hometown he ran away from a generation before. He decides to sail eastward, through the Mediterranean, the Suez Canal and the Red Sea. He has two barrels of ship's bread soldered up in tin cans. He has flour and baking powder. He has salt beef, salt pork, ham and dried codfish— slabs of it, "thick as a board and broad as a side of sole leather." He has condensed milk, butter in brine and muslin, eggs hermetically sealed, potatoes that he will roast in their jackets, sugar and tea, and coffee beans that he will grind himself.

*July 2, 1895.* Slocum and *Spray* clear Yarmouth harbor at a fast eight knots, scurrying past Sable Island to get clear of the track of the ocean liners which might run them down at night. He has designed a self-steering mechanism and discovers that it is successful beyond his wildest dreams. He can lash the helm and sleep while the sloop holds her course. But he cannot shake off the realization that he is totally alone. He shouts commands, fearful that in the long days ahead he may lose his ability to speak.

He reaches the Azores in just 18 days. He has some letters to mail and he takes on a cargo of fruit, the gift of the islanders. Later he harpoons a turtle, which he roasts with fried potatoes on the side. He reaches Gibraltar on August 4, more than pleased with the speed of his little sloop.

And here he learns that he must turn back. The British officers who wine and dine urge him to avoid the Red Sea. This narrow waterway is infested with pirates for whom he would be an easy victim. So Slocum sets *Spray*'s course westward for Brazil.

Irony of ironies! He is scarcely back in the Atlantic before he encounters pirates in a Spanish felucca. He changes course, but the felucca, a swift and slender sailboat, continues to close. Slocum prepares for an unequal fight; and then a monstrous wave strikes both ships. Slocum snatches up a rifle to ward off his attackers—only to find that the same wave has torn away the felucca's rigging. Exhausted but safe, he sets the sloop on course and rolls into his bunk.

It takes 40 uneventful days to recross the Atlantic. Later the dauntless Nova Scotian runs into furious seas along the coast of Argentina. A towering wave, masthead high, roars down, swamping *Spray*. She reels under the impact, rights herself and sails on. In the Strait of Magellan, he sails into a southwest gale. "I had only a moment to douse sail and lash all solid when it struck like a shot from a cannon. . . . For 30 hours it kept on blowing hard." Finally he puts into Punta Arenas.

*February 19, 1896.* Back in the fury of the strait, he has encountered the dreaded williwaws, "chunks" of wind that strike vertically down the mountain slopes. He reaches Cape Froward, the southernmost point of the South American mainland; then he meets a group of pirates led by one Black Pedro, notorious as the worst murderer on the bleak islands of Tierra del Fuego. Shrieking, they attack *Spray* in canoes but, as they try to close, Slocum fires a shot across the bow of the nearest boat, then one close to the pirate chief himself. Black Pedro and his gang turn tail.

*Spray* clears Cape Pilar and enters the Pacific. But a violent storm drives her down the coast of

Tierra del Fuego toward Cape Horn. She runs for four days before the gale, her mainsail in rags. Slocum rigs up a square sail to replace it. The seas are mountainous and in the distance he can hear the deafening roar of tremendous breakers. As dawn lightens the sky, he somehow guides *Spray* through a maze of rock and foam to the comparative safety of some small islands in the Cockburn Channel. "Jaded and worn," he eats a meal of venison stew; then, after sprinkling his deck with tacks, he turns in. At midnight he is awakened by shrieks. Some natives have boarded *Spray*; terrified by the tacks, they leap into their canoes and flee into the night. Slocum goes back to sleep.

Two days later, the gales temporarily abated, he sails into the Strait of Magellan—19 days after he first anchored there. Again attacked by Fuegians, Slocum seizes his rifle and drives them off. Several times he is driven off course again by gales. Black Pedro makes another appearance, but Slocum's rifle keeps him at bay. Near Langara Cove, Slocum salvages a barrel of wine and an entire cargo of tallow from the wreckage of a doomed ship. The tallow comes in 800-pound casks, which he must winch aboard by hand. But the old sea trader knows its value. His cargo aboard, Slocum sails on through a blinding snowstorm to Port Angosto. An Argentine cruiser offers to tow him east to safety; but that would mean giving up and that he will not do. He tries one more time to enter the Pacific, and succeeds.

*April 1, 1896.* As *Spray* sails out into the Pacific, a giant roller washes over her. Slocum has been at the helm for 30 hours without rest. But soon the sloop is under full sail. Next stop: Juan Fernandez, the island of Alexander Selkirk, the real-life castaway who was Daniel Defoe's model for Robinson Crusoe.

On this "blessed island," a boatload of natives greets the mariner, who treats them to a breakfast of coffee, and doughnuts cooked in the salvaged tallow. They are delighted. He shows them how to make doughnuts and then sells them the tallow; they reward him with a pile of gold coins salvaged from a sunken ship. He scampers about the hills with their children, picking ripe quinces that he will preserve as he sails out again across the empty Pacific on the 72-day leg to Samoa.

*July 16, 1896. Spray* casts anchor in Samoa. Three lissome women approach in a canoe. But Slocum is far more interested in the widow of his hero, Robert Louis Stevenson. She comes down to greet him and presents him with her husband's sailing directories, which he accepts with "reverential awe." He is invited to use her husband's desk to write his letters, but he cannot bring himself to sit in that hallowed spot.

After an idyllic month in Samoa he sails for Australia, where enthusiastic welcomes await him. There he recoups his finances, moving from Sydney to Melbourne to Tasmania, lecturing as he goes to paying audiences. Then he swings north again.

*May 24, 1897. Spray* moves gingerly through the Great Barrier Reef opposite New Guinea. The newspapers soon report that Slocum is lost at sea. Not until he arrives in September at Mauritius, in the Indian Ocean, are they able to correct the error.

Meantime, he has been the chief actor in a comic-opera scene on the remote island of Rodrigues, some thousand miles east of Madagascar. The local abbé has been filling the islanders' heads with tales of the approaching Antichrist, a piece of sermonizing calculated to keep them on the narrowest of pathways. Suddenly, into the harbor comes *Spray*, scudding before a heavy gale, her sails all feather-white and her gaunt occupant holding down the deck like a bearded prophet. Down to the jetty

flock the faithful, crying that the Antichrist has
truly arrived. The islanders soon recover, however,
and entertain him royally. On he sails to Durban
in South Africa, where he is introduced to the
explorer Henry Stanley. Livingstone's savior is fascinated that the ship has traveled through treacherous waters without any built-in buoyancy compart-
ments. What would happen, he asks, if *Spray* should
strike a rock. Slocum's answer: "She must be kept
away from the rocks."

*March 26, 1898.* Slocum sails from South Africa
for St. Helena, the island of Napoleon's exile in
the south Atlantic. A celebrity now, he dines with
the island's governor and unwisely accepts the presence of a goat put on board by a friend. Once
aboard, the goat begins to eat his way through
the ship. No rope can hold him; he devours them
all. Then he turns his attention to the charts of
the Caribbean. Finally he munches Slocum's straw
hat. Slocum suffers the ravenous goat for almost
a thousand miles until, at Ascension Island, he
kicks him ashore.

Off the coast of Brazil, the U.S. battleship *Oregon*
speeds up behind him and hoists a puzzling signal:
*Are there any men-of-war about?* Slocum is baffled.
He doesn't know that war has broken out between
the United States and Spain. *Let us keep together
for mutual protection,* he signals back. The *Oregon*
ignores this badinage and steams away.

Chartless, Slocum racks his memory of wind
and water as he approaches Trinidad. He moves
from island to island, packing lecture halls with
accounts of his adventures. He is becalmed for eight
days north of the Bahamas, in seas so smooth that
each evening he can read by candlelight. A three-
day gale follows the calm, and he begins to weary
of the ocean—"tired, tired, tired, of baffling squalls
and fretful cobble-seas."

*June 26, 1898.* Slocum reaches Newport, Rhode
Island, and journey's end. Because of the war, the
harbor is mined and he must hug the rocks as he
brings his sloop into port. At one the following
morning he casts anchor. He cannot suppress a
sense of triumph: *Spray* is sound as a nut and hasn't
leaked a drop (since leaving Australia he hasn't
even rigged his pump). But no bands greet him. No
civic dignitaries clamber aboard. No reporters seek
him out. People's minds are on the war, not *Spray*.

Slowly, the extraordinary character of his feat
sinks in. He writes an account of his adventures,
which the *Century Illustrated Monthly* publishes in
seven installments. Later, as a book, *Sailing Alone*

Impossible! "You don't mean sailing *around* the world," South Africa president Stephanus "Oom Paul" Kruger told Joshua Slocum. "You mean sailing *in* the world." This cartoon, from an 1898 issue of the Cape Town *Owl*, illustrates Kruger's conviction that the earth is flat.

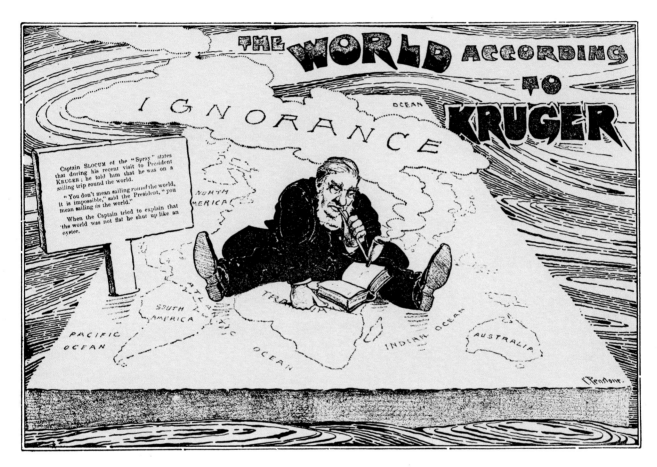

*Around the World* is translated into six languages, and becomes one of the classic stories of the sea.

But for Joshua Slocum, life begins to go slightly sour. There are no more seas to sail. With his earnings, he buys a farm at Martha's Vineyard in Massachusetts and plants fruit trees. But the years pass, and Slocum is running down, like a leaky schooner, his personality increasingly waspish, his appearance more and more slovenly, his sloop, once so trim and shipshape, filthier and filthier. He is withering away, an old salt clinging to the past.

He must have one more adventure. Together he and *Spray* will penetrate the mysteries of the Amazon River. He will sail his sloop to Venezuela, follow the Orinoco and the Rio Negro to the headwaters of the great river, then set his course downstream into the unknown jungle.

*November 14, 1909.* Joshua Slocum sets sails from Bristol, Rhode Island. Soon *Spray* is driving into the teeth of an easterly gale. The little sloop scuds along, white sails billowing in the wind, until she vanishes beyond the horizon. And that is the last that anyone sees of her. She and her master vanish without a trace. His ship—his faithful and sole companion and his last, true love—is with him to the end.

# A Rightful Place Among the Heroes

By George Ronald

"Be self-reliant. Take a hand in shaping the fate of mankind," Rear Adm. Leonard Murray once told a group of students. Murray followed his own advice. As Commander-in-Chief Canadian Northwest Atlantic he was instrumental in the Allied victory during the Battle of the Atlantic, one of the most fiercely waged campaigns ever fought at sea. The Allies relied heavily on the corvette (left), a doughty little vessel that escorted merchant convoys and terrorized German submarines. The corvette was manned by 88 sailors—the same number as the keys on a piano and, as Murray observed, "each with his own note."

Out to sea, the kind of fog that used to greet wartime convoys hung off Nova Scotia's Chebucto Head. A bright sun warmed the old city of Halifax and a gentle wind teased the flags at the Canadian Forces chapel. A ship's bell tolled as Rear Adm. Leonard Murray, former Commander-in-Chief Canadian Northwest Atlantic, bowed his head and listened to the roster of sad, familiar names.

*Fraser.* Destroyer, one of the originals, first to go. *Bras D'Or.* Converted lightship, foundered and sunk with all hands. *Otter.* Patrol vessel, destroyed by fire off Halifax. *Levis.* Corvette, torpedoed, North Atlantic . . .

At 73, fit as a midshipman and looking every inch a sailor, Murray had come from voluntary exile in England to lead a 25th-anniversary tribute to Canada's World War II seamen.

It was May 3, 1970, Murray's day of vindication. One of the chief architects of Allied victory in the Battle of the Atlantic and the only Canadian ever to command a theater of war, he had been robbed of his just acclaim by a victory celebration! In Hali-

For sighting a German submarine which his ship, *St. Croix*, sank in July 1942, a seaman receives a $10 award from Rear Admiral Murray. Murray had unflagging faith in his men. "His overwhelming concern was for your difficulties," said an officer who knew him. Murray also greatly admired merchant seamen (below, right, with navy ratings at St. John's, Nfld., in 1942). Battling weather and enemy vessels, the merchant marine ferried vital supplies between Canada and Britain. "Make no mistake," said Murray, "the real victors in the Battle of the Atlantic were not navies or air force but the Allied merchant seamen."

fax on May 7, 1945—25 years before—as ship's sirens suddenly whoop-whoop-whooped, signal flags celebrating the war's end were run up with colorful disregard for meaning. That night, rambunctious sailors wrecked a streetcar and, as fun subtly turned to riot, they were joined by civilians, soldiers and airmen. Mobs burned a police car, smashed windows, raided liquor stores.

Next day, in parks and on the Citadel slopes, wrote Thomas H. Raddall in *Halifax, Warden of the North*, "drunken seamen and workmen capered and sang, sprawled with drunken or merely hilarious women, eased themselves, and made unabashed love in the full blaze of the afternoon sun." The riots caused an estimated five million dollars dam-

age and spawned a royal commission which put the blame squarely on "the naval command."

Few Canadians know anything about Leonard Murray except that he drove into the wild heart of Halifax that day and ordered the rioters to go home. "My purpose was simply to help the mayor of Halifax carry out his responsibility to maintain law and order," said Murray later. "I was sticking my neck out. If the troops had not heeded the voice of authority, I'd have had to resign then and there." But his neck was out farther than he knew.

Supreme Court Justice R. L. Kellock, the royal commissioner, found that "the naval command" should have kept sailors off the streets at the first sign of trouble. (Charges for other than drunkenness were brought against 19 airmen, 41 soldiers, 34 sailors–and 117 civilians.) But Kellock, said Murray, "failed to appreciate that naval personnel had, that very day, been released from the haunting knowledge that every moment outside protected harbors they were liable to sudden death without warning." In any case, of 18,000 naval ratings in Halifax on VE-Day, reported Murray, "fewer than half were in ships and barracks and subject to immediate disciplinary control. The greater number were already in the town, quartered with families or friends or in billets."

Murray paid the price of being in command, says A. G. S. Griffin who had served as a lieutenant under Murray in the Battle of the Atlantic. "Six years of neglect and expediency by a government that made not the slightest gesture toward providing proper outlets for naval personnel in Halifax, bad housing, high rents, lack of restaurants and drinking establishments were all part of it. No wonder the men were ready for a blowup."

"Len Murray made himself the sacrificial lamb," said retired Rear Adm. C. J. Dillon. "He took all the blame."

After the Kellock report, naval feeling ran high. Murray avoided big gatherings at which sailors might demonstrate on his behalf and heighten tension between the city and the navy. Some outspoken officers talked of "taking the navy apart" for Murray. "I couldn't allow that," he said. "So I withdrew as quietly as I could, removing the bone of contention from the scene of conflict." But Murray paid a heavy price, forgoing honor and recognition that were his due. He retired from the navy at 49–and lost his rightful place among Canadian heroes.

Until VE-Day he'd held "the best job the Royal Canadian Navy ever had, in one of the decisive battles of history." He'd trained for it from boyhood. In Pictou Landing, N.S., where his father ran a coal shipping pier, Leonard Warren Murray was taught a profound respect for religion, a high regard for education and a deep love of the sea. At 17, the youngest of the first 21 cadets graduated from the naval college in Halifax, he was sent to the Royal Navy for training. World War I brought him a rich variety of assignments–as a cipher officer in Ottawa, in command of boarding parties from HMCS *Niobe* on patrol off New York and as aide to the Royal Navy's fleet navigating officer.

One memorable day in 1917, an exhilarating experience taught Murray that, to find what a man is capable of, you need only give him a chance. HMS *Agincourt*, the biggest battleship of the Grand Fleet, was exercising with the 4th Battleship Division in Scotland's Firth of Forth. Her navigator was in hospital, her captain was down with lumbago, and the second-in-command had no experience in handling the ship. So Murray, a 22-year-old lieutenant, took over. When the admiral was summoned by the commander-in-chief–and departed in his flagship–*Agincourt* became senior ship. "It fell to me, temporarily in charge," said Murray, "to lead the three other battleships up harbor and under the Forth bridge, then anchor them in new berths on a flooding tide."

Opportunities were few in peacetime. By 1922 the Royal Canadian Navy had been cut to 366 officers and men and to two destroyers and four minesweepers. But with periods of service in the Royal Navy, Murray's career progressed. At various times, he was assistant to the master of the Atlantic Fleet, navigator in the battle cruiser *Tiger*, a duty commander in the operations room at the Admiralty in London.

By the uncertain summer of 1939 he was a four-stripe captain and deputy chief of staff under Rear Adm. Percy Nelles who ran a growing Canadian

navy of 1,700, with 1,800 reservists, six destroyers and five minesweepers. Lacking clear-cut government instructions, Murray recalled, "we carefully read the papers and acted as we thought best. When obviously the balloon was about to go up, we ordered two destroyers around from the West Coast. They cleared the Panama Canal on September 10–the day Canada declared war–and arrived on the 15th. Next day, when the first convoy sailed from Halifax, one of those destroyers was in the escort."

A year later Commodore Murray went to sea in the destroyer leader *Assiniboine* as commander of all Halifax-based warships. When the RCN took over from the British in Newfoundland in mid-1941, Murray moved to St. John's. Escort ships were streaming from the builders–and the shortage of skippers steadily worsened. For want of an experienced captain, the four-month-old corvette *Pictou* lay idle. Murray summoned Lt. A. G. S. Griffin,

who was temporarily in charge of *Pictou*'s crew. Griffin had had 13 weeks of navigation, gunnery, signals, torpedo and submarine detection. He'd *instructed* another class of embryo officers for the next 13 weeks, then joined *Pictou* as first lieutenant. "Just want you to know I'm doing all I can to find another CO and get you to sea," said Murray.

"Sir–" Griffin swallowed hard. "Let me have her."

Murray reached a decision in seconds. "She's yours," he said, making a corvette captain of a life-insurance man. Now, with only eight weeks' sea time, the "old man" at 28, Griffin took *Pictou* to sea on a dull, rainy day. "I remember the hands on the fo'c'sle looking up at the bridge, and my wife on the jetty trying to smile. It was the blind leading the blind."

After this short training patrol, Griffin found himself in one of the worst convoy battles of the war; 19 merchant ships were sunk in two nights.

The war is over! And on VE-Day—May 7, 1945—
thousands gathered in Halifax to celebrate the end of six
years of conflict. But the wartime port soon became
turbulent as civilians and servicemen went on a two-day
binge of drinking, revelry—and rioting. Despite
attempts to control unruly celebrants (bottom), stores were
looted and property smashed and burned.

*Pictou* opened fire on a surfaced submarine, dodged
two torpedoes, depth-charged the diving enemy
and scored a "probable damage." When *Pictou*
returned to St. John's, Griffin was confirmed in
command.

Murray's Newfoundland Escort Force eventually
comprised 70 ships—Canadian, British, French,
Norwegian, Polish, Belgian, Dutch—with seldom
fewer than 55 at sea. They worked a 35-day cycle.
Off Newfoundland they met merchant convoys
from Canada, sheep-dogging them to Iceland waters
where escorts from Britain took over. Murray's
ships spent four days in galeswept Hvalfjord on
Iceland's west coast, with no provisioning and little
rest. Bridge and engine room were manned constantly to permit instant action if anchors dragged.
Then, picking up a westbound convoy, they made
the long beat back.

The worst time was the bloody winter of 1942-43,
when the Germans almost won. "Those merchant

captains knew that probably 25 percent might not reach the United Kingdom in their own ships, and perhaps 15 percent might not arrive at all," said Murray. "They never faltered. No ship missed a convoy from Halifax because of malingering."

By 1943 the RCN was the third biggest Allied navy and Murray became Commander-in-Chief Canadian Northwest Atlantic. He directed, controlled, routed and defended all but troop convoys to a point midway between New York and Liverpool, where they were turned over to the British.

As commander-in-chief, Murray identified completely with the seagoing branch. As soon as possible after entering harbor, each warship—by Murray's order—had mail, fresh food and a coterie of dockyard types looking for things to mend. He took responsibility for subordinates' errors, believing that a senior officer should conduct his affairs so that he was *always* informed. When Halifax operations sent an unclear signal in the commander-in-chief's name (although Murray hadn't seen it) to an escort group commander, the commander did what he *thought* was wanted. He guessed wrong and detached a ship. It was torpedoed. Deeply distressed by his wrong decision, he saw Murray in Halifax. "The fault," said Murray, a finger tapping his own desk, "was right here. No ambiguous signal should ever leave this headquarters."

In five and a half years of war the RCN grew from 11 ships to almost 400, from fewer than 2,000 men to nearly 100,000. Under Canadian escort, on 25,343 merchant-ship voyages, 181,643,180 tons of cargo were carried from North America to Britain. In 1944, from early May to mid-September, Canadian ships provided all trade convoy escort in the North Atlantic, plus some of the roving attack groups. Sixty-seven Canadian ships, including minesweepers from Murray's command, joined in the invasion of Normandy.

Nobody regretted more than the sailors themselves what the VE-Day riots did to Murray. When he left by ship for England, more than a thousand lined the Halifax jetties and cheered him. Murray's departure, said retired Rear Adm. H. F. Pullen, "was a tragedy—for him, for the RCN, for the country."

With one career behind him, Murray started a second. At 53 he became a student member of the Middle Temple in London, read law and was called to the British Bar in 1949. He practiced at the Admiralty Division of the High Court for a few years, then retired to Buxton in Derbyshire.

In Canada he was forgotten by all but a few contemporaries—men long out of the navy—and by wartime junior officers risen to high rank. One was Vice-Adm. J. C. O'Brien, in 1970 chief of Maritime Command. He had met Murray only once—in 1945 when Murray inspected a signals school where O'Brien was an instructor. He lent enthusiastic support when the Naval Officers Association of Canada invited Murray to unveil a memorial window in the Canadian Forces chapel in Halifax.

That morning, Battle of the Atlantic Sunday, Murray went with O'Brien for a 700-man march-past at the Sailors' Memorial in Point Pleasant Park. O'Brien, only 51 but a full rank higher than Murray, nodded in deference, then stepped back. Murray took the salute. "It was his day," said O'Brien, "as it should have been. I hope it signified to others, as it did to me, the continuity that is the very fiber of the navy."

At the unveiling, the old commander-in-chief stood deeply moved as O'Brien read the names of the 24 Canadian warships whose crews were part of the price of victory in World War II.

... *Windflower*. Corvette. Fresh from the builders, when armament was scarce, she sailed to war with a wooden gun. And died a year later ...

At a memorial service in the
Canadian Forces chapel in Halifax on
May 3, 1970 (Battle of Atlantic
Sunday), Rear Adm. Leonard Murray
listens as Vice Adm. J. C. O'Brien
reads the names of Canadian warships
lost during World War II. That
morning, Murray had gazed out at the
fog off the Nova Scotia coast.
"How often have we sailed through
that," he said sadly, "and so many
never returned."

... *Shawinigan*. Corvette, disappeared, no survivors. *Esquimalt*. Minesweeper, last to go, torpedoed in the Halifax approaches three weeks before VE-Day ...

"We meant it as tribute in full measure for his war services," said retired Cmdr. W. A. Manfield, another of Murray's sailors. "And as vindication for the black day in 1945."

At a reception in Ottawa a few days later, Murray beamed as he described his Halifax visit. "Does this wipe the slate clean, sir?" he was asked.

"I don't think that's possible," said Murray. "But this is not a personal thing, you know. What sticks in my gullet is what was done on VE-Day to the good name of the navy."

In November 1971, Leonard Murray died at the age of 75. Representatives of the French, British and Canadian navies, and a group of friends whose names took up two columns of the Buxton newspaper, attended the funeral. The newspaper recalled a statement made in 1945 by Douglas Abbott, then minister of naval services: "It would be regrettable if the truly great services of this officer were to be forgotten by the people of Canada." In Halifax, 25 years later, the navy had remembered. Rear Adm. Leonard Warren Murray had come home.

# She Was Big, Safe, Fast—and Doomed

## By F. J. Woodley

*On May 29, 1914, the liner* Empress of Ireland, *rammed by a collier in a St. Lawrence River fog, sank within minutes. It was the worst disaster in Canadian maritime history. More than 1,000 of the 1,477 persons on board perished, including 167 members of the Salvation Army—officers and bandsmen bound for an international congress in Britain. Among the 26 Salvation Army survivors was Lt. Col. Alfred Keith, whose vivid memories of that terrible day never faded.*

The afternoon of Thursday, May 28, 1914, was bright and sunny as the 1,057 passengers and 420 crew boarded *Empress of Ireland* in Quebec City for the six-day voyage to Liverpool. The party of 200 Salvationists, including some wives and children, had come from Toronto by train. Headed by Commissioner David M. Rees, they were looking forward to several weeks at the Salvation Army's Second International Congress in Britain.

At about 4:30 p.m., the *Empress* eased out from under the shadow of Quebec's massive Citadel and turned downriver toward the Atlantic. In eight years of service—and 95 Atlantic crossings—the sleek 14,191-ton liner had earned a reputation as the fastest and safest ship in the Canadian trade. Her lifeboats could hold 1,860 persons. The crew held weekly lifesaving drills. Fog patches had been reported on the lower river, but as the *Empress* glided past the picturesque villages of rural Quebec, Capt. Henry George Kendall had no reason to believe this voyage would be anything but routine.

*For dinner that night we were instructed to wear our full-dress uniforms—red with black trim,* recalls Lieutenant Colonel Keith. *Though we were traveling second class, Captain Kendall had invited us to be his guests in the first class dining saloon. He had a long table set up for us, and he sat at the head of it.*

The Salvation Army contingent had within its ranks many close relationships. Commissioner Rees was traveling with his daughter Ruth and his son Harding, both officers (ministers), as well as his wife and another daughter. Most of the group knew Bandsman Kenneth McIntyre, an ex-New Yorker who had moved to Toronto six months earlier and joined the Canadian Staff Band. All basked in the reflected happiness of Bandsman Tom Greenaway and his new bride, Margaret. Tom's brother Bert, also a band member, was aboard.

Deck lights burned brightly as the steamer proceeded downriver. By midnight most passengers had settled down for the night. Around 1:30 a.m., the crew on the bridge watched the river pilot board a tender and set off toward the lights of Father Point, visible on the south shore. The temperature was just above freezing. The vessel picked up momentum and headed for the open sea.

*I was awakened by a bump . . . and immediately noticed something strange—we were leaning over! I jumped out of my berth. The floor was at a strange angle. I went down a little corridor, and saw water coming in an open porthole. My first instinct was to close it, but the water was coming in much too fast.*

With Father Point less than 30 minutes astern, the routine voyage had suddenly become a nightmare. Minutes earlier, a lookout had spotted another vessel coming upstream, several miles ahead. Whistle signals were exchanged. A swirl of dense fog hid the other ship momentarily. As visibility returned, horrified eyes on the *Empress* saw the other boat looming out of the mist to starboard—a ship's length away, on a collision course. Captain Kendall desperately hailed it through his megaphone, but his frantic warning came too late. The steel-clad bow of the Norwegian collier *Storstad* sliced deeply into the *Empress'* hull.

*The ship was listing quickly. I ran back to the cabin and got the other fellows up. We tugged on sneakers, put pants on over our pajamas and ran to the stairway.*

Capt. Henry George Kendall commanded the ill-fated *Empress of Ireland* (left) when she was rammed and sunk in 1914 by the Norwegian collier *Storstad* (below, with bow crumpled by the collision). Kendall had intended to go down with his ship but he was flung from the bridge as the *Empress* listed and clung to drifting wreckage until rescued.

*By the time we got there it had tilted so badly that we had to pull ourselves up the rails to the deck.*

Captain Kendall used his megaphone again to ask *Storstad*'s master, Capt. Thomas Andersen, to keep his bow in the gaping hole it had punched in the liner's hull. But *Storstad*'s momentum tore the two ships apart, and water flooded in through the *Empress*' gashed side.

It was pitch black below the *Empress*' decks; the electrical system had failed almost upon impact. In partial shock, the terrified passengers began a silent struggle for life. Few made it. Many perished in the rush to safety through flooded passageways and up perpendicular stairways.

*Strange to say, there wasn't too much panic. I can clearly remember that, and it impressed me afterward. Many were trapped belowdecks. A lot more in the starboard cabins were killed and their bodies mutilated by the collision itself.*

*By this time the boat was going over very quickly. The deck was awash, and I made my way to the back of the ship hanging on to the railings along the side.*

As SOS signals crackled through the ether, Kendall ordered full steam ahead in a final effort to

The bodies of children, fished from
the icy St. Lawrence, are carried
from the government rescue vessel
*Lady Evelyn*, docked at Quebec City.

save his passengers by running the vessel ashore. But the *Empress* never made it. The crippled liner remained afloat only 15 minutes.

Only a handful of lifeboats were launched. Hundreds of passengers, clad only in night attire, threw themselves into the frigid St. Lawrence and clung desperately to life belts and floating debris.

Acts of heroism were many. Sir Henry Seton-Karr, a distinguished British statesman and author, gave his life belt to another passenger, and himself perished. Noted actress Mabel Hackney and her

husband, actor Laurence Irving, were seen to embrace as they went down with the ship. A Toronto man, able to find only two life belts, put them on his wife and young son; when it became apparent the belts wouldn't keep all three afloat, he quietly let go and disappeared in the darkness.

*When I hit the water, I thought 'I won't last long here.' There was still ice floating in the river. I got my pants and sneakers off, and began swimming in my pajamas.*

*I ran up against a couple of our group. We stuck*

Frank Tower's nickname was "Lucks," and the stoker and oiler aboard *Empress of Ireland* had earned it. He survived not only the sinking of the *Empress* but also that of *Titanic*, which struck an iceberg and went down in 1912 with the loss of more than 1,500 lives. In 1915 Tower was aboard *Lusitania* when she was sunk by a German submarine. More than 1,100 drowned—but "Lucks" was rescued.

Commissioner David M. Rees (right), who commanded the 200 Salvation Army members aboard *Empress of Ireland*, and chief secretary Col. Sydney Maidment wait on deck shortly before the *Empress* set sail on her last voyage. Both men perished.

*together for awhile in the water, but I got separated from them. Exhausted, I turned over on my back to rest, and saw the Empress go down. I was starting to wonder how long I could last, when, bang, I hit a floating log. I got my arms around it and hung on.*

Only a handful of Salvationists ever made it up from their cabins. Bandsman Kenneth McIntyre strapped his life belt on a frightened mother before she and her child went over the side. Both were rescued, and McIntyre himself swam around in the icy water until assistance came. Bert Greenaway made his way topside and prepared for the worst. Just as death seemed inevitable he spotted an empty lifeboat in the water. Calmly sliding down the side of the listing liner, he dropped 15 feet into the small craft—without even getting wet.

His brother Tom, meanwhile, had become separated from his bride. Reaching deck, he cried her name over and over again. As he clutched a railing, the *Empress* plunged into the cold depths. Miraculously, the force of the descent tore him loose and he rose to the surface, where a table floated up

295

beneath him. Others were not so lucky. Commissioner Rees and his entire family perished.

*Storstad* lowered her lifeboats and began the grim task of gathering in the liner's passengers, dead and alive. The government boats *Eureka* and *Lady Evelyn* also steamed to the scene. By the time they arrived, nothing of the *Empress* was visible except lifeboats, debris, and bodies dotting the river's surface.

*The log helped, but my arms and legs soon became numb. I saw a lifeboat and yelled 'Help!' It went past. I yelled some more, and one big, tall sailor saw or heard and they came back. The boat was so full that when he pulled me in, water started coming over the sides. We made it to* Storstad *and I was helped up to the deck.*

*Several of us were put in the captain's cabin and we lay close together for warmth. Then to put some life back into me, I had the only drop of alcohol I've ever had—before or since. I thought I was going to burn to death.*

*They took us from there onto* Lady Evelyn. *The only covering I had was a tablecloth taken from the table in the captain's cabin.*

The two government boats helped recover the *Empress'* passengers from the dark waters, then took aboard those already on *Storstad*. Corpse after corpse was gently laid on the cold decks. Distraught survivors scanned the dead faces for relatives and friends. Sailors wept.

The two vessels cruised back and forth until their captains were certain none remained to be saved, then headed upriver to Rimouski.

*Next to me when we got to Rimouski was Frank Brooks, one of our bandsmen. His wife, Mary, and little daughter were missing. "Alf," he said, "why didn't I go down? There's nothing left for me." I was looking around, and all of a sudden I said, "Look, Frank ... look! There's Mary!" She was sitting in one of the buggies farther down the line.*

*A number of us were taken from the dock to the Hotel St. Germain. I was sitting in the lobby, still draped in my tablecloth, when they called us to breakfast. The only other Salvationist I saw at the St. Germain was Tom Greenaway's bride of two weeks. She didn't know whether he was alive or not. I was back in the lobby after breakfast when in rushed Tom. "Alf," he cried, "where's Margaret? She's here, they say." I took him to her and discreetly left them alone.*

The dead, meanwhile, were moved to another government boat, *Lady Grey*. She steamed slowly into Quebec City harbor on Sunday morning, flag at half-mast. Coffins three and four deep covered her deck. She tied up at Pier No. 27 where a huge warehouse had been converted into a mortuary. There, anxious relatives moved silently from casket to casket, lifting the lids to identify the contents. Newsmen brushed their own tears from notebooks as they recorded the grim tableau being enacted in the gloomy shed.

*Those who survived were sent home by train. When we arrived in Toronto, the station concourse was thronged with thousands of people. The Salvation Army party was whisked off to the T. Eaton store on Albert and Yonge streets to be outfitted, from top to toe, at the firm's expense.*

The final death toll was 1,015. As Canadians mourned, they asked how such a tragedy could happen. A formal inquiry opened on June 16 and a month later the seven-man commission delivered its verdict: while commending *Storstad*'s crew for its rescue work, it placed full blame for the accident on the Norwegian vessel. Her first officer, Alfred Toftenes, had changed course in the fog, and had failed to call Captain Andersen to the bridge when the fog descended.

Burial and memorial services were held across Canada and around the world. Some 7,500 mourners attended the funeral for the Salvation

Burial services for the Salvation Army dead were held at Toronto's Mount Pleasant Cemetery. Each casket bore a silver plate with the victim's name and the single word: "Promoted." Although more than a half-century has passed since the *Empress* sank, the dead are not forgotten. Each year, on the anniversary of the tragedy, Salvationists gather at the cemetery's Empress Memorial (right) to pay tribute to the victims.

Army dead in Toronto's Mutual Street Arena. There, 16 bodies, each draped with a Salvation Army flag, lay in state, a small proportion of the 167 Salvationists who had perished. One casket contained the tiny body of Dolly Brooks, infant daughter of Bandsman and Mrs. Frank Brooks whom Alf Keith had helped reunite at Rimouski.

Meanwhile, Bandsman Kenneth McIntyre had made his way by another steamer to Britain and the International Congress. In the vast Strand Hall, the Canadian delegation was represented by remnants who had crossed on other ships. But in a great parade through the streets of London, McIntyre marched alone, behind draped flags, representing the Canadian Territorial Staff Band.

*Every year for the next 40 years, we survivors held our own private memorial service at Mount Pleasant Cemetery in Toronto. It was never advertised, but it got to be known, and it grew. Hundreds of people came. In the mid-'50s we felt it should be something more than an* Empress of Ireland *memorial, and it became a national day of remembrance for all Salvationists. We always read the 46th Psalm, which was read by the chief secretary, Colonel Maidment, at our last meeting before we sailed.*

Colonel Maidment and his wife were among those who went down with *Empress of Ireland*, but the 46th Psalm lives on. It says, "God is our refuge and strength, a very present help in trouble. Therefore will not we fear . . ."

# Lost!

## By Joseph P. Blank

**R**onald Woodcock sat on the trunk of a fallen tree, stared at the ground and tried to think. He was lost in the trackless, unspoiled wilderness of northwestern British Columbia. He marked the date on the calendar that he kept in his backpack: "June 5, 1971."

Woodcock wasn't worried about himself. He felt comfortable in the wilderness, and figured he had plenty of time to find the cabin that he had been using. But he was concerned about his family; he had been out of touch with them now for 40 days. His wife and six children were living in a rented house in Endako, more than 200 air miles to the south. The February before, his home and possessions—all uninsured—had been destroyed by fire. Financially, he had been wiped out.

That really was why he had made this trip to the wilderness. He needed more money than he was earning at his railroad job, so he had taken a leave of absence to trap beaver. A good pelt brought $20. In late April he flew to Damdochax Lake, after arranging for a bush pilot, Bill Jenkins, to pick him up eight weeks later.

Woodcock, 48, was brown-haired, blue-eyed and stocky at 170 pounds. This venture was his third trip to the bush in ten years, and he loved it. He often thought, "If there was a way to have my family with me, I'd spend my life here. You're at peace. You're your own boss. Fish and game are plentiful. You're in a world you're making for yourself, and no other world exists."

The trapping went smoothly, and Woodcock garnered more than 50 pelts in his first three weeks. On May 31 he left his cabin to retrieve skins that he had cached 20 miles north. He wore rubber boots, a wool shirt and a light jacket. His 30-pound backpack included a sleeping bag, an ax, food, a rifle and 15 rounds of ammunition.

He worked his way up Slowmaldo Creek and into Groundhog Pass, where he located his skins and spent several days cleaning them. Then he packed half the skins, a 60-pound load, and his remaining three-day supply of food. Because of the weight he was carrying, he decided to seek a shorter route back to Slowmaldo Creek.

After trudging south for six hours through high underbrush, he came upon a creek backed up by several unfamiliar beaver dams—and from which he had a stunning view of strange mountains. For a long minute he was hypnotized by the beauty of the panorama. Then, sitting down, he faced the fact that what had happened to other woodsmen had now happened to him. He was lost. He had no means of knowing whether Slowmaldo Creek was east or west. In this land of untapped mineral deposits, he thought his compass might not register true. He couldn't backtrack because there was nothing to follow. His best course, he reasoned, was to stick with this unfamiliar creek downstream to the south. It might bring him to recognizable land or a river. And south was the general direction of the closest town, Hazelton, 125 air miles away.

Woodcock pushed along the creek, still carrying the heavy beaver pelts. The creek was so overgrown along its banks that there was no simple path to follow. He was continually climbing and descending hills and fighting through underbrush; worse, he met an obstacle course of windfalls—dead trees that had accumulated over the years and sometimes built themselves into impasses 25 feet high.

On the evening of the second day, Woodcock reluctantly abandoned his furs. He cooked a handful of rice and climbed into his sleeping bag. As he lay awake, he realized that he was in trouble; other men in his predicament, he knew, had panicked, exhausted themselves and not survived. This would not happen to him. He resolved to pace himself and be finicky-careful. He *would* make it out.

Ron Woodcock, writes his mother, "much prefers the quiet of the woods to the gabble of the human race." Yet in the summer of 1971 those woods became his enemy. Lost and low on food, Woodcock trekked for 57 days through the forbidding wilderness of northwestern British Columbia—and survived.

Although he plodded on for about 13 hours a day, he always stopped when he was tired, rather than spent. He doled out his food sparingly, always on the lookout for game. He shot a woodchuck and a grouse, and on the tenth day he shot a moose. He spent the following day dressing a hindquarter and cooking it down to some 20 pounds of meat to pack with him.

About six o'clock that evening, as he prepared his campsite, he looked up to see a giant grizzly approaching the moose carcass. Although he was 100 feet downwind from the carcass, he knew he had to kill the bear. "The grizzly must have stood nine feet tall and weighed more than a thousand pounds," he remembered. "Those bears are touchy in the spring, and inclined to attack. I couldn't have him around my camp while I was sleeping."

Woodcock's first shot slammed into the bear's neck, paralyzing him. Reluctant to use another bullet, he waited for the wounded animal to die. Finally, as light grew dim, he had to finish off the bear with a second shot.

On the 14th day Woodcock's path toward home was blocked by an icy river too broad and deep

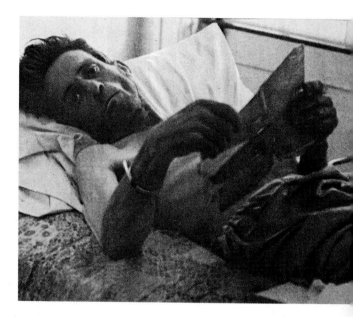

to ford. He worked westward for a day until he encountered a wildly running creek. He felled two trees across the water, but the current swept each away. Now he was blocked to the south and the west, so he moved north along the creek, hoping that it would narrow enough to enable him to cross.

On the evening of the 15th day a storm struck. The wind howled, trees crashed and rain slashed down. He fixed a shelter and a high "mattress" out of spruce limbs. For two days, while the storm raged, he lay in his sleeping bag, hardly moving. He thought about his family and about what the bush pilot, Bill Jenkins, would think and do when he returned for their rendezvous at the Damdochax Lake cabin and found no one.

(The pilot did return on schedule. Alarmed at Woodcock's absence, he searched the area for two days, went home and then came back again with Woodcock's brother and brother-in-law. In four days they found only an overturned raft, where the lake emptied into a creek. They concluded that Woodcock must have been on the raft when it capsized and that he had drowned.)

After the storm subsided, Woodcock, still lost, continued northward, looking for a place to cross the creek. "Take it easy," he told himself. "You'll get out." He found a narrowing of the stream, managed to cross and turned back southward.

On about the 25th day he ate the last of his food. Exertion already had chipped about 20 pounds off him. "Have to eat what grows," he ruminated. "But be careful. Don't get sick." He tried the young tender shoots of the Solomon's Seal plant; he had watched dairy cows munch on them. Squawberries, savored by moose, made his mouth pucker, but he assumed they contained some nourishment.

One morning, as he worked through the underbrush, he suddenly caught a glimpse of a rotting pole—a telegraph pole! He knew he had chanced on an abandoned telegraph trail, put through the wilderness by government packhorse expeditions in the late 1800s. If he could follow signs of the trail—a pole here and there, a piece of telegraph wire still nailed to a tree—the clues would lead him to Hazelton.

Although the trail was overgrown now, it had been trampled for many years by men and animals. Woodcock cut himself a walking stick. By poking it gently into the ground, he could differentiate between the packed earth of the old trail and the soft virgin soil on either side of it.

Now his odyssey became a step-by-step ordeal as he kept prodding the earth and looking for old poles and pieces of wire. Frequently he lost the trail in foot-high moss, dense brush and trees. He had to detour for swamps and stands of impenetrable willows. When he lost the trail, he patiently zigged to the east, zagged to the west, sometimes repeating the pattern for days until he picked up the trail again. All movement was a struggle.

During one two-week period he estimated that he had progressed no more than 20 miles.

By about the 43rd day his stamina was ebbing, and he couldn't remain on his feet more than six or seven hours a day. Since the 25th day he had eaten only wild berries and leaves. His belt could no longer hold up his tattered trousers, so he removed the sling from his rifle and fashioned a single suspender out of it. In climbing, he had to pause after three or four steps, and he relied increasingly on his rifle and a walking stick for support. The sole flapped off one boot, and he tied it to the upper with a piece of string from his pack. His clothing was progressively shredded by the sharp brush. Mosquitoes were turning his forehead into raw, bleeding meat. He found nothing to eat except heavily seeded highbush cranberries. The seeds lodged immovably in his intestines, doubled him up with cramps that shot through his middle like electric shocks.

On what he figured was about the 50th day, he lay on the ground, writhing and panting in pain. "Maybe it's time to give up," he thought. But that was not what he wanted to do; he wanted to see his family. "Rest awhile," he told himself. "You don't have much farther to go." He knew that somewhere ahead lay the dirt road to Hazelton.

So he got up and stumbled on. His rubbery legs felt boneless. He had to squint to focus his eyes. Saliva thickened in his mouth and throat, and he choked when he tried to scrape it out with his fingers. He knew he couldn't climb each new incline, but somehow he did. He had to make it in two more days. He could not last a third day. Yet, even in his condition, he did not let himself indulge in hopeless thoughts.

Suddenly, around noon of the 57th day, he found himself in the open, on a road—the dirt road to Hazelton! The scene around kept wavering and swimming. He tried to lock his knees so they wouldn't buckle.

A car approached him. The two men in it, intent on an afternoon of fishing, stared at the mangy scarecrow of a human being and continued past him. One hundred and fifty feet down the road the car stopped, then backed. Woodcock staggered toward it. He opened his mouth to talk, but he couldn't utter a sound. He weakly motioned for a pencil and paper.

"I need water," he laboriously scrawled. One man opened a bottle of beer and handed it to him. He slowly got it through the saliva that clotted his mouth. Then he wrote, "If it's not too much trouble, please take me to my mother in Hazelton." Her house was closest.

The two men helped him into the rear seat. He felt a mild sense of satisfaction and relief. He had made it. The fishermen helped him to the door of his mother's house. She couldn't believe the apparition before her. Woodcock's face was gaunt behind a three-inch beard. His eyes were glazed. He had lost 70 of his 170 pounds. The rips in his trousers revealed thighs that looked like white sticks.

He was hospitalized two weeks for treatment of malnutrition, exposure and intestinal disorders, and it took an additional two months for him to recover his health and strength. In the hospital, it was three days before he could talk even in a whisper. His wife sat by his bed and asked no questions. After four days Woodcock's feelings surfaced. When friends asked him about his experience, he began whispering the details, then broke into tears, not even aware that he was going to cry. The visitors misunderstood his tears. He couldn't explain that he had passed through a great adventure. It had given him a conviction that all human beings seek: that he had the courage to face and deal with whatever test life brought.

# Red Alert: Avalanche in Rogers Pass

By Roland Wild

Fred Schleiss stood on the Trans-Canada Highway and looked up at the mountains towering above Rogers Pass. It was 10 a.m. on Sunday, January 13, 1974, and it had been snowing heavily since midnight. Before it blew itself out, the storm would dump 21 inches onto the road. But it was the state of the mountains, not the highway, that concerned Schleiss. Through the curtain of falling snow, the bluffs and shoulders of Hermit Mountain, Grant Peak and Swiss Peak filled the northern

Winter avalanches sometimes close Rogers Pass for days—despite the efforts of soldiers and Parks Canada personnel to trigger slides before they become big enough to block the road. An avalanche in 1974, with winds reaching 135 m.p.h. and the temperature down to 28 below, broke fir trees two feet in diameter.

sky. From the tree line, giant firs marched in green and white ranks down the mountainside almost to the highway. It was a scene of Christmas card beauty—and also of danger.

Just six hours before, Fred, chief avalanche fore-

caster in Glacier National Park, and his brother and assistant, Walter, had sent out a red alert: the 27-mile Rogers Pass section of the highway snaking through the park in British Columbia's Selkirk Mountains had been closed to traffic. Now the

303

Avalanche forecaster Fred Schleiss, who relies on experience and instinct to anticipate where dangerous slides are likely, points out a target to Reg Wannamaker, a Royal Canadian Horse Artillery officer. Throughout the winter, gunners fire shells into areas of unstable snow accumulation, trying to avoid full-scale avalanches such as this one (opposite) thundering down a slope in Rogers Pass.

pass was silent as a graveyard as Fred Schleiss scanned a ridge overlooking a deep gash cut through the tree-lined slopes–the slide path of Single Bench, one of 160 carefully mapped areas where avalanches can start. There had already been one heavy slide at another site half an hour ago and the situation looked critical here. It was time for a shoot.

Schleiss got into his truck, made a U turn in the deepening snow and drove to the nearby Crossover gunsite, where a Royal Canadian Horse Artillery howitzer crew was waiting. "Fire when ready," he ordered. Within 60 seconds the crack of a howitzer echoed along the valley and the gun crew ran to their vehicles and shut the windows, a standard precaution that this time may have saved their lives.

As the 33-pound shell hit, enormous puffs of snow came boiling and rampaging down the slide path like thunderclouds, swept through the static defenses–earthen defense mounds 25 feet high and trenches dug into the mountainside–and onto the highway. Meanwhile, the air blast which always precedes an avalanche had suddenly lifted Schleiss' truck up like a toy and tossed it 30 feet away. One army truck was spun around and shoved into the other. Miraculously, no one was seriously hurt. But the gun position was buried in five feet of snow and the howitzer was out of action.

At the Lens snowshed, half a mile to the east, another dangerous situation was developing. Because of the red alert, some 20 motorists had been held in the snowshed by the park warden. But now snow blocked both ends of the 675-foot-long shed. The warden radioed for help. Then, after digging themselves out, the travelers walked eastward, to be picked up by park personnel.

Back at the Crossover site, Schleiss faced a new problem. He dared not call for snowplows and trucks to clear the highway until the slide area was stabilized; the vibrations might trigger another avalanche. A new gun would have to be brought in from Camp Wainwright, Alta., 500 miles away. Schleiss and the soldiers dug themselves out, clambered over the slide and were taken to their base two miles away.

Delayed by icy roads and heavy snow, the new gun did not reach Rogers Pass until Wednesday night at six o'clock. Schleiss put it to work immediately. Throughout the night, the soldiers lobbed shells into the snow, gradually working their way west along the highway from one position to another. By dawn Thursday, the plows could move in. Finally, at 6:55 that evening, five days after the red alert, Rogers Pass was reopened to traffic.

All winter long avalanche forecasters must watch the mountains from one end of the pass to the other. When they spot an unstable area that looks dangerous, the bombardiers swing into action, removing the snow overburden in a series of small, short slides before it can build into a bigger menace.

Located in one of the world's busiest avalanche zones, Rogers Pass provides the most direct route through the Rockies. An estimated two million persons and more than 30 million tons of freight move through it each year on the Trans-Canada Highway and CP Rail's transcontinental line. Delays at the pass can mean ruined delivery schedules for trucks, late arrivals in railway stations across the country, and ships swinging idly at anchor in Vancouver when they should be outward-bound with vital export shipments of grain or coal.

The CPR route, opened in 1886, has since 1916 avoided some of the worst slide areas. After years of wrestling with avalanches, including a slide in 1910 that killed 58 workmen, the CPR burrowed the five-mile Connaught Tunnel under Mount Macdonald. Automobiles came to the pass when

305

This concrete snowshed is one of eight sheds built to deflect slides over parts of the 27-mile Rogers Pass section of the Trans-Canada Highway. Right: a mangled steel guardrail is testimony to the fury of an avalanche.

the Trans-Canada Highway was put through in 1962, lopping 100 miles off the distance between Vancouver and Calgary. Today Parks Canada spends some $800,000 on maintenance and snow removal in the pass, and at least $300,000 a year on research and direct avalanche control (including more than $140 a round for the ammunition the army uses). But the payoff is that Canadians are linked by a coast-to-coast highway open year-round.

Tourists coming here in summer are treated to a feast of lordly and tranquil splendor. The park abounds with animal and plant life, hiking and riding trails, and breathtaking views of mountains, streams and meadows. "Such a sight; never to be forgotten," said engineer-surveyor Maj. A. B. Rogers in 1881 when he beheld the summit of the pass later named for him. Commented a European visitor in the *BC Motorist* in 1973: "I have driven the Amalfi in Italy, the Corniche in France,

the road to Srinagar in Kashmir, and the Arlberg in Austria. Rogers Pass ranks with any of them."

But even a motorist enjoying the beauty of Rogers Pass in 90-degree summer sunshine can glimpse its other face as he drives past the crunched guardrails, big broken trees and other debris that mark a severe previous winter. Mess or no mess, the tourist will be reminded of winter as he drives through the eight concrete snowsheds, each between 500 and 1,000 feet long and built at a cost of $1,500 a foot, which cover the highway near the slide paths. Open on the downhill side, the sheds are designed to deflect snow over their roofs into the valley. On one occasion a slide cascaded into the valley with such momentum that it triggered a slide on the opposite slope; the impact caused the first avalanche to roll back uphill into the open side of the shed. Fortunately, at the time, the road was closed.

Average annual snowfall in Rogers Pass is a whopping 400 inches. In the winter of 1966-67, almost double this—727 inches—fell. Such heavy falls combine with wind and temperature changes to produce continuous avalanche threats, sometimes requiring a gun crew to be on the firing sites for two or three days with only a few hours' sleep.

The army has been in on the avalanche control program since it began in 1962. A detachment of one officer and nine other ranks, rotated every six weeks, is provided from Camp Shilo in Manitoba. Despite long hours, urgent summonses from sleep, and blizzards, the duty is so popular that bombardiers often volunteer for it again. "The men feel that this is an important and exciting duty," says one detachment commander. Quartered at the summit of the pass, they can get their gun into action at any of the 17 firing positions on an hour's notice.

The artillery is aimed at an avalanche area's critical or "trigger" point. If forecasters have "read" the snow and the atmosphere correctly, the gunfire will roll the avalanche down a known path into designated areas short of the highway. The man-made mounds and trenches help to break up and scatter the slide.

Backing up forecasters and soldiers is the park's staff of wardens, technicians, mechanics, heavy-equipment operators, laborers and administrators. Because of the heavy snowfall, men must work almost around the clock to keep the highway clear, often running out of holes to dump the snow in before winter ends. Driving in the pass one winter, I saw snow piled as high as 30 feet on the valley side of the highway, shutting out the view.

Park wardens enforce the road closing whenever it is in effect, and look out for stranded motorists. Unavoidably, animals are sometimes disturbed by the slides. Former park superintendent P. Winston Smith recalls one slide when "a hibernating bear and her cub found themselves on the highway, blinking at the daylight."

Avalanche control really begins in summer when the snow researchers climb and tramp through the mountains studying the terrain, inspecting the previous year's debris, and augmenting their knowledge of slide areas and trigger zones. "By the time we finish our reports," says Schleiss, "it's almost time for the avalanches again."

In an office at the 4,200-foot summit of the pass, an array of graphs and machines provides forecasters with wind velocities, humidity and temperature readings, including reports sent down from a station manned around the clock on 7,434-foot Mount Fidelity. But intuition—based on experience—is the main instrument in assessing avalanche conditions.

The forecasters usually position themselves directly in the slide path to gauge the effect of the shooting and to tell whether the snow has been stabilized. Since nature in her fury is never easily predictable, running for their lives is routine for forecasters, who sometimes have to be dug out of the snow. Peter Schaerer, a Swiss avalanche researcher with the National Research Council who helped to develop the control program, recalls a narrow escape he had in 1969. "I was on skis setting up instruments to measure the impact of an avalanche, just above a snowshed. I looked over the slide area and decided it was too early for it to go. Then suddenly, it hit. The air blast carried me over the shed and into soft snow 300 feet below. I was lucky not to be buried. I lost both skis and my rucksack, and found one ski in the spring."

Hundreds of such slides occur annually in the British Columbia interior, but most of them don't matter. In Rogers Pass, it's different. Says Schaerer: "This unique system of warning and control is another case where Canada has fought a giant battle with its climate—and won."

# Index

313

# T

Tantramar marshes (N.B.), 227
Tarnava, Rita, 51
Taylor, Billy, 141
Taylor, E.P., 33, 38, 116
Tedder, Lord, 78
Temperance Act (Ontario), 122, 124
*Tempo VI*, 162, 165
Terhune, Charlie, 124
Terry, Walter, 154
Tex Rorschach, Frontier Psychiatrist (Wayne and Shuster), 169
Thames River (Ont.), 165
*Thank You, Canada*, 127
Thomas-Flyer, 35
Thompson, R. W., *The 85 Days*, 127
Thompson, Tommy, 75
Thunder Bay, Ont., 215
Tickle Cove, Nfld., 243
*Tiger*, 287
Tilley, Ross: awarded OBE, 266; and Guinea Pigs, 263, 264, 267; as plastic surgeon, 265-66; and saline baths, 264
*Titanic*, 29, 295
Toftenes, Alfred, 296
Toho Zinc Co., Ltd., 59
"Tonight Show," 157, 160
Toni Home Permanents, 169
*Topdalsfjord*, M.S., 66
Toronto, 20, 34, 54, 105; CN Tower, 14-19; Harbord Collegiate, 168; Hot Stove Club, 136; Kensington market, 211; Maple Leaf Gardens, 132-37, 138, 139, 140; McLaughlin Planetarium, 14; Metro Centre, 14; Metro Zoo, 68-75; Mount Pleasant Cemetery, 297; Ontario Science Centre, 211; Riverdale Zoo, 69-70; Royal Ontario Museum, 211; St. Lawrence Centre, 152; Symphony Orchestra, 211; University of, 168, 250; Woodbine Race Track, 116, 118, 119, 121
Toronto-Dominion Bank, 59
Toronto Hunt Club, Red Cross Horse Show, 118
*Toronto Star, The*, 139
*Toronto Sun, The*, 19
Toronto Turf Club, 116
Totem poles, 102, 107, 185
Touchstone, 118
Tower, Frank "Lucks," 295
Town, Harold, re CN Tower, 19
Trail of '98, 53
*Trails of a Wilderness Wanderer* (Russell), 98
Trancred, Sir Thomas, 53
Trans-Canada Highway, 305, 306
Travers-Smith, Brian, *Cowichan Lake*, 95
Tremblay, Mrs. Jacques, 272, 277
Trenholme, Edward, 26
Trois-Rivières, Que., Gentilly I, 23
Trudeau, Pierre Elliott, 48, 50, 94
Trudeau Sanatorium (Saranac Lake, N.Y.), 250
True, J. D., 54, 56
Tuktoyaktuk (N.W.T.), 40, 178
Tulips, in Ottawa, 126-30
Tupper, Lady, 152
Turboelectric drive, 26

Turcotte, Ron, 119-21
*Two Water Mills, The* (Hobbema), 130-31

# U

Ucluelet, B.C., 102
Underground railway, 113
UNESCO, 89
Ungava Bay (Que.), 43
*Unicorn, the Gorgon and the Manticore, The* (Araiz), 153
United Fruit Company, 29
United States, nuclear energy in, 22, 23
U.S. Army Corps of Engineers, 55, 56
U.S. National Association of Recording Merchandisers, 160
U.S. Weather Bureau, 28
University of Guelph (Ont.), 38
University of Manitoba (Winnipeg), 152
University of Montreal, 38
University of Toronto, 168, 250
*Unknown Country, The* (Hutchison), 91, 92-93
Uranium, 20-25

# V

Val-David, Que., 66
Vallée-Jonction, Que., 270
Vancouver, Capt. George, 186
Vancouver, B.C., 56, 305, 306; Chinatown, 186; Stanley Park, 186
Vancouver Island (B.C.), 102
Van Horne, William, 114
Vatcher, Georges, 277
Verdun, Que., 251
Victoria, Queen, 116, 118
Victoria, B.C., 93, 102, 104, 105, 106, 188
Victoria Cross, 112
Victoria Island (N.W.T.), 40
Victoria Park, 116
Victoria Song, 119
Victoria Tea Shop (Ottawa), 157
Victorious, 116
Volkova, Vera, 155

# W

Wageningen, Netherlands, 110
Waldorf-Astoria Hotel (New York), 165
"Walk for the Animals," 70
Wallace, George, 133
Wannamaker, Reg, 305
Wares, Eddie, 140
Waring, Fred, and his Pennsylvanians, 163
War of 1812, 113
Warren, Patricia *née* Brennan, 263
Warren, Paul, 263
Wascana Lake (Sask.), 198
Wascana Waterfowl Park (Regina), 198
Waskesui Lake (Sask.), 198
Waterton Lakes National Park (Alta.), 100
Wavell, Lord, 81
Wayne, Johnny, 166-71; "Cinderfella," 167; comedy sketches, 169; early career, 168-69; early life, 168; on "The Ed Sullivan Show," 166, 169; "The Elsinore Kid," 169; family life, 169-70; *Invasion Review*, 168;

"The Picture of Dorian Wayne," 169; stays in Canada, 166, 169; wins Silver Rose of Montreux, 170; writes own material, 170-71
Webb Zerafa Menkes Housden Partnership, The, 14
Weeks, Peter, 264
Wells, H. G., 81
Western Brook Pond (Nfld.), 240
West Nova Scotia Regiment, 131
Wetaskiwin, Alta., 263
"Whiskey Boat," 122-25
White, Paul Dudley, 81
Whitehorse, Y.T., 53, 54, 55, 56, 57, 59, 181, 277
Whiteman, Paul, 161, 163
White Pass and Yukon Corporation Limited, 56
White Pass & Yukon Route, 52-56, 57, 60; accidents on, 54; completion, 54; concept of, 53; construction, 53-54; containerization on, 53, 56; finances, 53, 55; keeping track clear, 54; modernization program, 53, 56, 59
White Pass Summit (Y.T.), 53, 54
White Pass Trail, 53
"White-Seek-Grace." *See* Bethune, Henry Norman
*Whoops-de-doo, Les*, 154
Wickes Canada, Ltd., 49, 51
*William D. Lawrence*, 230
Willie Wonder, 116-18
Wilson, J. O., 95
*Windflower*, 290
Winnipeg, Man., 202, 205; "Golden Boy," 206; Manitoba Centennial Concert Hall, 152; Playhouse Theatre, 152; Royal Ballet, 144, 150-55; University of Manitoba, 152
Winnipeg Ballet Club, 152
Woensdrecht, Netherlands, 129, 130
Wolfe, Gen. James, 113
Women Farmers' Circle (Saint-Joseph-de-Beauce, Que.), 270
Woodbine Race Track (Toronto), 116, 118, 119, 121
Woodcock, Ronald, 298-301; abandons furs, 298; financially wiped out, 298; finds road to Hazelton, B.C., 301; finds telegraph trail, 300; kills game, 299; lost, 298, 301; returns to mother, 301; traps beaver, 298
*Wood Interior* (Carr), 106
World Championships for Handicapped Skiers, 260, 261
World War I, 118
World War II, 55
Worthington, Peter, re CN Tower, 19
Wright, Frank Lloyd, 78
Wrigley's Chewing Gum, 164

# Y

Yarmouth, N.S., 279, 280
Yellowknife, N.W.T., 179
Yoho National Park (B.C.), 189
York University (Toronto), 38
Young, Winston, 17
YWCA, 38
"You're Having My Baby" (Anka), 157
Ypperciel, Pierre, general manager, Glendale (Que.), Ltd., 268, 270, 271
Yukon, 174-83; gold, 179, 180; minerals, 180
Yukon River, 54, 55, 59

# Acknowledgments

The condensations reprinted in this book are used by permission of, and special arrangement with, the publishers holding the respective copyrights.

**A Poet's View of Canada**, by Alden Nowlan, *Reader's Digest,* October '71, condensed from *Maclean's* (June 1971), © 1971 Maclean-Hunter Ltd., Toronto, Ont.

**"Bravo CN Tower!"** by Larry Collins, *Reader's Digest,* November '75 (Toronto's Cloud Nine).

**Canada's CANDU: A Nuclear Triumph**, by Robert Collins, *Reader's Digest,* March '75 (CANDU: The Nuclear Gamble That Came Off).

**"By His Genius Men Sail Unafraid"**, by Ormond Raby, *Reader's Digest,* December '72 (Canada's Most Extraordinary Inventor).

**One Grade Only and That the Best**, by Robert Collins, *Reader's Digest,* November '72.

**Inuit Co-ops: The Little Five-Cent Idea**, by Lois Neely, *Reader's Digest,* June '76 (Eskimo Co-ops: New Dawn in the Arctic).

**Enterprise at Stand Off**, by Fred McGuinness, *Reader's Digest,* January '74 ("Sell the Grass, Not the Land").

**"The Railroad That Couldn't Be Built"**, by Paul Friggens, *Reader's Digest,* January '73 (Happy Days for the Gold Rush Railway).

**Anvil! Tapping the Yukon's Great Wealth**, by Paul Friggens, *Reader's Digest,* March '73 (Anvil! The Yukon's Fabulous Mine).

**Being Fully Alive, *That's* the Thing!** by W. J. Lederer, *Reader's Digest,* March '72 (He Blazed a Trail—on Skis), condensed from *Ski Magazine* (February '72), © 1972 by Universal Publishing and Distributing Corp., New York, N.Y.

**The Zoo That Aims to Be Best of All**, by Anker Odum, *Reader's Digest,* March '77 (Toronto's Wild Kingdom).

**The Many Faces of Yousuf Karsh**, by Adrian Waller, *Reader's Digest,* March '76; Churchill, Einstein, Khrushchev, Hemingway and Riopelle captions adapted from *Faces of Our Time,* by Yousuf Karsh © University of Toronto Press 1971.

**Gentle Genius of the Screen**, by Lawrence Elliott, *Reader's Digest,* August '71 (Norman McLaren: Gentle Genius of the Screen).

**All That's Best in a Reporter**, by David MacDonald, *Reader's Digest,* January '72 (Bruce Hutchison: The Sage of Shawnigan Lake).

**Trying to Save What's Left**, by Robert Collins, *Reader's Digest,* April '75 (The Wild, Free Life of Andy Russell), condensed from *Outdoor Canada* (April '75), © by Outdoor Canada Magazine Ltd., Toronto, Ont.

**"Crazy Old Millie Carr"**, by David MacDonald, *Reader's Digest,* April '72.

**Where the Past Shapes the Future**, by Hartley Steward, *Reader's Digest,* June '73 (Storehouse of the Nation's History), adapted from an article by Evan Hill.

**As Much a Mood As It Is a Race**, by Bill Surface, *Reader's Digest,* June '74 (The Pageantry and Passion of the Queen's Plate).

**"That Could Be a Whiskey Boat!"** by Robert Collins, *Reader's Digest,* October '74 (The Day the Whiskey Ship Ran Aground).

**The Message of the Tulips,** by George G. Blackburn, *Reader's Digest,* May '71.

**A Battlefield Letter,** by Douglas How, *Reader's Digest,* November '72 (The Letter on the Battlefield).

**The House That Smythe Built,** by Robert Collins, *Reader's Digest,* October '72 (Where Hockey Night In Canada Was Born).

**The Hockey Final *Everyone* Was In,** by Foster Hewitt, *Reader's Digest,* May '75 (My Most Memorable Stanley Cup).

**Not Just a Dancer—a Star,** by Susan Carson, *Reader's Digest,* October '77 (Karen Kain: Canada's Prima Ballerina).

**"Canada's Bolshoi",** by Martin O'Malley, *Reader's Digest,* December '71 (The Ballet That Came In From the Cold), condensed from *The Globe Magazine* (July 24, '71), © 1971 The Globe and Mail Ltd., Toronto, Ont.

**Cheek, Charm and Audience Command,** by Adrian Waller, *Reader's Digest,* October '76 ("Lonely Boy" on Top of the World).

**Mr. New Year,** by Adrian Waller, *Reader's Digest,* January '76 (Meet Mr. New Year).

**They Do It *Their* Way,** by Robert Collins, *Reader's Digest,* February '74 (Wayne and Shuster: Canada's Stay-at-Home Clowns).

**After a Life of Storm, a State of Grace,** by Harold Horwood, *Reader's Digest,* January '75 (Norman Bethune: the Rebel China Reveres).

**"I Can Ski Again!"** by Diane Alder, *Reader's Digest,* April '75.

**The Guinea Pigs' Lost Weekend,** by George Ronald, *Reader's Digest,* September '71, adapted from an article by Oscar Schisgall.

**"Everybody to the Corvée!"** by Louise Cousineau, *Reader's Digest,* August '75.

**The Quebec Town That Disappeared,** by Joseph P. Blank, *Reader's Digest,* December '71 (The Town That Disappeared).

**First to Sail Around the World—Alone,** by Pierre Berton, *Reader's Digest,* January '77 (The Magnificent Voyage of Joshua Slocum), condensed from *My Country,* © 1976 by Pierre Berton Enterprises Ltd., published by McClelland & Stewart Ltd., Toronto, Ont.

**A Rightful Place Among the Heroes,** by George Ronald, *Reader's Digest,* August '72 (The Day Admiral Murray Came Home), condensed from *The Atlantic Advocate* (January '72), © 1972 by The University Press of New Brunswick, Fredericton, N.B.

**She Was Big, Safe, Fast—and Doomed,** by F. J. Woodley, *Reader's Digest,* August '75 (Last Voyage of the "Empress of Ireland").

**Lost!** by Joseph P. Blank, *Reader's Digest,* April '72 (Ron Woodcock's Long Walk Home).

**Red Alert: Avalanche in Rogers Pass,** by Roland Wild, *Reader's Digest,* February '75 (The Never-Ending Battle of Rogers Pass).

# Picture Credits

The following abbreviations have been used:

BCI  Bruce Coleman Inc.
BF   Bryce Flynn
CH   Chic Harris
DW   Daniel Wiener
IBC  Image Bank of Canada

JK   J. A. Kraulis
JdeV John de Visser
MF   Menno Fieguth
PvB  Paul von Baich
PAC  Public Archives of Canada

Credits are left to right, top to bottom. A single credit means that all pictures are from the same source.

1 David Steiner; 2 Lowell Georgia/Photo Researchers; Wilbur S. Tripp; MF; 3 Barry W. Gray; PvB; Mary Ferguson; 4-5 JdeV; 7 J. Chris Christiansen; 8-9 PvB; 10 BF; 13 Lowell Georgia/Photo Researchers; 15 Canadian National Railways; 16 Peter Reid, Canadian National Railways; Canadian National Railways; 18-19 Canadian National Railways; 20-21 ©Bill Brooks/IBC; 21-22 Ontario Hydro; 23 Réal Lefebvre; 25 Ontario Hydro; 27-31 State Dept. of Archives and History (Raleigh, North Carolina); 32 PAC PA-57611; 33 Canadian Automotive Museum; 34-38 courtesy General Motors of Canada Ltd.; 39 Royal Ontario Museum; M-H Specialty Sales; Marty Sheffer; 41-43 JdeV; 44 Lois Neely; 44-45 JdeV (2); 47 Glenbow-Alberta Institute; Terry Bland Photography; 48 Terry Bland Photography; 49 Terry Bland Photography; Dept. of Indian and Northern Affairs (2); Terry Bland Photography; 50 Terry Bland Photography; 52 Yukon Archives; 55 PvB; 56-61 courtesy Anvil Mines; 63 John Birkett; 64 courtesy H. Smith-Johannsen; 65 Gerald Birks; 66 Michael Drummond; 67 courtesy Karen Austin; 68 Bill Lowry; 70-71 CPS Film Productions; 71 Bill Lowry; 72 CPS Film Productions; Bill Lowry (2); 72-73 CPS Film Productions (2); 74 Metro Toronto Zoo; 75 Metro Toronto Zoo; Ken Elliott/Canadian Magazine; 77 Wilbur S. Tripp; 79-83 courtesy Yousuf Karsh; 84-88 N.F.B. Photothèque; 90 CBC; 93 courtesy Bruce Hutchison; 94 courtesy Bruce Hutchison/photo Eric Skipsey; 95 courtesy Bruce Hutchison; 96-101 Andy Russell; 103-105 Archives of British Columbia; 106 Archives of British Columbia; "Above the Gravel Pitt" (oil c. 1936) collection of the Vancouver Art Gallery; "Wood Interior" (oil c. 1932) collection of the Vancouver Art Gallery; 107 "Kitwancool Totems, 1928" courtesy of the Art Gallery of Ontario, Hart House Permanent Collection; "Alert Bay" Private Collection; 109 MF; 111 PAC; 112 Bob Anderson; 114 PAC; 115 Bob Anderson; 117 H. Barclay/Miller Services; Michael Burns Photography Ltd.; 118 Michael Burns Photography Ltd.; 119 Lutz Dille; 120-121 Michael Burns Photography Ltd.; 123 from "Picturesque Canada"; 125 PAC PA-118728; Steamship Historical Society Library, University of Baltimore; 126 Malak, Ottawa; 128 PAC C-4908; 129 Malak, Ottawa; 130 National Art Gallery of Canada, Ottawa; 132 John Maiola; 133 Hockey News; Graphic Artists; 134 R. Mitchell/Miller Services Ltd.; 135 The Globe and Mail, Toronto; 137 John Maiola; 139 Roy Mitchell/Alexandra Studio Archives; UPI Photo; 140-141 UPI Photo; 143 Barry W. Gray; 144 Christopher Darling; 146-148 from KAIN & AUGUSTYN, published by Macmillan Co. of Canada, photos Christopher Darling; 149 Christopher Darling; 151 Barry W. Gray; 153 photo Peter Garrick/courtesy Royal Winnipeg Ballet; 154 ©Bob Anderson/IBC; 155 photo Peter Garrick/courtesy Royal Winnipeg Ballet; 156 Max Tobin/Globe Photos; 158-159 Paul Anka Productions; 161 CBC; 162 UPI Photo; 164 Paramount Studios; 165 Max Hirshfeld; 167 CBC; 168 Ken Bell; 169 CBC/photo Robert C. Ragsdale; 170-171 CBC; 173-175 PvB; 176 Fred Bruemmer; 176-177 Paolo Koch/Photo Researchers; 177 Danny Singer; 178 René Fumoleau; 178-179 Lorne Smith; 180 PvB; 181 PvB; Crombie McNeil; PvB; 182-183 George Hunter; 183 PvB; 184-185 Jack Fields/Photo Researchers; 185 PvB; 186 JdeV; ©Ivor and June Sharp/IBC; 186-187 Allan Harvey; 188 Ulrich Kretschmar; Allan Harvey; PvB; 188-189 JdeV; 189 ©JK/IBC; S.R. Cannings; 190-191 Lowell Georgia/Photo Researchers; 192 JdeV; David Steiner (2); 192-193 Lowell Georgia/Photo Researchers; 194 ©JdeV/IBC; ©Toby Rankin/IBC; 195 Lowell Georgia/Photo Researchers; 196 Saskatchewan Government Photo; 196-197 Lorne Scott; 198 Richard Knelsen; MF; Lorne Scott; 199 E. Otto/Miller Services; 200 Richard Vroom; 200-201 MF (2); 202-203 JdeV; 204 Pierre Gaudard (2); Dennis Fast; 205 Manitoba Tourism; CH (2); 206-207 E. Otto/Miller Services; 208 ©Bill Brooks/IBC; 208-209 Bill Brooks/BCI; 209 BF; O. J. Dell; 210 JK; 210-211 ©JdeV/IBC; 211 Rudi Christl; 212 Rudi Christl; Rudi Haas; 212-214 BF; 215 Danny Singer; BF; 216 CH; JK; Dunkin Bancroft; 217 JK; 218 JK (2); ©Ivor and June Sharp/IBC; 218-219 PvB; 219 Paul Lambert; CH; ©Bill Brooks/IBC; Dunkin Bancroft; 220 JK; 221 PvB; CH; Pierre Gaudard; George Dineen/Photo Researchers; Ray Webber; 222-223 CH; 224 Doris Mowry; Charles Steinhacker/Black Star; 225 N.B. Dept. of Tourism; CH; N.B. Dept. of Tourism; 226 Mike Saunders; 227 Stephen Homer; 228 DW; 229 Nicholas de Vore III/BCI; 230 DW; CH (2); 231 Owen Fitzgerald; 232 DW (2); Ron Webber; 232-233 Owen Fitzgerald; 234-235 JdeV; 236 Sherman Hines; 236-237 George Zimbel; 237 CH; 238 Wayne Barrett; Richard Vroom; J. C. Hurni; 239 JdeV; 240 Nicholas de Vore III/BCI; 241 Dan Guravich; 242 Nicholas de Vore III/BCI; 243 Ray Webber; DW; Nicholas de Vore III/BCI; 244 Nicholas de Vore III/BCI; 244-245 Dan Guravich; 247 Mary Ferguson; 249 courtesy Dr. J. Wendell MacLeod, Bethune Memorial Committee; 250 courtesy Frontier College; 251 courtesy Roderick Stewart; 252-253 PAC/Hazen Sise Collection; 254-255 courtesy Roderick Stewart; 256-257 Diane Alder; 259 Diane Alder; Simon Hoyle; 260 Simon Hoyle; 262 Private Collection; 264 Private Collection; Dr. Ross Tilley; 265 Dr. Ross Tilley; 266-267 Private Collection; 269-271 courtesy Glendale (Quebec) Ltd.; 273-276 Marc Ellefsen; 278 Historical Pictures Service, Chicago; 282 NYT Pictures; 283 from "Sailing Alone Around the World" (1901), courtesy Sheridan House; 284 PAC 0-1004-5; 285 Maritime Command Museum; 286 PAC PA-37456; PAC L-5524; PAC PA-37424; 288 Public Archives of Nova Scotia; 289 Public Archives of Nova Scotia (2); The Halifax Herald Ltd.; 291 courtesy Nina Murray; 293 Canada Wide; ILN Picture Library, England (2); 294 Wide World/Canada Wide; 295 7 C's Press; courtesy The Salvation Army; 297 courtesy The Salvation Army; 299 courtesy Mrs. Irene Woodcock; PvB; 300 courtesy Mrs. Irene Woodcock; 302-303 Parks Canada; 304 Parks Canada/photo Fred Schleiss; 305 Canadian Armed Forces; 306 Parks Canada; 318 Pierre Gaudard; 320 Dennis Fast.

Color separation: Herzig Somerville Limited
Typesetting: The Graphic Group of Canada Ltd.
Printing: Metropole Litho Inc.
Binding: Volumex Limited

Editor: Keith Bellows
Art Director: Val Mitrofanow
Photo Research: Viki Colledge, Rachel Irwin
Production: Holger Lorenzen